MW01000113

APPROPRIATION & INVENTION

APPROPRIATION & INVENTION

Three Centuries of Art in Spanish America

Selections from the Denver Art Museum

Edited by Jorge F. Rivas Pérez

With contributions by Olga Isabel Acosta Luna, Luisa Elena Alcalá, Elsa Arroyo Lemus, Carla Aymes, Michael A. Brown, James M. Córdova, Gustavo Curiel Méndez, Carmen Fernández-Salvador, Raphael Fonseca, Philippe Halbert, Ricardo Kusunoki Rodríguez, Natalia Majluf, Franziska Martha Neff, Janeth Rodríguez Nóbrega, Sofía Sanabrais, and Luis Eduardo Wuffarden Revilla

HIRMER

Rº. x D. Thomas Mariª. Joachin Villas.r y Gomez, hijo Lexit.mo
de D. Lorenzo Xavier de Villas.r Regidor, y Alcalde
Ordinario q. fuè d esta Ciudad æ Guadalax. y de Dª
Maria Josepha Gomez. muriò à los 5 aº. y 8. m.s de
su edad à 23 de Junio de 1760.

CONTENTS

Introduction

CAT. 1 **Marcos Zapata and his workshop**
Peruvian, active 1741–1776, *Adoration of the Magi*,
Cuzco, Peru, ca. 1760. Oil paint and gold leaf on canvas,
6 ft. 2 in. × 49⅝ in. (188 × 126 cm). Gift of Mr. and Mrs. Frank
Barrows Freyer II for Frank Barrows Freyer Collection, 1969.347

Director's Foreword

A 1936 gift of southwestern *santos* from Anne Evans seeded the Denver Art Museum's illustrious collection of Latin American art. Since then, our collection of art objects created between 1600 and 1900 in Mexico, Central and South America, the Caribbean, and the southwestern United States has grown to over three thousand objects. Ours is the largest and most complete such collection in the United States and one of the best in the world.

The museum established the New World department in 1968, and the gift of the Frank Barrows Freyer Memorial Collection of seventeenth- and eighteenth-century Peruvian colonial art (CAT. 1) inspired additional donations, including colonial silver from the Robert C. Appleman family (CAT. 2), about four hundred objects collected in northern South America—silver, sculpture, jewelry, and furniture—from the Stapleton Foundation of Latin American Colonial Art (made possible by the Renchard family) (CAT. 3), and the bequest from Robert J. Stroessner (CAT. 4)—the first curator of the department. Two transformational gifts greatly expanded the department's holdings—the Frederick and Jan Mayer collection of colonial Mexican art in 2014 (CAT. 5) and a selection of Venezuelan and South American artworks from the collection of Patricia Phelps de Cisneros in 2019 (CAT. 6)—which allow the museum to exhibit paintings, sculptures, and decorative objects that represent the broad range of artistic production from a vast territory once ruled by the Spanish Crown. More recently, the museum has begun to acquire modern and contemporary Latin American art to better bridge the cultural narratives of past, present, and future.

In 2001, longtime museum trustee and benefactor Frederick Mayer and his wife, Jan, endowed the first curatorial position exclusively dedicated to Spanish colonial Latin American art in the United States. In 2003, the Mayers established another generous endowment for the New World department staff, programs, and research, creating the Mayer Center for Ancient and Latin American Art, which sponsors symposia, educational and scholarly programming, and publications, including this collection highlights book. Though Frederick left us too soon in 2007, we offer our heartfelt thanks to Jan and her continued generosity, enthusiasm, and her ongoing dedication to the museum as a whole and to the study of the arts from Latin America in particular.

I must thank Jorge Rivas Pérez, the Frederick and Jan Mayer Curator of Latin American Art, not only for his thoughtful and careful selection of works to highlight in this book but also for his reimagining, strengthening, and broadening the museum's Latin American art collection.

I would also like to thank the Carl and Marilynn Thoma Foundation for their generous support of this catalog.

Christoph Heinrich
Frederick and Jan Mayer Director

CAT. 2 **Unknown artist, *Crown***
Mexico, ca. 1740. Silver, 8 × 7 in. dia. (20.3 × 17.8 cm dia.). Gift of the Robert Appleman family, 1992.393

CAT. 3 **Unknown artist, *Saint John with Holy Family***
Colombia or Ecuador, 1600s. Oil paint on canvas, 15½ × 12¼ in. (39.4 × 31.1 cm). Gift of the Stapleton Foundation of Latin American Colonial Art, made possible by the Renchard family, 1990.515

CAT. 4 **Nicolás Rodríguez Juárez, Mexican, 1667–1734, *Saint Joseph***
Mexico City, Mexico, late 1600s–early 1700s. Oil paint and gold on canvas, 13¼ × 13¼ in. (33.7 × 33.7 cm). Gift of Robert J. Stroessner, 1991.1158

CAT. 5 **Luis Lagarto, Spanish, active in Mexico, ca. 1550–1624, *The Annunciation***
Mexico, 1611. Gouache (opaque watercolor) and gold leaf on parchment, 12⅜ × 9¾ in. (31.4 × 24.8 cm). Gift of the Collection of Frederick and Jan Mayer, 2014.212

CAT. 6 **Unknown artist, *Archangel Michael***
Bolivia or Peru, 1700s. Oil paint on canvas, 71¾ × 45 in. (182.2 × 114.3 cm). Gift of Patricia Phelps de Cisneros in honor of Gabriel Pérez Barreiro, 2017.122

Appropriation and Invention in the Arts of Spanish America

Jorge F. Rivas Pérez

In 2021, the Denver Art Museum reinstalled its permanent collection galleries, allowing us to show more of our Latin American art collection than ever before. In addition to the colonial art and modern and contemporary galleries, a gallery dedicated exclusively to nineteenth-century Latin American art is the only one of its kind in the United States (CATS. 7 AND 8). A number of the pieces have never been exhibited, and now we can tell more inclusive stories, incorporate voices from artists and community members, and provide more social and historical context for our visitors. Although this volume does not include all of the remarkable artworks in the collection, the present selection provides an excellent overview of the collection's importance, depth, and range, and we hope that this volume will serve as a starting point for all those interested in exploring the complex historical circumstances that gave rise to the arts of Latin America, the extraordinary originality and inventiveness of its artists, and the richness of its artistic heritage.

In the interest of clarity, this book is organized by region and media, and the essays illuminate the complex artistic landscape, with its porous borders and overlapping questions, of a vast territory once ruled by the Spanish Crown. The texts by renowned scholars from the United States, Latin America, and Europe provide deep historical insights and context for the artworks from the Caribbean—the place of origin of the Spanish colonial enterprise—and the enormous viceroyalties of New Spain (present-day Mexico, Central America, the US Southwest and California, and the Philippines) and Peru (present-day Spanish-speaking South America).

Dazzling and surprising, colonial art invented a new, different, and extraordinary type of art that challenged and disrupted traditional European aesthetics and displayed ingenuity and subtle but powerful nuances that contested the colonial authority. The Denver Art Museum is fortunate enough to have an unparalleled collection that allows us to tell this fascinating and nuanced story. This volume presents a more plural art history focusing on cross-cultural artistic currents and the resulting ruptures with established models.

* * *

Everything changed in the Americas after the arrival of the Europeans in the 1490s, as profound processes of readjustments and transformations ensued from the conquest and colonization of the land. For the Indigenous peoples, the European invasion permeated all facets of life, bringing political change, the destruction of their cities and monuments, diseases, and slavery—and the forced labor of the *encomiendas*—which led to catastrophic demographic losses and devastated their civilizations. For the Europeans, it was challenging to deal with the new realities resulting from settling and administering those vast territories and incorporating the many different populations that inhabited the Americas into the new order. It took several generations

1 In his memoir, Toribio de Benavente (Motolinía) describes the abilities of Mexican Indigenous craftsmen in learning Spanish trades by watching Europeans at work. Toribio de Benavente (Motolinía) and Daniel Sánchez García, *Historia de los indios de la Nueva España: escrita a mediados del siglo XVI* (Barcelona: Herederos de J. Gili, 1914), 79.

to assimilate the magnitude of change; however, new artistic expressions, often with significant contributions by Indigenous artists, arose from that protracted process. The arrival of enslaved Africans in the early 1500s, followed by trade and immigration from Asia later that century, further complicated the already multilayered relationship between European and non-European visual cultures in the Americas.

In an effort to create continuity across the empire, European settlers organized their daily lives and administration following Spanish customs, including a deeply intertwined connection with Roman Catholicism, but different local conditions and contexts kept them from fully supplanting Indigenous customs. European artists had to adapt to local resources, market conditions, and, in particular, deal with many heterogeneous societies, which included skilled Indigenous artists who competed with Europeans.[1] Native artists and those of multiracial Native descent were not a homogeneous group. They mirrored the racial complexities, diversity of origins, and class distinctions of the colonial society. The rich artistic output from the period resulted from protracted cultural negotiation, accommodation, and appropriation, processes that led to the invention of visual vocabularies that reflected the continuities and ruptures with ancient artistic traditions and the social and cultural dynamics of each community.

The artistic production in Spanish America was more than a unidirectional exercise of copying, translating, and adapting European models. In the process of transference and relocation from one cultural framework to another, artistic creation acquired new contexts and meanings. Colonial cultural exchange is not just the circulation of art

CAT. 7 **Attributed to Luis Montero, Peruvian, 1827–1869, *Una Imitación Antigua (An Ancient Imitation)***
Peru, 1868. Oil paint on canvas, 53⅝ × 32⅞ in. (136.2 × 83.5 cm). Gift of Drs. Sydney G. & Virginia M. Salus, 1979.179

CAT. 8 **Unknown artist, *La Gran Ñusta Mama Occollo (The Grand Ñusta Mama Ocllo)***
Peru, ca. 1850–70. Oil paint on canvas, mounted on board, 18⅛ × 14⅞ in. (45.9 × 37.8 cm). Gift of Dr. Belinda Straight by exchange and New World Department Acquisition Funds, 1996.18

and ideas but their inexorable reinterpretation and resignification within a cross-cultural situation. When studying material culture, for example, religious artifacts have different connotations and meanings according to context and users. For instance, the retooled prehispanic emerald beads mounted on a gold cross that once embellished the crown on a statue of the Virgin Mary in Colombia had different connotations depending on the worshiper in front of it (CAT. 9). For an Indigenous convert, the emerald beads likely were charged with sacred, symbolic value—associated with life and fertility—transferring some prehispanic, ancient religious meaning to the Christian image. For a European, those green gems were valuable offerings to the Virgin Mary but likely did not hold other symbolic associations. We find a similar example in colonial Mexican featherwork images, for which artists adapted ancient techniques and materials to produce Christian images (CAT. 13). Charged with sacred meaning and associated with power and the ruling elites, feathers were incorporated into many aspects of Aztec material culture.[2] The repurposing of this artistic tradition suggests that the material itself, imbued with ancient symbolic value, played an important role in the development of colonial cross-cultural art forms.

Ancient object types associated with religious practices were sometimes transformed during the Spanish age and partially deprived of their symbolic connotations as they became used as everyday objects. For example, Andean ritual drinking vessels called *keros* (CAT. 10) were decorated with European motifs after the conquest (CAT. 11), and in other cases, their shape and incised geometric decoration served as models for colonial drinking bowls.[3] In this example, Spanish-style handles were added (CAT. 12). In Mesoamerica, a similar transformation process occurred. The ancient type of chocolate drinking cup made from gourds (*xicalli* in Nahuatl) becomes the colonial *jícara,* or chocolate cup. Initially made from gourds (CAT. 14), and later from coconut seeds (CAT. 15), the cups were painstakingly incised and carved. Their decoration and forms often depict a fusion of European and ancient ornamental motifs, and frequently they display the engraved name of their original owners.

In the case of painting and sculpture, European styles and aesthetics had no parallels in the visual cultures of the Ancient Americas; consequently, their combination with Indigenous styles and practices created new visual vocabularies appropriate to the multicultural world that developed after the conquest. Artists in Spanish America often relied on printed sources or copies of well-known European

2 On colonial featherwork, see Alessandra Russo, Gerhard Wolf, and Diana Fane, *El vuelo de las imágenes arte plumario en México y Europa* (Ciudad de México: Instituto Nacional de Antropología e Historia, 2011).

3 Ritual drinking vessels (*keros*) were very important symbolic objects among all Andean culture. See Tom Cummins, "Representation in the Sixteenth Century and the Colonial Image of the Inca" in *Writing Without Words: Alternative Literacies in Mesoamerica and the Andes*, edited by Elizabeth Hill Boone and Walter D. Mignolo (Durham, NC: Duke University Press, 2004), 188–219.

4 Matthäeus Merian, *Icones biblicae; praecipuas sacrae scripturae eleganter & graphice repraesentantes; Biblische Figuren, darinnen die Fuernembsten Historien, in Heiliger und Goettlicher Schrifft begriffen* (Strasbourg: L. Zetzners, 1629). On European printed sources, see Thomas B. F. Cummins, "The Indulgent Image: Prints in the New World," in *Contested Visions in the Spanish Colonial World*, edited by Ilona Katzew (Los Angeles: Los Angeles County Museum of Art, 2011), 203–225;

masterworks for their compositions, such as Antonio Enríquez's *King Solomon and the Queen of Sheba* (CAT. 16) based on a print of the same subject from the *Icones Biblicae*, a popular illustrated bible published by Matthäeus Merian before 1630 (FIG. 1).[4] In other cases, artists' interpretations were rather loose, such as in a pair of modest Peruvian *países* (landscape paintings) in the collection (CATS. 17 AND 18), which were likely inspired by European prints but unmistakably executed in the color palette and stylistic features of late-colonial Andean painting.

Although printed sources led to a close adherence to European artistic canons and iconographies for artists who had never set foot in Europe, many painters went beyond those, challenging the canon and inventing new styles and types of representation. Juan Rodríguez Juárez's *Saint Rose of Lima with Christ Child and Donor* exemplifies Spanish American artists' sophistication and inventiveness (CAT. 19). As a hint of his familiarity with Spanish art, Rodríguez Juárez references a well-known painting of the saint by the Spanish master Bartolomé Estebán Murillo (FIG. 2), but the artist included a portrait of a donor at the bottom—an aspiring nun richly dressed—and reworked many details, including the fine rug on which the donor kneels and the copious amount of blood trickling down the saint's forehead.[5] During the Spanish era, representations of blood recalled preconquest cultures for which blood was central to religious rituals and often represented in art.[6] Colonial artists depicted blood with an astonishing realism and exaggerated abundance far exceeding European artistic conventions. Both gorgeous and gruesome, religious art from the period can be shockingly graphic in its representation of Christ's sufferings and crucifixion (CAT. 20), the exertions of saints (CAT. 21), and the allegories of the Holy Eucharist (CAT. 22).

In other cases, the inventiveness of artists was less ambitious and limited to subtler gestures, such as the substitution of a European element in a Cuzco painting that depicts the Virgin Mary as the Immaculate Conception with an Indigenous donor (CAT. 23). The Native artist transformed the European cypress tree (symbolic of immortality) into the more familiar giant Andean bromeliad plant (*titanka* in Quechua).[7] The portraits of Indigenous

and Kelly Donahue-Wallace, "Picturing Prints in Early Modern New Spain," *The Americas* 64 (2007): 325–49.

5 For a detailed study of this painting see Jaime Cuadriello, "Transoceanic Depictions and Fictions: Marian Representation as Social Personification," in *Return Journey: Art of the Americas in Spain*, edited by Rafael López Guzmán (Madrid: Museo Nacional del Prado, 2021), 71–75.

6 On prehispanic blood rituals, see Giuseppe Orefici, "Bleeding Hearts, Bleeding Parts: Sacrificial blood in Maya society," in *Blood: Art, Power, Politics, and Pathology*, edited by James M. Bradburne (Munich: Prestel, 2002), 41–54.

CAT. 9 **Unknown artist, *Cross Finial*** Colombia, ca. 1600. Gold, pearls, and emeralds, 4 × 1⅝ × ½ in. (10.2 × 4.1 × 1.3 cm). Gift of the Stapleton Foundation of Latin American Colonial Art, made possible by the Renchard family, 1990.526

donors, often wearing a mix of Indigenous and European-style garments, also showcase how artists adapted European models to better fit the colonial society and its complex structure (CAT. 24).

The artworks discussed in this short text embody more than three centuries of appropriation and invention in the arts. They showcase the ingenuity of local artists and their efforts in creating original expressions that mirrored the complex society in which they lived and worked. They also speak to the ways artistic ambitions fueled identity formation and the ideas of nationalism that eventually led to the independence from Spain.

7 Endemic to the high Andean valleys, the *titanka* (Puya raimondii Hams), also known as "queen of the Andes," is the world's largest species of bromeliad.

CAT. 10 **Unknown Inca artist, *Kero (ceremonial cup)***
Southern Highlands, Peru, ca. 1300–1500. Wood, 5⅛ × 4⅜ in. dia. (13 × 11.1 cm dia.). Gift of Lindsay A. Duff, 1984.634

CAT. 11 **Unknown artist, *Kero (ceremonial cup)***
Peru, 1700s. Wood and pigmented resin inlay, 7½ × 6½ in. dia. (19.1 × 16.5 cm). Bequest from the Estate of Leon H. Snyder, 1978.289

CAT. 12 **Unknown artist, *Double-Handled Drinking Cup***
Ecuador or Peru, ca. 1800. Silver, 3¾ × 7 in. overall dia. (9.5 × 17.8 cm. overall dia.), Gift of the Stapleton Foundation of Latin American Colonial Art, made possible by the Renchard family, 1990.374

CAT. 13 **Unknown artist, *Saint John the Evangelist***
Mexico, 1600s. Feathers glued on paper, mounted on copper, 12⅛ × 8⅞ in. (30.8 × 22.5 cm). Gift of the Collection of Frederick and Jan Mayer, 2013.389

CAT. 14 **Unknown artist, *Silver-Mounted Gourd Cup (jícara)***
Guatemala, 1740s. Gourd and silver, 4½ × 3⅞ × 2¾ in. (11.4 × 9.8 × 7 cm). Gift of the Robert C. Appleman family, 1992.406A-B

CAT. 15 **Unknown artist, *Silver-Mounted Coconut Cup (jícara)***
Guatemala, mid-1750s. Coconut shell and silver, height 3⅝ in. (9.2 cm). Funds from Ethel Sayre Berger by exchange, 2019.553

CAT. 16 **Antonio Enríquez, Mexican, active 1722–1787,** ***King Solomon and the Queen of Sheba***
Mexico, 1732. Oil paint on canvas, 40¾ × 66 in. (103.5 × 167.6 cm). Gift of the Collection of Frederick and Jan Mayer, 2015.552

FIG. 1 Matthäus Merian, the Elder, *The Queen of Sheba Visiting King Solomon* from the series *Icones Biblicae*, ca. 1626. Etching. Courtesy The State Hermitage Museum, Russia, ОГ-97833.

CAT. 17 **Unknown artist, *Landscape (país)***
Peru, early 1800s. Oil paint on wood panel, 8¼ × 9⅛ in. (21 × 23.2 cm). Gift of Frank B. Freyer II for Frank Barrows Freyer Collection at the Denver Art Museum, 1971.423.1

CAT. 18 **Unknown artist, *Landscape (país)***
Peru, early 1800s. Oil paint on wood panel, 8⅛ × 9⅛ in. (20.6 × 23.2 cm). Gift of Frank B. Freyer II for Frank Barrows Freyer Collection, 1971.423.2

FIG. 2 Bartolomé Esteban Murillo, *Saint Rose of Lima*, Spain, 1670. Oil paint on canvas, 57 × 37 in. (144.8 × 94 cm). Museo Lázaro Galdiano, Madrid, Spain, 05310. Bartolomé Esteban Murillo, Public domain, via Wikimedia Commons.

CAT. 19 **Juan Rodríguez Juárez, Mexican, 1675–1728, *Saint Rose of Lima with Christ Child and Donor***
Mexico, ca. 1700. Oil paint on canvas, 66 × 42 in. (167.6 × 106.7 cm). Gift of the Collection of Frederick and Jan Mayer, 2014.216

CAT. 20 **Unknown artist, *The Flagellation of Christ***
Mexico, 1680–1725. Oil paint on canvas, 41 × 26 in. (104.1 × 66 cm). Gift of Mr. and Mrs. John Bunker, 1977.165

CAT. 21 **Unknown artist, *Saint Peter of Alcantara Penitent***
Quito, Ecuador, early 1700s. Painted wood with glass and metal, 12 × 6 × 3½ in. (30.5 × 15.2 × 8.9 cm). Gift of the Stapleton Foundation of Latin American Colonial Art, made possible by the Renchard family, 1990.332

CAT. 22 **Juan Correa, Mexican, ca. 1646–1716, *Allegory of the Holy Sacrament***
Mexico, ca. 1690. Oil paint on canvas, 64½ × 41⅝ in. (163.8 × 105.7 cm). Gift of the Collection of Frederick and Jan Mayer, 2015.570

PATER IGNOSCE ILLIS

CAT. 23 **Unknown artist, *Immaculate Conception with Indigenous Donor***
Cuzco, Peru, ca. 1700. Oil paint and gold leaf on canvas, 39¾ × 35¼ in. (101 × 80.5 cm).
Gift of Mr. & Mrs. Frank Jager, 1978.118

CAT. 24 **Unknown artist, *Virgin of Ocotlán***
Mexico, 1789. Oil paint and gold leaf on canvas, 13 × 9¾ in. (33 × 24.8 cm). Gift of the Collection of Frederick and Jan Mayer, 2013.402

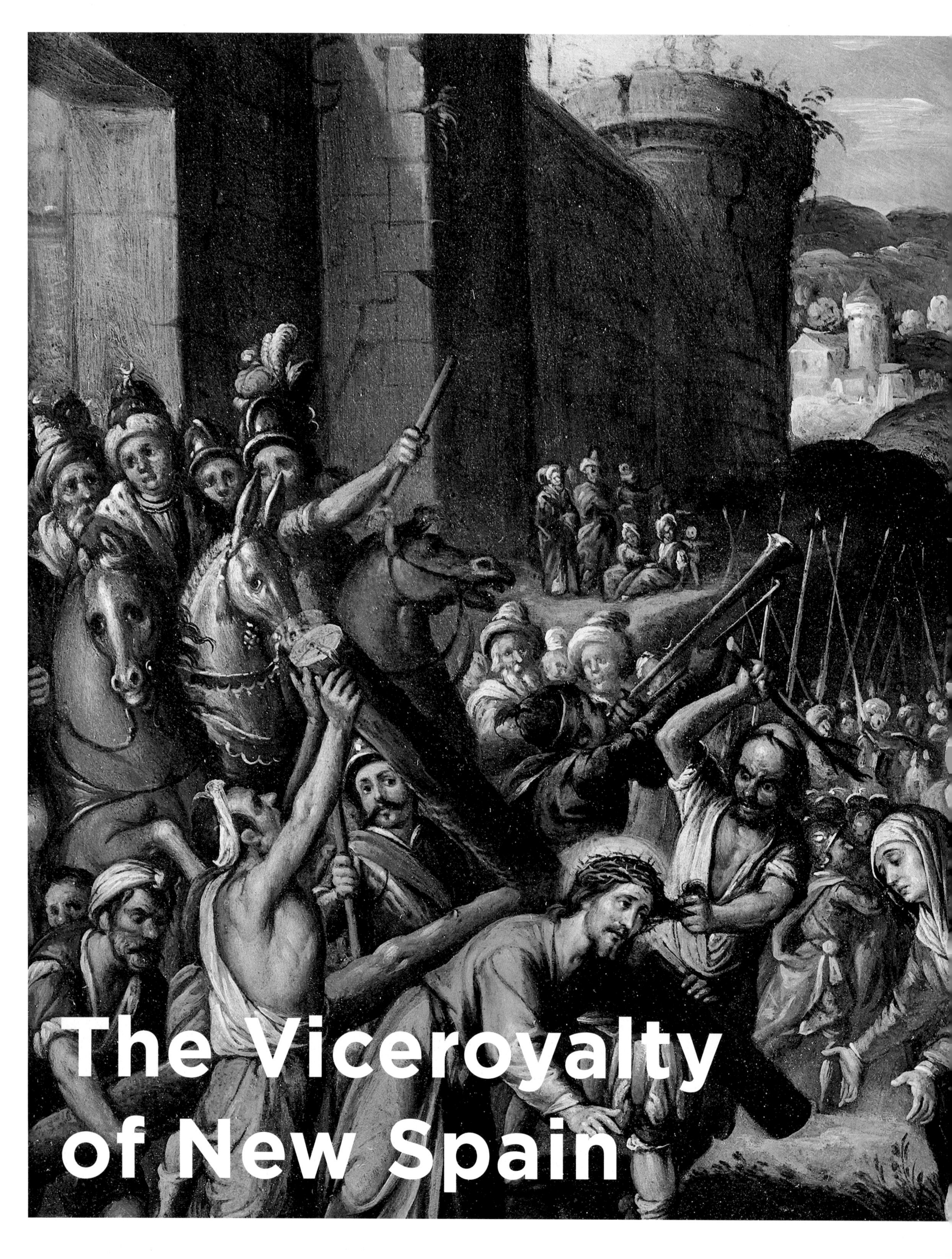

The Viceroyalty of New Spain

S.P.Q.R

Materiality and Innovation in Seventeenth-Century Painting of New Spain

Elsa Arroyo Lemus

The Denver Art Museum's collection offers a heterogenous selection of paintings from New Spain by prominent artists who did not hesitate to display their technical and artistic ability, and by anonymous artists who painted themes that dominated intellectual concerns and their audience's beliefs.

At the dawn of the seventeenth century, painting in New Spain began to define its identity, thanks to the establishment of workshops organized by European or Creole painters who understood the demands of a local elite willing to demonstrate its power.[1] Master craftsmen who specialized in religious imagery began to demand that their work be recognized as an intellectual activity.

The Basque painter Baltasar de Echave Orio (ca. 1558–1623) was crucial in projecting the demands and claims of his guild.[2] He headed one of the most prominent artistic dynasties, was adept at flattering the taste of the clientele of the Viceroyalty of New Spain, and reinvented himself within a vast, booming local market. Additionally, works produced by Indigenous artists circulated in this market to the same extent as artworks that were highly regarded by the intelligentsia and the modern European courts.

The paintings on copper plates by Baltasar de Echave Ibía, *The Crucifixion* and *The Road to Calvary* (CATS. 25 AND 26), exemplify the skill that prevailed in the art market of New Spain, as artists had to compete with the numerous shipments of Flemish works supplied to the Latin American clientele via the port of Seville. Oil painting on copper plates occupied a privileged place within this universe of portable images, due to their resistance to environmental conditions and to the difficulties in transporting the paintings across the Atlantic. Other pieces in the collection such as *The Birth of the Virgin* by Luis Juárez (CAT. 28) and *Saint Anthony and the Christ Child* by Alonso López de Herrera (CAT. 27) attest to artists' preference for using the same formats and materials that serviced a global commercial circuit.[3]

Strategies in the utilization of color were also crucial in the evolution of the painting of the period. In Echave Ibía's work we have identified an important innovation: the use of reddish and dark primers. This change in the palette served to expand the Baroque style.[4] Although the role of color in the development of painting in New Spain is still not well studied, some recurring formulas allow us to interpret the artists' decision making process. When the Sevillian Sebastián de Arteaga painted the *Apparition of Saint Michael on Mount Gargano* (CAT. 29), he chose a varied palette of bright and translucent colors to configure the image of the monumental angel. It is probable that these loose and expressive swaths of fabric of translucent tonalities were created using mixtures of cochineal red, a popular, traditional dyeing material in New Spain employed in the Puebla-Tlaxcala region since before the Spanish conquest.[5] By taking advantage of this "carmine of the Indies,"

1 The arguments for the beginnings of a pictorial tradition in New Spain have been supplied by Rogelio Ruiz Gomar, "La tradición pictórica novohispana en el taller de los Juárez" and Nelly Sigaut, "El concepto de tradición en el análisis de la pintura novohispana. La sacristía de la catedral de México y los conceptos sin ruido," in *Tradición, estilo o escuela en la pintura iberoamericana. Siglos XVI-XVIII*, ed. María Concepción García Sáiz and Juana Gutiérrez Haces (Ciudad de México: Universidad Nacional Autónoma de México/ Instituto de Investigaciones Estéticas/ Fomento Cultural Banamex, 2004), 151–72 and 219–21.

2 Jaime Cuadriello, Elsa Arroyo, et al., *Ojos, alas y patas de la mosca. Visualidad, técnica y materialidad en* El martirio de san Ponciano *de Baltasar de Echave Orio* (Ciudad de México: Universidad Nacional Autónoma de México, 2018), 83–7.

3 I take up the notion of an early globalization from Dennis O. Flynn and Arturo Giráldez, "Los orígenes de la globalización en el siglo XVI," in *Oro y plata en los inicios de la economía global: De las minas a la moneda*, ed. Bernd Hausberger and Antonio Ibarra, (Ciudad de México: El Colegio de México, 2014), 29–76.

4 We have confirmed this during the technical analysis of the *Immaculate Conception* (Museo Nacional de Arte, inv. 3068) and, more recently, of the panel *Pentecost* (Pinacoteca de la Profesa). See Elsa Arroyo, Manuel Espinosa, et al., "Variaciones celestes para pintar el manto de la Virgen," *Anales del Instituto de Investigaciones Estéticas* XXXIV, no. 100 (2012): 85–117 and Miguel Pérez, E. Arroyo-Lemus, et al., "Technical Non-invasive Study of the Novo-Hispanic Painting *The Pentecost* by Baltasar de Echave Orio by

CAT. 25 **Baltasar de Echave Ibía, Mexican, 1585–1650, *The Crucifixion***
Mexico, 1637. Oil paint on copper, 16½ × 16½ in. (41.9 × 41.9 cm).
Gift of the Collection of Frederick and Jan Mayer, 2013.397

an expensive material with enormous visual qualities, Arteaga celebrated the inscribing of his production in a local route of circulation of images, aware of his distance from European models, and was able to take advantage of the viceroyalty's economic development, already apparent in the production of raw materials "from the earth."[6]

It is also in the works of the Sevillian master that we notice the practice of leaving the outlines free and unpainted, a way of separating the figures from the backgrounds.[7] This technique was shared by contemporary artists such as Diego de Borgraf, as seen in his *Saint Catherine of Alexandria* (CAT. 30). Creating paintings with these free areas became a leitmotif in subsequent painting styles.

Yet the most significant approach in relation to pictorial strategies and color effects during this period is undoubtedly manifested in the oeuvre of Cristóbal de Villalpando (ca. 1649–1714), one of the most prestigious artists in New Spain.[8] His ingenuity

CAT. 26 **Baltasar de Echave Ibía, Mexican, 1585–1650, *The Road to Calvary***
Mexico, 1638. Oil paint on copper, 16⅜ × 16⅜ in (41.6 × 41.6 cm).
Gift of the Collection of Frederick and Jan Mayer, 2013.398

Spectroscopic Techniques and Hyperspectral Imaging: In Quest for the Painter's Hand," *Spectrochimica Acta Part A: Molecular and Biomolecular Spectroscopy* 250 (2021): 1–16.

5 Baltazar Brito Guadarrama, "La grana en Hujotzingo. Lugar del pequeño huejote," in *Rojo Mexicano. La grana cochinilla en el arte,* ed. Georges Roque (Ciudad de México: Instituto Nacional de Bellas Artes/ Museo del Palacio de Bellas Artes, 2017), 74–91.

6 Arteaga intentionally used cochineal lake in works such as *Virgin with Child* and *Marriage of Mary,* which belongs to the collection of the Museo Nacional de Arte de México. Elsa Arroyo Lemus, Manuel Espinosa Pesqueira, and Witold Nowik, "Paños labrados de carmín en la pintura novohispana," in *Rojo Mexicano,* 158–77.

7 For an introduction to the visual effects of the artist see Elsa Arroyo, "Sebastián de Arteaga y la construcción de un lenguaje pictórico en contexto." https://www.sebastiandearteaga.esteticas.unam.mx/, accessed April 22, 2022.

8 Juana Gutiérrez Haces, Pedro Ángeles Jiménez, et al., *Cristóbal de Villalpando ca. 1649-1714. Catálogo razonado* (Ciudad de México: Fomento Cultural Banamex/ Instituto de Investigaciones Estéticas, UNAM, 1997).

and modes of painting, in which the qualities of transparency and opacity converge, distinguish his work from others. Villalpando used a palette rich in tonalities, composed of raw or minimally processed materials, such as indigo, charcoal, and mineral pigments, as well as organic dyes. Similarly, minerals and other pigments derived from chemical synthesis are present in his paintings: azurite, malachite, gypsum, enamel blue, vermilion, verdigris, and those obtained from the oxidation of lead.[9]

In *Joseph Claims Benjamin as His Slave* (CAT. 31), Villalpando incorporates several simultaneous actions. One of them, the surprised gesture of a figure looking through his glasses in the background, acts as an invitation to discover the forms constructed by superimpositions of thin, fluid layers of paint. Shifting shimmers and golden glints highlight the folds of the textiles, lending this devotional scene a luxurious and extravagant character. This peculiarly fast and effective system with which Villalpando vaunts his coloration skill becomes a sort of trademark, especially in the last phase of his artistic career. In my opinion, it becomes his public defense of a color theory based on light variations and technical mastery.

If Villalpando's representational strategies constitute a recognizable code, it is then necessary to review some of the works attributed to his brush. In particular, the *Virgin of Valvanera* (CAT. 32) invites us to begin an open discussion about the artistic environment and modes of painting during the 1680s in New Spain. This work reveals a different logic in the use of color and its visual effects, distinguishing it from the Villalpando's masterful color work. Here, the artist seems to repeat formal conventions found in the work of the same subject painted by multiracial artist Juan Correa, although the former is loaded with iconographic details, rendered with greater skill, care, and precision (FIG. 1). This painting, then, is likely by Correa or his workshop and not by the hand of Villalpando.

The Denver Art Museum's collection brings together diverse examples of the rich artistic heritage of New Spain, allowing us to disentangle

CAT. 27 **Attributed to Alonso López de Herrera, Spanish, ca. 1580–1675, active in Mexico, *Saint Anthony and the Christ Child***
Mexico, ca. 1640. Oil paint on copper, 22¼ × 16 in. (56.5 × 40.6 cm). Gift of the Collection of Frederick and Jan Mayer, 2014.213

enigmatic invention from the expressive and semantic role played by art's materiality and to expand the geographic and cultural borders of formulas that were once conceived only as practices transplanted from the Old World.

9 In recent years, the specialized bibliography on Villalpando's technique has notably increased: Mari Carmen Casas, "Técnica pictórica utilizada por Cristóbal de Villalpando en la cúpula de la Capilla de los Reyes," in *La catedral de Puebla en el arte y en la historia*, ed. Montserrat Galí Boadella (Puebla: Secretaría de Cultura, 1999), 255–61; Elsa Arroyo, "Transparencias y fantasmagorías: La técnica de Cristóbal de Villalpando en *La Transfiguración*," appendix to the exhibition catalog *Cristóbal de Villalpando, pintor mexicano del Barroco* (Ciudad de México: Fomento Cultural Banamex, 2017), 1–14; Dorothy Mahon, Silvia A. Centeno, et al., "Cristóbal de Villalpando's *Adoration of the Magi:* A Discussion of Artist Technique," *Latin American and Latinx Visual Culture* 1, no. 2 (2019): 113–21; Mirta Insaurralde Caballero and María Castañeda-Delgado, "At the Core of the Workshop: Novel Aspects of the Use of Blue Smalt in Two Paintings by Cristóbal de Villalpando," *Arts* 10, no. 25 (2021): 1–18.

CAT. 28 **Luis Juárez, Mexican, ca. 1585–1639,**
Birth of the Virgin
Mexico, ca. 1620. Oil paint on copper,
39 × 32½ in. (99.1 × 82.6 cm). Gift of the
Collection of Frederick and Jan Mayer, 2011.425

CAT. 29 **Sebastián López de Arteaga, Spanish,**
1610–1652, active in Mexico, *Apparition of Saint*
Michael on Mount Gargano
Mexico, ca. 1650. Oil paint on canvas, 75 × 61 in.
(190.5 × 154.9 cm). Gift of Frank Barrows Freyer Collection
by exchange and gift of Frederick and Jan Mayer, 1994.27

CAT. 30 **Diego de Borgraf, Flemish, 1618–1686, active in Mexico, *Saint Catherine of Alexandria***
Mexico, 1656. Oil paint on canvas, 65¾ × 45¾ in. (167 × 116.2 cm). Gift of the Collection of Frederick and Jan Mayer, 2011.426

CAT. 31 **Cristóbal de Villalpando Mexican, ca. 1649–1714, *Joseph Claims Benjamin as His Slave***
Mexico, 1700–14. Oil paint on canvas, 59⅞ in. × 6 ft. 10⅝ in. (152.1 × 209.9 cm). Gift of the Collection of Frederick and Jan Mayer, 2009.761

Virgen el Robleestays
fuente pura
za gracia ydulc

CAT. 32 **Attributed to Juan Correa and workshop Mexican, ca. 1646–1716, *Virgin of Valvanera***
Mexico, ca. 1710. Oil paint on canvas, 6 ft. 7½ in. × 57⅝ in. (201.9 × 146.4 cm). Gift of the Collection of Frederick and Jan Mayer, 2008.832

FIG. 1 Juan Correa (Mexican, ca. 1646–1716), *Virgin of Valvanera*, Mexico, ca. 1665–1700. Oil paint on canvas, Museo Franz Mayer, Mexico City

Innovation, Tradition, and Style in Eighteenth-Century Mexican Painting

Luisa Elena Alcalá

The museum's collection of eighteenth-century Mexican painting has long been recognized for its breadth and quality. It includes works by the most famous artists of the period, as well as some by lesser-known names currently drawing scholarly attention. The collection strikes a balance between paintings made in Mexico City, the capital and dominant artistic center, and those from regional centers in other areas of the viceroyalty. Eighteenth-century colonial painting differed from the previous period. The early decades of the century reveal a conscious desire on the part of the leading painters to shift their palette to lighter tonalities, study anatomical drawing, follow academic ideals, explore the narrative potential of gestures and expressions, and respond to models from Italy and France impregnated with Baroque classicism.

Juan Rodríguez Juárez paved the way for these transformations through his superior talent. His lucid portrait of the French Jesuit Saint John Francis Regis (CAT. 33) exemplifies his skill in a genre in which portraiture and religious painting converge.[1] Juárez models the figure with his trademark elegance, adding a subtle glow about the head to signal his status. In contrast to the crucifix and lilies—generic attributes—the wheat and the mound of grain on the table allude to a miracle during the famine of 1638 in Le Puy, France: St. Regis had organized a beneficiary granary, and when it was depleted, it replenished itself miraculously.[2]

The modeling of the figure in this work reflects Juárez's leadership in the informal academy of painting created in Mexico in the 1720s. Little is known about it, but painters gathered to practice drawing the human figure and correct each other's work. The artistic effects of this academy are reflected in numerous paintings of narrative themes which include multiple figures, complicated poses, or else require the presence of a nude, such as in Christ's Passion.[3] An illuminating example is Juan Patricio Morlete y Ruiz's *Lamentation Over the Dead Christ* (CAT. 37). The way he stretched Christ's body before the viewer, parallel to the picture plane, invites contemplation while also displaying the artist's signature use of blues and whites. Against the nocturnal sky, intricate folds of white fabric lead the eye from the lower right corner, across Christ's body, into the Virgin's dress, and finally upward to the Cross. Poignant and delicately painted, Morlete's painting simultaneously inspires devotional prayer and displays his skill, also evident in the intense treatment of the isolated shiny objects in the foreground.[4]

Although religious themes from the New Testament and the lives of Christ and the Virgin dominate pictorial production in the Hispanic world, the Old Testament captured the imagination and offered opportunities to depict exotic places and fantastical stories. An example is Antonio Enríquez's *King Solomon and the Queen of Sheba* (SEE RIVAS PÉREZ, CAT. 16) with its throne lined with gilded lions, camels parading through

1 The specific iconography of this work suggests that Rodríguez Juárez must have played an important role in developing the saint's iconography in the viceroyalty. News of his beatification in 1716 traveled quickly from Rome to America, and by 1722 several altarpieces had been dedicated to him in Jesuit churches in Mexico City. See Luisa Elena Alcalá, "El Espejo pintado: retórica y práctica en el mundo hispánico," in *La mirada extravagante. Arte, ciencia y religión en la Edad Moderna. Homenaje a Fernando Marías*, eds. María Cruz de Carlos, Felipe Pereda, and José Riello (Madrid: Marcial Pons, 2020), 542, 551–52.

2 Beyond didactic intent, this attribute may have resonated with Mexico City's inhabitants given their own grain and maize supply problems as well as epidemics during the 1720s and 1730s. See América Molina del Villar, *Por voluntad divina: escasez, epidemias y otras calamidades en la Ciudad de México, 1700-1762* (Mexico City: Centro de Investigaciones y Estudios Superiores en Antropología Social, 1996), 129–36.

3 For an introduction to the leading artists and the development of style in this period, see, among others: Rogelio Ruiz Gomar, "Unique Expressions: Painting in New Spain," in *Painting a New World: Mexican Art and Life, 1521-1821*, ed. Donna Pierce, Rogelio Ruiz Gomar, and Clara Bargellinie (Denver: Denver Art Museum, 2004), especially 69–75; Paula Mues Orts, "Illustrious Painting and Modern Brushes," in *Painted in Mexico, 1700–1790: Pinxit Mexici*, ed. Ilona Katzew (Los Angeles and Mexico City: Los Angeles County Museum of Art and Fomento Cultural Banamex A.C., 2017), 52–75, as well as the catalog entry, 259–60; and Ilona Katzew, "Valiant

CAT. 33 **Juan Rodríguez Juárez**
Mexican, 1675–1728, *Saint John Francis Regis*
Mexico, ca. 1716. Oil paint on canvas, framed 42¼ × 31½ in. (107.3 × 80 cm). Gift of the Collection of Frederick and Jan Mayer, 2013.383

streets, and plaza with obelisk.[5] Enríquez's surviving works suggest that he made a name for himself on similar ambitious compositions populated with vivid crowds and distant vistas, and even branched out into mythological painting, a rarity for these artists but one also represented in the collection.[6]

Enríquez is one of several painters in the museum—like Pedro Noriega in Querétaro and Miguel Jerónimo Zendejas in Puebla—to have worked in a regional center, in his case in Guadalajara.[7] Capital of the wealthy region of Nueva Galicia, Guadalajara flourished in the eighteenth century. Artists born in the 1600s, such as Francisco de León, found a growing market there.[8] His *Birth of the Virgin* (CAT. 36), bright in color as was typical of this artist, is stylistically reminiscent of the late seventeenth century, although the dazzling curtains are also consonant with the dominant taste of the early 1700s, when ornament was much appreciated in the arts. Miguel Cabrera's version of the same theme, painted decades later (CAT. 38), maintains the reds while introducing a classic, muted tonal combination more typical of this period in the pink and light blue garments of the servant woman on the lower left. In addition, Cabrera emphasizes the role of St. Joachim following the rise of the cult of the extended Holy Family.[9]

The quieter tonalities introduced in Cabrera's work became the norm by the 1780s and 1790s. A number of paintings in the collection attest to this transformation, which is often associated with the founding of the Royal

Styles: New Spanish Painting, 1700-1785," in *Painting in Latin America, 1550-1820*, ed. Luisa Elena Alcalá and Jonathan Brown (New Haven: Yale University Press, 2014), 149–203.

4 Such exercises in still life painting are also found in other works by Morlete, such as *Virgin of Sorrows* (ca. 1760) at the Convent of Nuestra Señora del Carmen del Santo Desierto, Tenancingo, Mexico), analyzed in Katzew, *Painted in Mexico*, 261–63.

5 Antonio Enríquez's signature and the 1732 date on this canvas were recently uncovered, bringing this work into the fold of the growing number of paintings known by this master. The

Academy of San Carlos in 1781–84 and the arrival of neoclassical taste. These changes are evident in the sober and soft brush of Juan Nepomuceno Sáenz's *Coronation of the Virgin* (CAT. 34) and in the restrained interpretation of the *Martyrdom of Saint Agatha* (CAT. 35) by José Guerrero. The background architecture in the latter is typical of many paintings of this period, although here it does more than simply anchor the figurative scene. The unusual detail on the wall behind the saint offers a symbolic foil for the martyrdom; the stone peels away to reveal red bricks, a second skin that echoes her bleeding body.

While the official academy attempted to control artistic education—and through it form and style—the earlier tradition continued to thrive thanks to consumer demand.[10] For example, Sáenz's painting depicts the Trinity in anthropomorphic guise, which was the favored interpretation in New Spain starting in the earlier part of the century. Even though it was bitterly critiqued in the Fourth Mexican Provincial Council of 1771, the iconography clearly persisted.[11] Similarly, densely symbolic images of the Good Shepherd reclining in a fanciful, allegorized garden of divine love, which were displayed in New Spanish convents for women since the 1740s, continued to be produced much later, such as this version by Andrés López (CAT. 39).

Some of these nuns also adorned their habits on special occasions with large painted badges, of which the museum has a rich collection (CAT. 40). Local cults, such as that of the Virgin of Guadalupe in Tepeyac, seen in the badge, flourished. Due to their popularity, images of the Virgin of Guadalupe became a staple of any given artist's output. While representations of cult images were supposedly meant to be a faithful copy of a miracle-working original to keep viceregal customers safe and inspire devotion, local taste was sophisticated, and painters lavished attention on the adornments surrounding the images, as is seen in the altar table presentation of the *Christ of Ixmiquilpan* by José de Ibarra (CAT. 41).

The eighteenth century was a defining period for local painting traditions, and Mexican painting overall

composition is based on an engraving by Matthäeus Merian I (1593–1650), which was reprinted and reworked in many later prints, extending into the eighteenth century. The print is illustrated in Almerindo Ojeda, Project on the Engraved Sources of Spanish Colonial Art (PESSCA), 2623B, accessed October 4, 2021, https://colonialart.org/artworks/2623b.

6 The mythological works are analyzed by Clara Bargellini and illustrated in Pierce, et al., *Painting a New World*, 203–5.

7 Enríquez worked in Guadalajara at least between 1747 and 1760: Alena Robin, "Antonio Enríquez, Felipe Pastor y san Ángel predicando: un cuadro desconocido en la colección del Museo Regional de Guadalajara," *Anales del Instituto de Investigaciones Estéticas* XLII, no. 17 (2020): 259–87. Some of the regional artists traveled to Mexico City and trained there before returning to their places of origin.

8 His connection to Guadalajara was proposed in the earlier historiography by Leopoldo I. Orendáin, "Francisco de León, pintor del siglo XVII," *Anales del Instituto de Investigaciones Estéticas* V, no. 17 (1949): 17–21.

9 See Gomar, catalog entry in Pierce, et al., *Painting a New World*, 212–15. The

CAT. 34 **Juan Nepomuceno de Sáenz Mexican, active late 1700s–early 1800s, *Coronation of the Virgin***
Mexico, ca. 1790. Oil paint on copper, 29¼ × 22½ in. (74.3 × 57.2 cm). Gift of the Collection of Frederick and Jan Mayer, 2013.325

CAT. 35 **José Guerrero, Mexican, active 1787–1803, *Martyrdom of Saint Agatha***
Mexico, ca. 1790. Oil paint on copper, 18¼ × 13¾ in. (46.4 × 34.9 cm). Gift of Valery Taylor and David Brown in honor of Jan and Frederick R. Mayer, 2000.218

CAT. 36 **Francisco de León, Mexican, active 1690–1730, *Birth of the Virgin***
Mexico, 1704. Oil paint on canvas, 80 × 47 in. (203.2 × 119.4 cm). Gift of the Collection of Frederick and Jan Mayer, 2015.556

acquired a stronger individualized character. Nowhere is this character more evident than in the great numbers of *casta* (caste) paintings that were produced throughout the 1700s. This new genre, initiated by Juan Rodríguez Juárez, was made up of series of paintings representing multiracial family units, identified through inscriptions (CAT. 42). The museum is particularly rich in casta paintings, holding the only complete set in the United States, which is signed by the Spanish painter Francisco Clapera (CAT. 43). Through this series, as well as individual works, including the recently cleaned painting attributed to José de Alcíbar (CAT. 44), one can follow the complex local view on racial mixing. At the same time, one can learn about Mexican material culture and its particular mix of Indigenous, Spanish, Asian, and African elements.[12] For his part, Rodríguez Juárez was sensitive to the rising pride in local identity, and he exploited the power of dress, specifically Mexican dress, early on, and beyond his casta paintings. This is evident in the way he labors over the embroidered *huipil* of the donor portrait in his famous *St. Rose of Lima* (SEE RIVAS PÉREZ, CAT. 19), one of the masterpieces in the collection.

Overall, Mexican painting in the eighteenth century thrived and demonstrated a tremendous capacity to innovate new subject matter, techniques, formats, and local styles and evolved with commercial interests, patron demands, and professional ambitions.

painting is part of a set in the Museo de América, Madrid, analyzed by Ana Zabía de la Mata, "La obra de Miguel Cabrera en España. La serie de la Vida de la Virgen del Museo de América de Madrid," in *Identidades y redes culturales. V Congreso internacional de Barroco iberoamericano* (Granada: Universidad de Granada, 2021), 353–64.

10 Jaime Cuadriello, "The Paintings Department of the Royal Academy of San Carlos: Origins, Development and Epiloque," in Alcalá and Brown, *Painting in Latin America*, 205–42.

11 On the iconography of the Trinity in New Spain, see María del Consuelo Maquivar, *De lo permitido a lo prohibido: iconografía de la Santísima Trinidad en Nueva España* (Mexico City: Instituto Nacional de Antropología e Historia, 2006); and, more recently, Cuadriello, catalog entry in Katzew, *Painted in Mexico*, 411–12.

12 For more on the role of costume, as well as the presence of chocolate in this painting, see Katzew's catalog entry in Pierce, et al., *Painting a New World*, 245. And for casta painting in general, see Ilona Katzew, *Casta Painting* (New Haven: Yale University Press, 2004).

CAT. 37 **Juan Patricio Morlete y Ruiz**
Mexican, 1715–1772, *Lamentation Over the Dead Christ*
Mexico, ca. 1760. Oil paint on copper, 21 × 16 in.
(53.3 × 40.6 cm). Gift of the Collection of Frederick
and Jan Mayer, 2013.305

CAT. 38 **Miguel Cabrera, Mexican,**
1695–1768, *Birth of the Virgin*
Mexico, 1751. Oil paint on canvas,
72⅜ × 52¾ in. (183.9 × 134 cm).
Gift of the Collection of Frederick
and Jan Mayer, 2014.210

EGO CLAMAVI, QUONIAM EXAUDISTI ME DEUS. Pſm. 41
TOTA PULCHRA ES MARIA. Cant. C. 4
Mich.l Cabrera pinxit Mexici anno 1751.

CAT. 39 **Andrés López, Mexican, 1727–1807,**
Divine Spouse
Mexico, ca. 1780. Oil paint on canvas,
18¼ × 23½ in. (46.4 × 59.7 cm). Gift of
the Collection of Frederick and Jan Mayer, 2013.385

CAT. 40 **Francisco Martínez**
Mexican, active 1717–1758, *Virgin of Guadalupe with Saints (nun's badge)*
Mexico, 1700s. Oil and gold leaf on copper with glass and tortoise shell frame, 1 × 8⅜ in. dia. (2.5 × 21.3 cm dia.). Gift of the Collection of Frederick and Jan Mayer, 2013.401

INRI
V.ro R.to del SXPTO. de Ixmiquilpan, colocado por el Ill.mo S.r Arcobiſpo D.n Juan dela Serna,
en el Convento antiguo de Carmelitas deſcalſas de S.r S.n Joſeph, de Mexico.
ſerenobo dicha Sagrada Imagen el ano de 1621. y ſe hizo esta copia el de 1731.
Joſephus ab Ibarra faciat

CAT. 41 **José de Ibarra, Mexican, 1685–1756,** ***Christ of Ixmiquilpan (Christ of the Chapel of Saint Teresa)***
Mexico, 1731. Oil paint on canvas, 7 ft. 6½ in. × 56¼ in. (229.9 × 142.7 cm). Gift of the Collection of Jan and Frederick Mayer, 2008.829

CAT. 42 **Juan Rodríguez Juárez Mexican, 1675–1728,** ***Otomi Indians on the Way to the Fair***
Mexico, ca. 1725. Oil paint on canvas, 32½ × 41 in. (82.6 × 104.1 cm). Gift of the Collection of Frederick and Jan Mayer, 2013.300

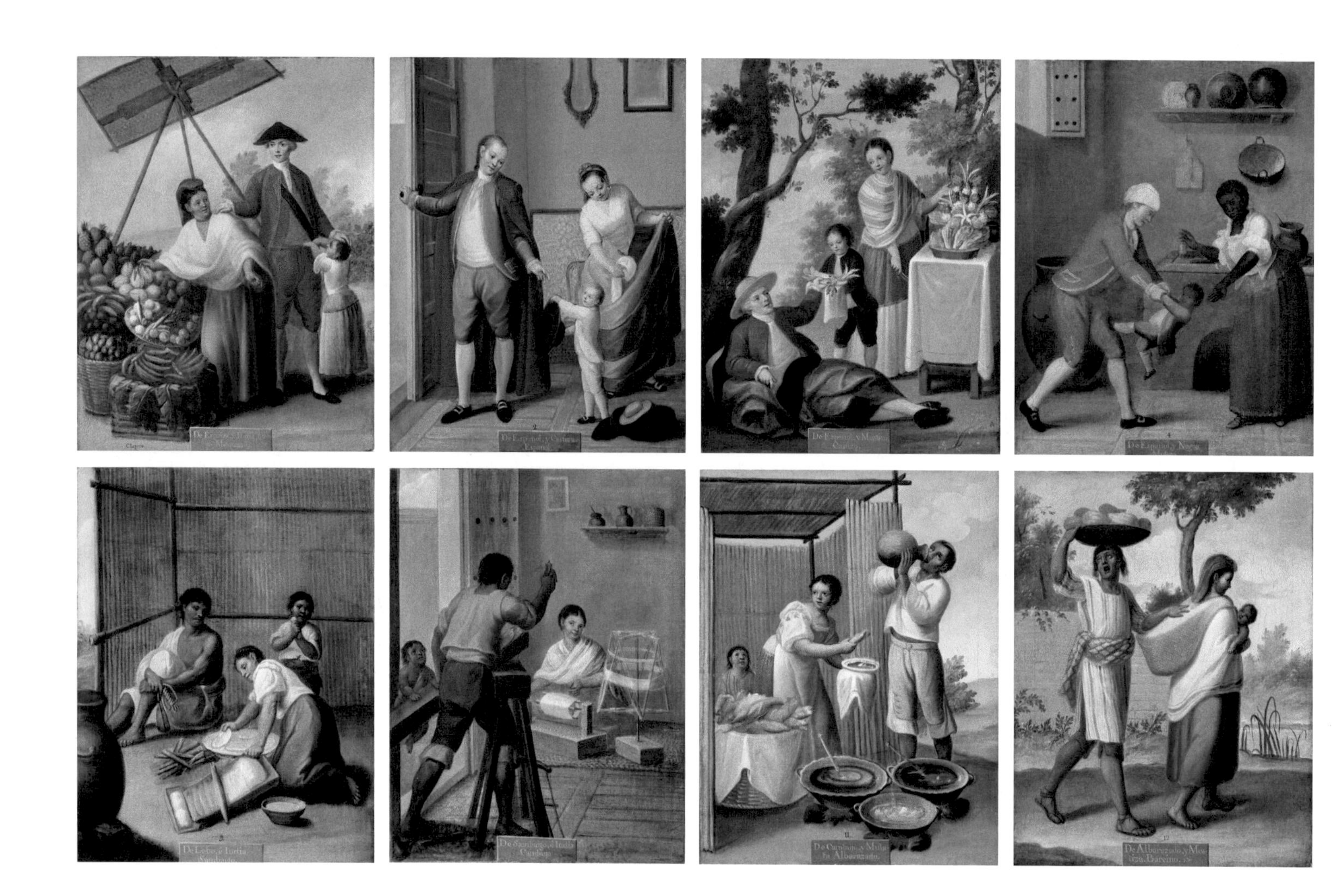

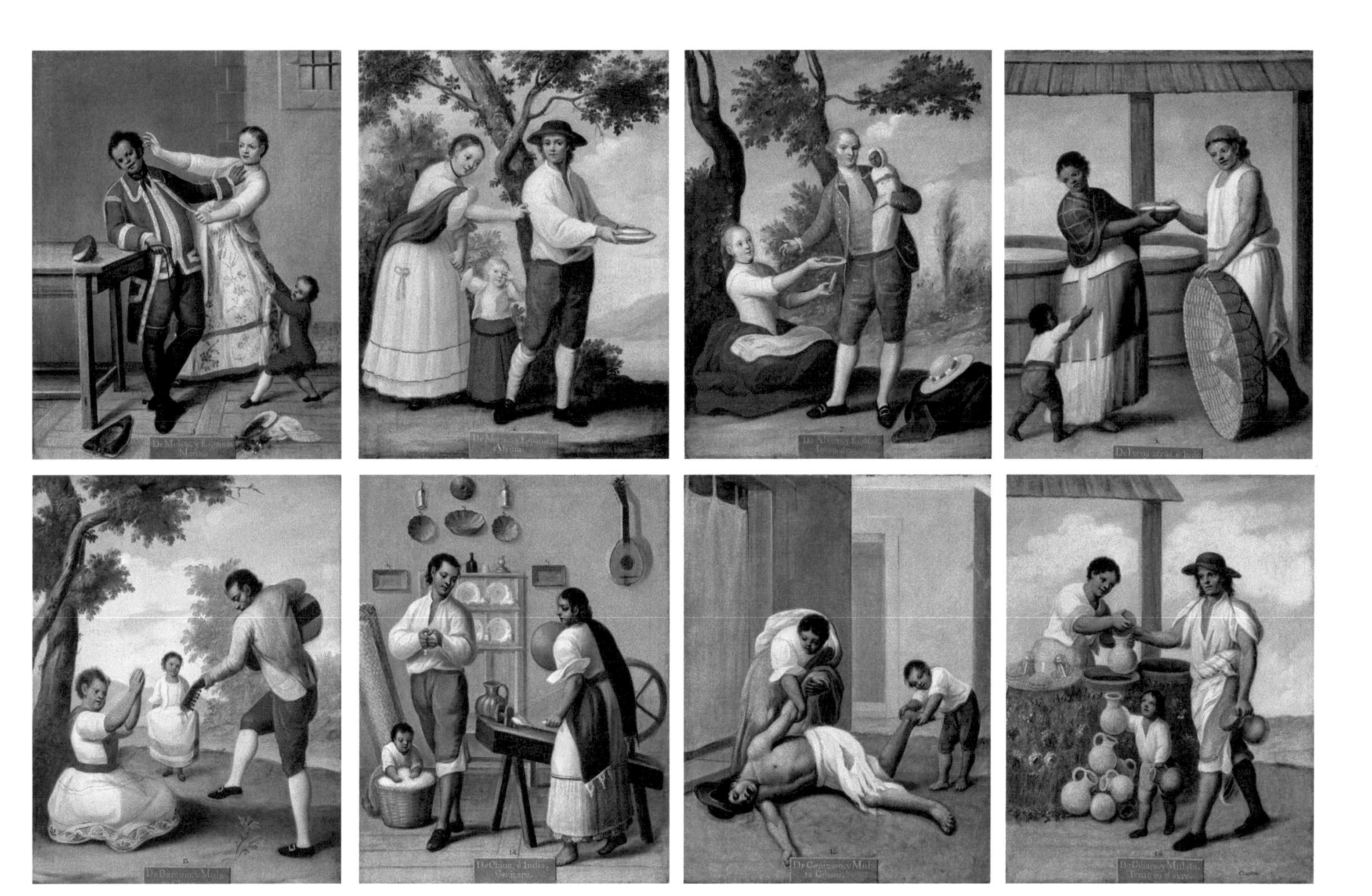

CAT. 43 **Francisco Clapera, Spanish, 1746–1810, active in Peru and Mexico, *Set of Casta Paintings***
Mexico, ca. 1775. Oil paint on canvas, each approx. 20⅛ × 15⅝ in. (51.1 × 39.7 cm). Gift of the Collection of Frederick and Jan Mayer, 2011.428.1-16

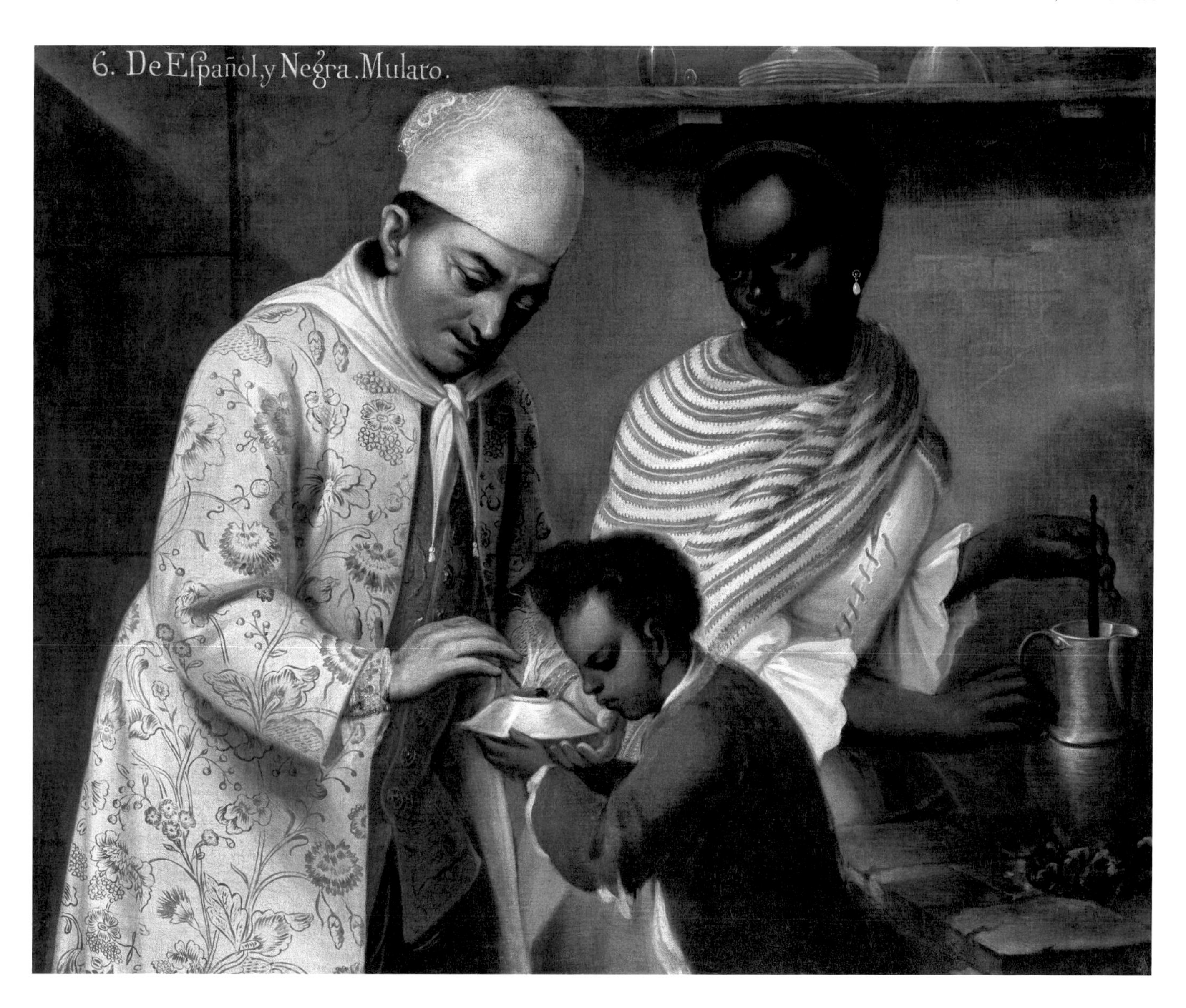

CAT. 44 **Attributed to José de Alcíbar**
Mexican, 1726–1803, *De Español y Negra, Mulato (From Spaniard and Black, Mulatto)*
Mexico, ca. 1760. Oil paint on canvas,
30⅝ × 38¾ in. (77.8 × 98.4 cm). Gift of the Collection
of Frederick and Jan Mayer, 2014.217

Inventing Identity: Portraiture and Society in New Spain

Michael A. Brown

While the soaring architecture, magnificent devotional painting, and—with origins in Indigenous techniques and materials—splendid decorative arts traditions flourished during the sixteenth and seventeenth centuries, portraiture developed fitfully in the early decades of the viceroyalty. It was not until the eighteenth century that this unheralded genre finally emerged in a glorious explosion of color and panache. To some degree, this remarkable transformation reflected changes in Spanish court taste following the monarchy's dynastic changeover in 1700 from the stolid Hapsburgs to the more extravagant Bourbons. More importantly, however, portrait paintings manifested the ascendant identity, individuality, and nascent independence of Mexican society.

In Hapsburg Spain, portraiture—apart from the pioneering outliers Titian (ca. 1488–1576) and Velázquez (1599–1660)—conformed to the impeccable but static court style established by Antonis Mor (1517–1576/77), Alonso Sánchez Coello (ca. 1531–1588), and Sofonisba Anguissola (ca. 1532–1625). It also reflected the sumptuary laws that restricted sartorial ostentation such as excessive jewelry, garish colors, and elaborate lace ruff collars. Established Spanish artists who traveled to New Spain early in the colonial endeavor, such as Baltasar de Echave Orio (ca. 1558–1623) and Alonso López de Herrera (ca. 1580–1675), imported this courtly tradition, especially in the corporate portrait series of statesmen and ecclesiastic authorities that were commissioned for the viceroy's palace, the city council, and cathedral chapter halls. By their very nature, these series, to which each subsequent officeholder would be added in perpetuity, enforced a consistent type of composition and range of symbolic attributes and served the specified political purpose of cementing the legitimacy of the office by showing its unbroken lineage.

Three examples of ecclesiastical portraiture stand out in the Frederick and Jan Mayer Gift to the Denver Art Museum: in chronological order, *Archbishop Fray Felipe Galindo Chávez y Pineda* attributed to Diego de Cuentas (CAT. 45), *Don Francisco José Pérez de Lanciego y Eguilaz* by Juan Rodríguez Juárez (CAT. 46), and *Don Fernando Navas Arnanz* by José de Páez (CAT. 47). The latter, whose nephew is the subject of a rare adolescent portrait also in Denver's collection (CAT. 48), served as chief financial officer of the cathedral of Morelia.[1] The first two works, depicting the archbishops of Guadalajara and Mexico, respectively, closely follow the full-length model initially founded by Echave Orio and López de Herrera for the first series of portraits commissioned for the Metropolitan Cathedral (later abandoned in favor of the extant half-length series that accords with that of the viceroys).[2] However, the portrait of Lanciego features a second figure and was apparently intended for export to the archbishop's family in Navarra, Spain.[3] Multiple likenesses of Lanciego were commissioned for the cathedral and other institutions; taken as a collective body, the portraits reflect the prelate's desire to project his political authority as delegate of Philip V and the monarch's policies in the Americas.

Before about 1700, portraits of lesser nobility were rare, and those of women or the emerging merchant classes even

1 The inscription at lower right notes that he was named to the position of prebendary (canon) of Valladolid (now Morelia) in 1757. The library of legal tomes relates to his academic training while the clock reflects the precision and efficiency with which he carried out his financial duties. The painter of Navas Arnanz's nephew, Fernando Fraile Navas, remains unidentified, although it would have been likely that the family turned once again to Páez or one of his circle for the commission.

2 Michael A. Brown, "La imagen de un imperio: el arte del retrato en España y los virrenatos de Nueva España y Perú," in *Pintura de los Reinos: identidades compartidas en el mundo hispánico*, edited by Juana Gutiérrez Haces, Jonathan Brown, and Cándida Fernández de Calderón (Mexico City: Fomento Cultural Banamex, 2009), 1474.

3 Paula Mues Orts identifies the attendant as José Ansoain y de los Arcos, Lanciego's secretary and liaison with papal authorities in Rome. See Ilona Katzew, ed., *Painted in Mexico, 1700–1790: Pinxit Mexici* (Los Angeles: Los Angeles County Museum of Art; Mexico: Fomento Cultural Banamex, 2017), 348–49. Elsewhere, I have suggested that the second figure is that of Miguel Angel Lanciego y Eguilaz, the archbishop's Jesuit nephew who accompanied him to Mexico and served as his uncle's co-eulogist with Juan Antonio de Fábrega in 1728. See Michael A. Brown, *Portraiture in New Spain, 1600–1800: Painters, Patrons and Politics in Viceregal Mexico* (PhD dissertation, New York University: 2011), 91.

CAT. 45 **Attributed to Diego de Cuentas Mexican, 1654–1744, *Portrait of Archbishop Fray Felipe Galindo Chávez y Pineda***
Mexico, ca. 1700. Oil paint on canvas, 6 ft. 8½ in. × 50½ in. (204.5 × 128.3 cm). Gift of the Collection of Frederick and Jan Mayer, 2015.544

more so. Echave Orio's *Portrait of Doña Inés de Velasco* (ca. 1600, Museo de Arte Nacional, Mexico), a tour-de-force likeness of a female donor in prayer, and the anonymous double portrait of Don Bartholome Andres and Don Agustín Pérez (CAT. 49), who are likewise shown in adoration, are noteworthy exceptions. In the latter's case, it is all the more remarkable in that the donors are Indigenous Tlaxcalan noblemen, one wearing the pre-Hispanic *tilma* (cape) while the other (at right) wears European-style attire, including a lavish gold- or silver-lined coat. Presumably, the sitters' female counterparts would have been similarly attired in the now-lost pendant canvas that would have hung on the right. The donors' decision to represent themselves inhabiting both worlds reflects not a crisis of identity but a powerful indicator of the sitters' status and their social and cultural mobility.

The core of Denver's portrait collection lies in an impressive group of civic—we might call them society—portraits, all made in the second half of the eighteenth century. Of these, five are among the finest examples produced in viceregal New Spain. The first (CAT. 50) depicts a young woman of pre-marriage age, whose identity, like that of the painter, is still unknown, standing by a harpsichord, wearing a sumptuous *bata abierta* (open robe) gown of imported silk (either from China or Valencia). The young woman's social standing and education are indicated by her musical aspirations, as she points to sheet music inscribed with the word *Sonata*. Female musicians and composers were much esteemed at the convents of Mexico, and allusions to the most famous of all sister-composers—Sor Juana Inés de la

CAT. 46 **Juan Rodríguez Juárez**
Mexican, 1675–1728, *Portrait of Don Francisco José Pérez de Lanciego y Eguilaz*
Mexico, 1714. Oil paint on canvas, framed
7 ft. 1¾ in. × 53⅜ × 2¼ in. (217.8 × 135.6 × 5.7 cm),
Gift of the Collection of Frederick and Jan Mayer, 2013.350

Cruz—would not have been lost on contemporary viewers. Perhaps she was destined for the religious life, as was the future Mother Ana Maria of the Precious Blood of Christ, depicted in 1770 on the occasion of taking her vows, crowned with flowers (typically made of fabric) for the ceremony (CAT. 51). The museum recently acquired an exquisite miniature portrait (CAT. 52) in oil on silver plate of a young woman in fine court dress. The artist rendered the silk and gold thread of the sitter's garment, as well as her silver tiara and black lace mantilla, with a mastery and deftness of touch that points to a highly developed yet overlooked tradition of miniature painting in Mexico.[4]

Rivaling the high fashion of the young ladies' lavish costumes is the remarkable 1761 likeness of *Don Francisco de Orense y Moctezuma, Count of Villalobos* (CAT. 53), whose winning personality and assuredness is captured brilliantly by an accomplished painter yet to be identified. In general, sitters assumed a gradually less formal comportment later in the century, which is the case with Juan Nepomuceno de Sáenz's *Portrait of Fernando de Musitu Zalvide*, made in 1795 (CAT. 54). Musitu, who came from a wealthy Basque family, is depicted in the height of Madrid's shabby-chic *majo* fashion, made famous in the depictions of Francisco Goya.[5] Indeed, the painter's connection to Goya was not far removed. Sáenz trained at the Royal Academy of San Carlos with director Rafael Ximeno y Planes, the Valencian artist who, in turn, had studied with Goya's teacher and father-in-law, Francisco Bayeu, at the academy in Madrid.[6] However, the brilliant palette and the sitter's *sprezzatura*, or nonchalance, set

4 See Mari Carmen Espinosa Martín and Soumaya Slim de Romero, *Santuarios de lo íntimo: Retrato en miniatura y relicarios: La colección de Museo Soumaya* (México: Telmex and Museo Soumaya, 2004).
5 See James Middleton, "Reading Dress in New Spanish Portraiture: Clothing the Mexican Elite, circa 1695–1805," in *New England/New Spain: Portraiture in the Colonial Americas 1492–1850: Papers from the 2014 Mayer Center Symposium at the Denver Art Museum*, ed. Donna Pierce (Denver: Mayer Center for Pre-Columbian and Spanish Colonial Art, Denver Art Museum, 2016).
6 Donna Pierce, "Portrait of Fernando de Musitu Zalvide," Denver Art Museum, 2015, https://www.denverartmuseum.org/en/object/2008.27.

the image apart from contemporary trends in Spain and from the stiff and regimented portraiture of earlier decades in Mexico. Independence from Spain—which came in 1821—was just around the corner, and the viewer has the sense that Fernando de Musitu, like many of his compatriots, was ready for it.

CAT. 47 **José de Páez, Mexican, 1720–1790,** ***Portrait of Don Fernando Navas Arnanz***
Mexico, ca. 1758. Oil paint on canvas,
67½ × 46 in. (171.5 × 116.8 cm). Gift of the Collection of Frederick and Jan Mayer, 2013.356

CAT. 48 **Unknown artist, *Portrait of Don Fernando Fraile Navas at Thirteen Years of Age***
Mexico, 1763. Oil paint on canvas, 56½ × 39¼ in. (143.5 × 99.7 cm). Gift of Collection of Frederick and Jan Mayer, 2013.357

CAT. 49 **Unknown artist, *Double Portrait of Donors (Don Bartholomé Andrés and Don Agustín Pérez)***
Tlaxcala, Mexico, late 1600s. Oil paint on canvas, 22¼ × 27½ in. (56.5 × 69.9 cm). Gift of the Collection of Frederick and Jan Mayer, 2014.219

CAT. 50 **Unknown artist,**
Young Woman with a Harpsichord
Mexico, 1735–1750. Oil paint on canvas, framed 72¼ × 50 × 3 in. (183.5 × 129.2 × 7.6 cm). Gift of the Collection of Frederick and Jan Mayer, 2014.209

CAT. 51 **Unknown artist, *Portrait of Mother Ana María of the Precious Blood of Christ***
Mexico, 1770. Oil paint on canvas, 45 × 35 in. (114.3 × 88.9 cm). Gift of the Collection of Frederick and Jan Mayer, 2014.215

CAT. 52 **Unknown artist,**
Portrait of a Lady in Court Dress
Mexico City, Mexico, ca. 1770. Oil paint on silver sheet with gilded silver frame, framed 3½ × 2¾ in. (8.9 × 7 cm). Funds from Carl Patterson in honor of Julie Wilson Frick, 2018.305

CAT. 53 **Unknown artist, *Portrait of Don Francisco de Orense y Moctezuma, Count de Villalobos***
Mexico, ca. 1761. Oil paint on canvas, 74 × 59 in. (188 × 149.9 cm). Gift of the Collection of Frederick and Jan Mayer, 2011.427

CAT. 54 **Juan Nepomuceno de Sáenz, Mexican, active 1768–1818, *Portrait of Don Francisco de Orense y Moctezuma, Count de Villalobos***
Mexico, 1795. Oil paint on canvas, 64¾ × 36¾ in. (164.5 × 93.3 cm). In memory of Frederick Mayer with funds from Lorraine and Harley Higbie, Marilynn and Carl Thoma, Patrick Pierce, Alianza de las Artes Americanas, and Department Acquisition Funds, 2008.27

Divine Mediators in Polychromed Wood: Sculpture in New Spain

Franziska Martha Neff

The varied sculptural production created from the sixteenth to the early nineteenth century in New Spain, a jurisdiction that incorporated present-day Mexico and Guatemala in the Spanish monarchy, is principally of a devotional character. These works privilege the relationship between work and observer more than that of artist and work, are usually unsigned, and emphasize their communicative power and cultic function. For these reasons, and because of the strategies chosen for these purposes, many nineteenth-century intellectuals denied them the category of sculpture, which had long-lasting implications. Nevertheless, they embody multiple discourses and stand as valuable testimonies to various aspects of viceregal life and society.

New Spain inherited from the Iberian Peninsula the tradition of sculpture carved in polychromed wood and characterized by the collaboration between sculptor and gilder,[1] thus leaving the mark of at least two hands on the work—and perhaps more, given the custom of reworking sculptures. During the sixteenth century, the first artists, like many of the sculptures themselves, arrived from Europe, but by 1557 and 1568 ordinances governing painters and sculptors had been approved, instituting guilds that oversaw these professions. Most of the artists in the guilds were Spaniards, but archival sources reveal that multiracial and Indigenous artists also participated in the guild system during the period of the viceroyalty.[2]

The *Saint John Nepomuk* of Guatemalan origin is exquisitely carved and polychromed (CAT. 59). Since the seventeenth century, workshops in the Captaincy General of Guatemala produced sculptures of a characteristic preciosity that combined a delicate round volume with a meticulous polychromy, demonstrating a wide formal repertory and making them successful exports. The patron saint of priests stands in *contrapposto*—made visible by the measured movements of the garments—with his head slightly inclined, contemplatively gazing at a crucifix originally held in his right hand. The use of realistic materials such as the application of fake eyelashes and glass eyes reinforce the detailed depiction of facial features: skin tones of subtle hues, *peleteado*,[3] and finely delineated eyelashes and eyebrows. Pressed brocade[4] evokes the opulent textiles of the epoch, although adapted to visual expression,[5] making use of techniques such as relief, punchwork, sgraffito,[6] and paint applied with the tip of the brush, the latter masterfully demonstrating the delicacy of the translucent lace of the surplice.

The *Crucifix*, belonging to the type of lightweight sculptures (*esculturas ligeras*), encourages contemplation (CAT. 56)[7] and was also destined for export on a large scale. A fusion of European and American sculptural techniques occurred in the early sixteenth century that resulted in works ideal for processions and reenactments during Holy Week. The dead Christ (although with half-open eyes that intensify the impact) exhibits his wounds, stirring and guiding the observer to reflect on the recognition of the sins that gave rise to

1 Although painters were allowed to paint canvases and apply polychromy to wood sculptures, frequently the polychromy was applied by a gilder, a professional who usually belonged to the painters' guild. At the same time, the sculptors' guild also included *talladores* (carvers of ornaments and smaller sculptural works) and *ensambladores* (builders of altarpieces). Often a master practiced various professions in the same guild or in several different ones.

2 The regulations for painters were renewed in 1687 (see Paula Mues Orts, *La libertad del pincel* (Ciudad de México: Universidad Iberoamericana, 2008), 378–92) and for sculptors in 1589 and 1703 (see María del Consuelo Maquívar, *El imaginero novohispano y su obra: Las esculturas de Tepotzotlán*, (Ciudad de México: INAH, 1999), 135–61). Puebla, too, preserves regulations and documents concerning the elections of representatives to the guild. See Franziska Martha Neff, *La Escuela de Cora en Puebla. La transición de la imaginería a la escultura neoclásica* (PhD diss., Universidad Nacional Autónoma de México, 2013).

3 Small hairs painted in areas of transition to carved hair.

4 Imitation of textiles in polychromy with the aid of metal foil. Although gold leaf is most frequent in sculpture in New Spain, silver foil was also employed, but it required being covered with a translucent coat of colored varnish (*corladura*) to prevent oxidation, thus creating an iridescent effect.

5 Because of the lack of signatures on sculptures, imitated textiles provide help in dating the polychromy. On the relationship between polychrome sculpture and textiles see Pablo F. Amador Marrero and Patricia Díaz Cayeros, *El tejido polícromo. La escultura*

the depicted suffering. The blood, presented in a dramatic manner, as well as the traces of blows and ropes on the body, including the back, emphasize the Passion. The reduced volume of the hair and loincloth indicate that the figure was adorned with a wig, a crown of thorns, and a garment of real cloth, all for the purpose of greater naturalism.

It was not only the exchanges between the different regions of the viceroyalties and with Europe that determined the new sculptural environment but also the products arriving on the Manila galleon that inspired local artistic production. This confluence of styles and traditions can be seen in a double-sided sculpture of *St. Michael, the Virgin, and Child, and Saints Dominic and John the Baptist*, made of alabaster in the style of Asian ivories (CAT. 57). While the figures have Asian features and some details recall Indian techniques, the iconography is based on the Christian repertoire forged in Europe. It is one of the few examples of a signed sculpture, although the words "Diego Reinoso inbentor" (Diego Reinoso inventor) on its base leave ambiguity as to whether he conceived the composition or actually did the carving.[8]

The majority of sculptures were situated in altarpieces and, therefore, within a contextual iconographic discourse. The altarpieces of the sixteenth century are characterized by a relief that runs through the center of the panel, as seen in the *Christ Washing the Feet of the Apostles* (CAT. 58), which belonged to a Passion or Eucharistic altarpiece.[9] The circular composition takes advantage of the entire space and integrates the position of the observer, drawing the gaze toward Jesus and the apostle whose feet he will wash. The implied dialogue suggests that this is Saint Peter at the moment of his denial, which explains the astonishment of the rest of the apostles, who communicate with their looks and gestures. Saint John, assisting with the jug, adds an additional narrative element.

Similarly, the *Saint Francis of Assisi* (CAT. 55), of good quality carving and press brocade, was part of an altarpiece, which emphasized the identity and mission of the religious orders, specifically the Franciscans.[10] Francis can be identified by the stigmata, the skull, and a crucifix (now lost), as well as by the characteristic facial features and beard. The sculptor's nods to verisimilitude include the mouth slightly open to reveal

CAT. 55 **Unknown artist, *Saint Francis of Assisi***
Mexico, ca. 1650. Painted and gilded wood, 47 × 22 × 15 in. (119.4 × 55.9 × 38.1 cm). Bequest of Robert. J. Stroessner, 1992.27

CAT. 56 **Unknown artist, *Crucifix***
Guanajuato, Mexico, 1700s. Tzompantle wood, corn paste, gesso, fabric, and oil paint, 72 × 47 in. (182.9 × 119.4 cm). Museum exchange, 1968.192

novohispana y su vestimenta (Ciudad de México: IIE-UNAM, 2013) and Pablo F. Amador Marrero, "A propósito de los estofados novohispanos del siglo XVIII," lecture held at the Seminario de Escultura Virreinal, August 3, 2020, https://www.youtube.com/watch?v=Ax-ZiAqexX7Q.

6 A paint layer was applied over the gilding that was later scratched off in certain areas to reveal the gilding, producing different effects.

7 Formerly known as *esculturas en caña de maíz* (corn-stem paste sculptures), nowadays the more generic name is preferred on account of the variety of materials employed (paper, celerin wood, corn-stem paste, etc.).

8 A similar piece exists signed by the same person, "Diego Reinoso Inventor

CAT. 57 **Diego de Reinoso**
Mexican, active late 1600s,
Double-Sided Carving of Saint Michael and the Virgin and Child with Saints Dominic and John the Baptist
Mexico, ca. 1696. Alabaster,
7 × 3⅜ × 3⅜ in. (17.8 × 8.6 × 8.6 cm).
Gift of Robert J. Stroessner, 1991.1150

the tongue, the big toe of the right foot protruding from the base, and the position of the hood to reveal the monk's tonsure. The figure wears a Franciscan habit made from fragments and girded with a four-knotted cord, but the delicate sgraffito enhances and embellishes the cloth.[11]

The press brocade also plays an important role in the life-size sculpture of *Saint Ferdinand* (CAT. 60), designated as a king by the imperial orb, the sword, and crown (the latter two now lost). The press brocade—thanks to the punch gilding, sgraffito, and brush drawing—highlights the different textures of the textiles, metals, and jewels worn by the figure. The naturalism of the flowers and the shell-like motifs of the press brocade refer to contemporary Rococo textiles, a departure from the usual depiction of this thirteenth-century figure.[12] The sculpture belonged to an altarpiece of kings, a sign of the royal patronage that the Spanish monarch exercised over the Latin American Church.[13]

Altarpieces continued to exist in nineteenth-century Mexico, although with a more sober aesthetic noticeable beginning in the mid-eighteenth century that was reinforced by the creation of the San Carlos Academy, which also modified the teaching and practice of the trade. Within this context, the door of a tabernacle (CAT. 61) illuminates the importance of prints as a visual source since it is based on an 1868 painting by Franz Ittenbach and engraved by Joseph Kohlschein (FIG. 1).[14] Both artists belonged to the Nazarenes, a movement of German Romanticism that had repercussions in Mexico. The lamb portrayed among the Holy Family alludes to the task of salvation that awaits the child Jesus as well as the sacred eucharist that was once kept in the tabernacle behind this door.

Sculptures also played a leading role in the domestic sphere, as inventories, wills, and dowry letters mention small-format objects, occasionally with valuable materials such as alabaster, ivory, ebony, precious metals, and stones, as well as luxurious textiles. Among these objects is an ingenious figure of *St. Michael* (CAT. 62) sculpted in *tecali*, the alabaster of Puebla. The sculptor intertwined wings, cloths, sword, feathers, and the dragon in such a way as to achieve a dynamic unity whose center is St. Michael, posing elegantly, almost as if dancing. The purple polychrome appears to be cochineal, which would increase the value of the object. This victorious warrior was a very popular patron saint, perhaps here for an ecclesiastical authority whose circular shield can be seen on the base.

Domestic altarpieces also provided a suitable setting for this type of sculpture. This anonymous altarpiece (CAT. 63) has Solomonic columns[15] with helicoidal shafts covered with gilded vines. The colorful polychromy of the whole harmonizes the gilding, the imitation of floral fabrics, and the different colored marbles. Special care is given to the painted

en México 1696," in the Victoria and Albert Museum, London.

9 Despite missing parts of the wood and polychromy, one can still see the characteristic press brocades of the sixteenth century. Maquívar, *El imaginero novohispano*, 107; Pablo F. Amador Marrero, "En busca de eslabones para el estudio de la policromía en la Nueva España: Tras los pasos de Pedro de Requena y Francisco de Zumaya," lecture held at the Seminario de Escultura Virreinal, YouTube, May 4, 2021, https://www.youtube.com/watch?v=FvuwvW1nI24.

10 It also could have belonged to a Dominican altarpiece, given the legendary brotherhood between the two orders. It was common for the founding saint of one of the orders to have a place in an altarpiece dedicated to the other.

11 Since it is catalogued as originating from the Puebla school, one presumes that it was acquired in that city, one of the centers of sculptural production in the viceroyalty, although the distinctive features of Puebla's sculptural production in the seventeenth century still need definition.

12 The engraving by Claude Audran the Elder (1630), inspired by *Los Santos Reyes y Nobles* (The Sacred Kings and Nobles) by Giovanni Battista Crespi (1587), is regarded as one of the first works to depict the official iconography of Saint Ferdinand, in which he wears armor, a royal ermine cape, and ruff collar. Manuel Jesús Roldán, "Un san Fernando sevillano, a subasta," June 26, 2017. https://sevilla.abc.es/pasionensevilla/noticias-semana-santa-sevilla/sevi-san-fernando-sevillano-subasta-113952-1498429319-201706260021_noticia.html.

13 According to information from the museum, the sculpture is from Querétaro (Denver Art Museum, *Saint Ferdinand*, https://www.denverartmuseum.org/en/object/1956.91a-b, accessed April 22, 2022). Its counterpart, a sculpture of Saint Louis of France, is found in a private collection in Mexico City. This same source indicates it was originally located in the Querétaro cathedral. Querétaro, however, only became the seat of a diocese in 1921, thus when the sculpture was created the city had no cathedral. The present-day cathedral is located in the church of the former Oratorio of Saint Philip Neri, inaugurated in 1805. Since the morphology of the sculpture and its press brocade allude to the middle of the eighteenth century, future research will have to determine if the work did in fact belong to the *Oratorio of Saint Philip Neri*.

14 The engraving by Joseph Kohlschein (1841–1915) was known from the diffusion of religious images in Düsseldorf, Germany. The painting by Franz Ittenbach (1813–1879), *The Holy Family in Egypt*, is currently in the National Gallery in Berlin. I am grateful to Israel Gutiérrez Barrios for informing me of the existence of this engraving.

CAT. 58 **Unknown artist, *Christ Washing the Feet of the Apostles***
Mexico, ca. 1600. Painted and gilded wood, 54 × 30 in. (137.2 × 76.2 cm). Gift of Mr. And Mrs. Morris A. Long, 1986.603

CAT. 59 **Unknown artist,**
Saint John Nepomuk
Guatemala, mid-1700s. Painted and gilded wood,
35⅜ × 14⅜ × 11¾ in. (89.9 × 36.5 × 29.8 cm). Gift of the collection of Jan and Frederick Mayer, 2008.831A

curtain of the niche, which unveils and conceals, a theatrical trope characteristic of the period. Although the *Virgin of Loreto* (CAT. 65) was not originally part of this altarpiece, it allows us to complete the domestic scene. This peculiar Marian advocation, introduced into New Spain by the Jesuits, is situated within the context of the Holy Family devotion during the eighteenth century. Its iconography is distinguished by the bell-shaped vestment that envelopes the Holy Child, the loose hair of the Virgin, and the jewels given to it by the devotees.

The Holy Child in different guises was a common devotion for religious believers and was strongly rooted in female convents.[16] This *Salvator Mundi* (CAT. 64) imparts a gesture of blessing and once held a globe in his left hand. All the power and meanings of the adult Christ are transferred to the child, with his nudity a sign of the mystery of the incarnate God.[17] The carving and polychromy highlight the characteristics of the child's body, arousing empathy. In addition, such figures were often dressed for special occasions, appealing to emotions and encouraging interaction with the sculpture.

Whether for public or private settings, life-size or miniature, made of precious or of everyday materials, to legitimize authority or comfort the soul, sculpture in New Spain attests to artistic creativity, networks of exchange, and transcultural processes, many of which have yet to be explored.

15 This type of column marked the production of altarpieces in the second half of the seventeenth and first decades of the eighteenth centuries. It was common for Christological ornaments such as grenades and bunches of grape to appear among the vegetal ornamentation and volutes.

16 A figure of the Holy Child was usually given to nuns during the ritual of the taking of vows, often depicted in nun portraits. Quite a few Holy Child sculptures are still preserved in convents' collections.

17 See Ramón Avendaño Esquivel, *En este tiempo con la demasía de cosas vaciadas: El Niño Jesús de plomo en la imaginería sevillana* (MA thesis, Universidad Nacional Autónoma de México, 2019), citing Michele Dolz, *El Niño Jesús: Historia e imagen de la devoción del Niño Divino* (Córdoba: Editorial Almuzara, 2010).

CAT. 60 **Unknown artist, *Saint Ferdinand***
Querétaro, Mexico, ca. 1750. Painted and gilded wood with cloth, 76 × 35 × 18 in. (193 × 88.9 × 45.7 cm). Gift from Sam Houston in honor of Helen Bonfils, 1956.91A-B

CAT. 61 **Unknown artist, *The Holy Family***
Mexico, ca. 1870. Gilded bronze, framed
15½ × 11¼ in. (39.4 × 28.4 cm). Bequest
of Robert. J. Stroessner, 1992.1014

FIG. 1 Josef Kohlschein (after Franz Ittenbach), *The Holy Family*, Germany, mid-1800s. Etching and engraving on *chine collé*; 21¾ × 15¾ in. (55.2 × 40 cm). The Metropolitan Museum of Art: Gift of Alice C. Taft, Hope Smith, Marianna F. Taft, Helen Head, and Brockholst M. Smith, 1945, 45.78.24.

CAT. 62 **Unknown artist, *Saint Michael Slaying the Dragon***
Mexico, ca. 1700. Painted and gilded Mexican alabaster *(tecali)*, 16⅛ × 8¼ × 4 in. (41 × 21 × 10.2 cm). Gift of the Collection of Frederick and Jan Mayer, 2015.561A-B

CAT. 63 **Unknown artist, *Altarpiece (retablo)***
Mexico, late 1600s or early 1700s. Painted and gilded wood, 8 ft. ½ in. × 6 ft. 6½ in. × 22½ in. (245.1 × 199.4 × 57.2 cm). Gift of Pauline Gano, 1958.148A-J

CAT. 64 **Unknown artist, *Standing Christ Child (Salvator Mundi)***
Mexico, 1700s. Painted and gilded wood,
33½ × 14½ × 9¾ in. (85.1 × 36.8 × 24.8 cm).
Museum purchase, 1977.188

CAT. 65 **Unknown artist, *Virgin of Loreto***
Mexico, early 1700s. Painted and gilded wood, 25¼ × 17½ × 9 in. (64.1 × 44.5 × 22.9 cm). Gift of the collection of Jan and Frederick Mayer, 2008.830

On Furniture in the Viceroyalty of New Spain

Gustavo Curiel Méndez

The famous Florentine Codex from the sixteenth century[1] depicts, in the illustration at the beginning of the twelfth book, the Spanish ships transporting the conquistador Hernán Cortés with his troops from Cuba and arriving at the coast of Veracruz. In the image, one can see a box and a trunk that have been unloaded (FIG. 1), the first European furniture on the continent, in what would subsequently be known as New Spain.

As illustrated in a scene from Lienzo de Tlaxcala, before arriving at the great city of Tenochtitlán, the Spanish conquistador gifted Moctezuma an X-chair, which the *tlatoani* of the Mexicas could sit on when the two men met (FIG. 2).[2] After the initial conquest, furniture began to be manufactured that was based on European models. The Franciscan chronicler Toribio de Benavente (known as Motolinía) reported that the "Indians make *bandurrias* [plucked string instrument similar to a mandolin], *vihuelas*, and harps, profusely decorated with ornaments and scrolls. They have made so many X-chairs that the houses of the Spanish are filled with them."[3]

On October 26, 1568, the Royal Court of Mexico approved the first ordinances for carpenters, sculptors, joiners, and luthiers (lute makers) in Mexico City.[4] Once the labor of woodworkers was regulated, a complex exchange of forms, techniques, materials, appropriations, and interpretations began, which led to the creation of unique types of furniture, still nourished by the forms of European art.

Beginning in 1571, luxury furniture arrived in Acapulco from Manila in the Philippines (via the so-called Manila galleons), a consequence of the first globalization of the world. Manila was a center for the collection and production of a multitude of types of furniture, especially from China, Japan, and India. This remarkable exchange led to the arrival of the first *biombos* (screens) in Latin America, which were soon adapted to the American reality. Painted screens displayed local themes and scenes of daily life (SEE SANABRAIS, CAT. 193). If anything characterizes the furniture of the viceroyalty, it is the coexistence of types and ornamentation derived from the locally produced furniture of the different cities of New Spain (*mobiliario de la tierra*), from Europe, Asia, and the Andean zone.

Many local woods were used for the new furniture, including ayacahuite (*pinus ayacahuite*), mahogany, *tapincerán* (*Dalbergia granadillo Pittier*), balsam, oyamel (*abies religiosa*), Montezuma pine, *xalocote* (*Pinus patula*), *tepehuaje* (*Lysiloma acapulcense*), linaloe (*Bursera linanoe*), and *ahuehuete* (*Taxodium mucronatum*). Imported furniture used European and Asian precious woods, including walnut, cedar, padauk (*Pterocarpus blancoi*), Chinese rosewood (*Dalbergia odorifera*), Chinese mahogany, sandalwood, ebony, rosewood, orange, pear, and ash.[5]

During the entire viceregal period, furniture from Spain, France, England, and Germany continued to arrive in Veracruz and was incorporated into the production of this new laboratory of

1 See *Historia general de las cosas de Nueva España por fray Bernardino de Sahagún* (Códice Florentino), Book XII: "De la conquista de México," accessed April 22, 2022, https://www.wdl.org/es/item/10623/view/1/1/. This codex was made between 1547 and 1577.

2 See Bernal Díaz del Castillo, *Historia verdadera de la conquista de la Nueva España*. Introduction and notes by Joaquín Ramírez Cabañas (Ciudad de México: Editorial Porrúa, 2019), 64. See also *Lienzo de Tlaxcala, Hernán Cortés and La Malinche meet Moctezuma II in Tenochtitlan, November 8, 1519*. Facsimile (ca. 1890) by Lienzo de Tlaxcala.

3 Fray Toribio de Benavente, (Motolinía), *Historia de los indios de la Nueva España. Relación de los ritos antiguos, idolatrías y sacrificios de los indios de la Nueva España, y de la maravillosa conversión que Dios en ellos ha obrado* (1541), ed. Edmundo O'Gorman (Mexico City: Editorial Porrúa, 2007), Third "Tratado," chapter 13, 246. "De los oficios mecánicos que los indios han aprendido de los españoles, y de los que ellos de antes sabían."

4 This set of ordinances stipulated that those who wanted to become master craftsmen had to make perfectly "a writing desk with two tops and its base with molding . . . , a French chair and an X-chair with inlay . . ., a field bed turned on the lathe and with inlay . . ., a table with six pieces with six *cuerdas* and inlaid chairs." For joiners *de lo blanco* (those who worked with lighter woods), the ordinances state: "In the examination a joiner who wants to have a shop has to know how to make a box with box joints . . . with its base of Roman molding; another box with rings of the mentioned molds and the ring half-carved. He must know how to make a table of six pieces, with its heads and hinges; know how to make doors with their wicket gates and

forms. Writing desks from Augsburg were prominent, giving rise to specific types of production, as can be seen in the furniture in San Ildefonso Villa Alta, Oaxaca, which used sgraffito inlays filled with a black paste known as *zulaque* (CAT. 66).[6] These pieces of furniture are adorned with images of local origin (including flora and fauna), which coexist with those from classical mythology and everyday life.

With the advent of the eighteenth century, furniture in New Spain was influenced by French Rococo repertoires. Later, the forms of Classicism and Neoclassicism were copied, but the furniture's legs, trimmings, aprons, backrest supports, and the arms of chairs and canapés retained a local character. Typically, traditional European techniques were used in assembling the furniture, although Chinese ones were also employed. Another decisive influence was the arrival of European furniture with chinoiserie, that is, with Western interpretations of Asian ornamentation. This style was reproduced in the viceroyalty both in *maques* (local lacquers) as well as in paintings.

Often, furniture in New Spain incorporated painting and gilding, a clear contrast to Castilian furniture, which is distinguished by direct carving and does not employ painting or gilding. With the passage of time, especially in the eighteenth century, polished furniture made of fine-grained wood varieties, including red mahogany, became as fashionable as in England, France, and Spain (CAT. 67).

The types of eighteenth-century European furniture include writing desks, mirrors, dressing tables, corner cabinets, armoires, chairs, stools, footstools, girandole mirrors, trunks, desks, beds, benches, small lap desks, writing cases, boxes, chests of drawers, shelves, small cabinets, small libraries, and tables. Sets of great beauty, including chairs, chests of drawers, and tables, mimicked the English Queen Anne style and were reproduced with great success (CATS. 68 AND 69). Influential Asian furniture included maque tables, Japanese lecterns (Nanban art), mother-of-pearl inlaid trunks, lacquer screens, gilded boxes, and Japanese desks. Lacquer furniture from China and Japan gave rise to copies in Latin American lacquerware and furniture that included painted imitations of imported lacquer furniture; the best were from Pátzcuaro and Peribán in Michoacán and those from Olinalá in Guerrero (SEE SANABRAIS, CAT. 191).[7] Similarly, furniture inlaid with mother-of-pearl shell was very popular (CAT. 70). Also famous are the Campeche *butaques* (ARMCHAIRS, CAT. 71) derived from

FIG. 1 Bernardino de Sahagún, The Spaniards approaching Veracruz, 16th century. Florentine Codex, Book XII. Ms. Med. Palat. 218–220, frontispiece. Biblioteca Medicea Laurenziana, Florence. Courtesy World Digital Library (WDL) and the U.S. Library of Congress.

FIG. 2 Scene from Lienzo de Tlaxcala. Hernán Cortés and La Malinche meet Moctezuma II in Tenochtitlan, November 8, 1519. Facsimile (1892), plate 11. Courtesy Smithsonian Libraries via Internet Archive.

half a molding with two faces." María del Consuelo Maquívar, *El imaginero novohispano y su obra: Las esculturas de Tepotzotlán* (Ciudad de México: Instituto Nacional de Antropología e Historia, 1999), 46, 140. The first ordinances were modified and updated in 1589 and 1703–04. One should not forget that the brotherhoods and the monastery schools also played a key role in the manufacture of carpentry work.

5 See Gustavo Curiel, *La mansión de los condes de San Bartolomé de Xala de la Ciudad de México. Inventario y aprecio de los bienes del caudal de don Antonio Rodríguez de Pedroso y Soria. 1792.* (Ciudad de México: Universidad Nacional Autónoma de México, Instituto de Investigaciones Estéticas, in press), especially Relación VII in Appendix X.

Caribbean *tures* (low chairs). Other important examples include the tortoiseshell veneered trunks and boxes from Campeche (CAT. 72) and Guadalajara, the magnificent furniture from Puebla, among which the geometric pieces derived from Mudéjar carpentry stand out (CAT. 73), as well as the alabaster tables and caskets from Tecali de Herrera, near Puebla.[8] Another important type of furniture with inlaid geometries and features excellent iron fittings is from Choapan, Oaxaca.

6 See Gustavo Curiel, ed., *Carpinteros de la sierra. El mobiliario taraceado de la Villa Alta de San Ildefonso, Oaxaca (siglos XVII-XVIII)*, volume I, Studies; volume II, catalog raisonné (Ciudad de México: Universidad Nacional Autónoma de México, Instituto de Investigaciones Estéticas, 2019).

7 In Pátzcuaro, the maque furniture from the workshop of Manuel de la Cerda, an Indigenous nobleman active in the second half of the eighteenth century, stands out.

8 On furniture from Puebla and Tecali, see Gustavo Curiel, "En el cruce de caminos: el mobiliario civil virreinal en la ciudad de Puebla de los Ángeles," in *El mobiliario en Puebla: Preciosismo, mitos y cotidianidad de la carpintería y la ebanistería*, ed. Francisco Pérez de Salazar Verea (Puebla: Fundación Mary Street Jenkins, 2009), 11–32. The quarries yielding the famous stone of Tecali, in Puebla, produced small-scale trunks and impressive coverings for tables. There was a very special taste for these types of pieces with multicolored veins.

CAT. 66 **Unknown artist,**
Chest with Engraved Decoration
Villa Alta de San Ildefonso, Oaxaca, Mexico, early 1800s. Spanish cedar with *zulaque*-filled engravings and wrought iron lock, 19⅜ × 35½ × 18⅞ in. (49.1 × 90.2 × 47.8 cm). Gift of the Patricia Phelps de Cisneros in honor of Plácido Arango Arias, 2017.118

CAT. 67 **Unknown artist, *Settee***
Mexico, ca. 1770. Mahogany and fabric upholstery, 36¼ × 71⅛ × 23⅛ in. (92.1 × 180.7 × 58.7 cm). Gift of the Collection of Frederick and Jan Mayer, 2015.571

CAT. 68 **Unknown artist, *Chest with Serpentine Front***
Mexico, 1770s. Hardwood and brass, 47¾ × 48¼ × 30½ in. (121.3 × 122.6 × 77.5 cm). Gift of the Collection of Frederick and Jan Mayer, 2015.551

CAT. 69 **Unknown artist, *Armchair***
Mexico, ca. 1775. Wood and fabric upholstery, 43½ × 25½ × 23¾ in. (110.5 × 65.8 × 60.3 cm). Gift of the Collection of Frederick and Jan Mayer, 2015.573

CAT. 70 **Unknown artist, *Cabinet***
Mexico, 1600s. Wood, mother-of-pearl, tortoise shell, and bone, 36½ × 36¼ × 19¾ in. (92.7 × 92.1 × 50.2 cm). Gift of the Collection of Frederick and Jan Mayer, 2015.564A-N

CAT. 71 **Unknown artist, *Butaque Armchair***
Campeche, Mexico, 1780–1820. Spanish cedar, leather, and metal, 36¼ × 27½ × 28¾ in. (92.1 × 69.9 × 73 cm). Funds from the Carl Patterson bequest, 2021.99

CAT. 72 **Unknown artist, *Writing Box***
Campeche, Mexico, ca. 1700. Wood, bone, tortoiseshell, and metal, 4¾ × 14⅞ × 14¾ in. (12.1 × 37.8 ×37.5 cm). Funds from Alianza de las Artes Americanas, 2018.598A-B

CAT. 73 **Unknown artist, *Casket***
Puebla, Mexico, late 1700s. Wood, bone, and gilded metal, 8⅛ × 11⅞ × 7¼ in. (20.6 × 30.2 × 18.4 cm). Funds provided by Carl Patterson, 2019.870

Silversmithing in New Spain

Carla Aymes

A great part of the history of Latin America is tied to the search for and extraction of precious metals in this territory, specifically of silver in the area of New Spain. It is interesting, therefore, to focus our attention on certain works in the Denver Art Museum's collection that allow us to highlight some aspects of the art of silversmithing, a craft that played a fundamental role in New Spain's life, economy, and arts during these three hundred years (1521–1821).

The viceregal world in New Spain was subject to a variety of cultural influences that lent it a particular, unique, and complex identity. Obviously, the production processes, the forms, and many of the ornamental models were inherited from the European world. Although this influence continued to be exerted in subsequent periods, silversmiths *de la tierra* (local) appropriated, transformed, and fine-tuned such influences—as well as others—to create objects that were purely from New Spain, even generating specific types that responded to local necessities and customs.

A selection of ten pieces from the Denver Art Museum's collection offers us a glimpse of the importance of this practice. The works have been selected because of their technical quality, type, marks, time period, or originality, and offer a balanced view of objects stemming from the religious world and from the civic sphere. Historically, liturgical pieces tend to abound in collections, while domestic ones are more scarce and rare. The types of sumptuous objects chosen from the civic sphere were produced for a privileged social group that, fascinated by pomp, flaunted their wealth, practically an obligation in their social hierarchy.

We begin with a spouted pitcher (CAT. 74) dated around 1600, of excellent workmanship, with suggestive chased and embossed work.[1] This form was known since the sixteenth century, although it is interesting that it appears in inventories only until the middle of the eighteenth century, probably due to changes in fashion.[2] According to the ordinances of the silversmiths' guild, four marks were to be placed on an object: that of maker, locality, assayer, and the *quinto real* tax, equivalent to one-fifth of the value of the piece. The pitcher has two partial marks. One of them, indicating locality, depicts a male head between crowned columns with the initial of the city (sometimes consisting of two letters) where it was marked below. Despite the poor legibility of the hallmark, it is presumed to be a piece from Mexico City since it resembles the marks of its silversmiths.[3] But other silversmithing centers used this same structure in their locality marks: Puebla de los Ángeles, Guadalajara, Zacatecas, Pachuca, Guanajuato, Querétaro, San Luis Potosí, Mérida de Yucatán, and Antequera de Oaxaca, just to mention some of the most important ones.

Also noteworthy is a raised salver (CAT. 75), most commonly known as a *salvilla* at the time, that would have been used as a tray for serving drinks in glasses or jugs.[4] Richly worked and with great personality, it displays a special preference for profuse decoration, in this case elaborated from a central medallion that generates eight radial sections with undulating vegetal motifs. It originates from the workshops of Mexico City and bears two marks: that of the senior assayer Juan de la Fuente (active between 1674 and

1 Chasing is one of the techniques in silversmithing that requires the greatest skill and knowledge of the artisan. It consists of adding textures and lines by means of smooth incisions with chisels and blows of the hammer on the surface of the silver. Lustre/chasing is a technique of texturized backgrounds. It consists of impressing and stamping a variety of designs with punches on the front surface of the metal with the aid of a hammer. These impressions are positioned closely and uniformly to one another to create a grainy effect with varying highlights and textures.

2 Carla Aymes, "La platería civil novohispana y decimonónica en los ajuares domésticos. Estudio documental 1600–1850" (MA thesis, Universidad Nacional Autónoma de México, 2010).

3 The second mark, also incomplete, displays a V. It is not known what it could refer to.

4 Aymes, "La platería civil novohispana y decimonónica en los ajuares domésticos."

5 Cristina Esteras Martín, *Marcas de platería hispanoamericana. Siglos XVI-XX* (Madrid: Ediciones Tuero, 1992), 24, 25, 108, and 180.

6 See Aymes, "La platería civil novohispana y decimonónica en los ajuares domésticos," 31.

7 See Cristina Esteras Martín, *La platería del Museo Franz Mayer: Obras escogidas, siglos XVI-XIX* (Ciudad de México: Museo Franz Mayer, 1992), 235, 236, 238, 239, 242, and 243. See alos Cristina Esteras Martín, *La platería en el Reino de Guatemala, siglos XVI-XIX*, 1st edition (Guatemala: Fundación Albergue Hermano Pedro, D.L., 1994).

8 This Captaincy oversaw the silversmithing centers of Almolonga (Guatemala), Santiago de los Caballeros de Guatemala, Nueva Guatemala de la Asunción, Quetzaltenango (Guatemala), León (Nicaragua), Ciudad Real (Chiapas, Mexico), and San Salvador (El Salvador).

9 Lince is identified by the mark LNC.

CAT. 74 **Unknown artist, *Pitcher***
Mexico, ca. 1600. Gilded silver, 7⅝ × 6⅛ in. (19.2 × 15.6 cm). Gift of the Collection of Frederick and Jan Mayer, 2013.314

1677), of whom few works are known, and that of the quinto real tax.[5]

Then we find a candlestick (CAT. 76) in the form of a turned baluster with claw-and-ball feet and vegetal ornamentation typical of the Baroque period with motifs of intertwined scrolls. It bears an inscription of 1727 that also attests to its patronage.

Made in the last third of the eighteenth century, an imperial crown, carved to adorn a religious statue, immerses us in the ornamental language of the Rococo (CAT. 77). The viceregal world was fond of this motif; it was used widely for a long period, and elaborate combinations were created with it.

Rocaille similarly adorns an alms purse (CAT. 78), a delicate piece with religious purpose. It is made of two carved silver plates with a core of rich silk fabric embroidered with gold threads. On one side, one can see the monogram of the Virgin Mary; on the other, a gilded monstrance flanked by two angels.

The *tachuela* (CAT. 79) is a type of footless drinking cup or bowl usually made of silver, with or without handles. It is a type that appears regularly in inventories from 1700 and later from Mexico City.[6] Most of the known examples are from Guatemala, which this example resembles.[7] (It should be remembered that the Captaincy General of Guatemala was administratively dependent on the viceroyalty of New Spain.)[8] This piece with two handles has been dated to around 1775 and has a wavy outline, in which thin concave double gadroons alternate with thicker convex ones.

An elegant serving dish (CAT. 81) from the last decades of the eighteenth century, with simple lines and a gentle undulating movement, illustrates that many of the pieces in New Spain are distinguished by the heavy use of silver; they tend to be works of a certain weight. Also known as a toilet tray, this particular one was marked by the celebrated assayer José Antonio Lince y González,[9] who worked in Mexico City between 1779 and 1788.[10]

A ciborium (CAT. 82) in gilded silver with refined faceted work on its surface is reminiscent of Guatemalan Rococo, which perhaps served as a model for the silversmiths of El Salvador; in fact, the ciborium bears the mark of this locality.[11] It is noteworthy that it has two sets of extemporaneous crowns in its mark, used to attest to the payment of the quinto real. One matches those

The object possesses three marks: that of Mexico City, that of the quinto real, and the last one, whose meaning is debated: the crowned R could refer to *plata de rescate* (silver that has been taxed at twenty percent). See Carla Aymes, "'R': La marca de la plata de rescate", in *Ophir en las Indias: Estudios sobre la plata americana. Siglos XVI–XIX* (León: Universidad de León, 2010), 241–48.

10 Esteras Martín, *Marcas de platería*, 180.

11 As mentioned above, this silversmithing center was dependent on the Captaincy General of Guatemala.

12 See the similar case of a dessert dish in Esteras Martín, *La platería en el Reino de Guatemala*, 176. For the mark see Esteras Martín, *Marcas de platería*, 126.

13 See examples of antependiums in plates 110, 115, and 126 in Cristina Esteras Martín, *El arte de la platería mexicana, 500 años* (Ciudad de México: Centro Cultural Arte Contemporáneo, 1989), 94–95, 102–3, 114–15.

14 See Esteras Martín *Marcas de platería*, 85–90, 110, and 179.

15 According to the *Diccionario de Autoridades de la Real Academia Española, 1726–39*: "a wide receptacle of silver, gold or crystal, with a round shape, with two lateral handles, and a small base. There are many sizes and they are usually made of a very thin sheet that appears to tremble, from which its name arose."

found in San Salvador, while the other is closer to those of New Guatemala, so it is possible that it may have been marked there.[12]

Dated around 1785, a large panel has in its center an ornamental motif of an urn decorated with vegetal and floral elements, framed by a decorated border (CAT. 83). It is intriguing to consider that it could be a panel for an altar frontal, given the dimensions and the type of ornamental motifs.[13]

We conclude with a piece (CAT. 80) originating in independent Mexico that demonstrates not only the mastery of its makers but also the survival of the craft in the face of the vicissitudes of the nineteenth century, at which time it gradually lost strength. In this case, the silversmith is unknown, but from the markings, we know that the piece was assayed by the celebrated Cayetano Buitrón, which allows us to date it to the years of his activity in Mexico City, between 1823 and 1843.[14] It is a vessel with a foot and two handles. Its shape raises the question of whether it is a fruit bowl or perhaps another type of vessel used at that time, such as a cup or a *tembladera*.[15]

In closing, it is interesting to note another aspect of this collection discovered when reviewing and selecting the most significant pieces: more than forty percent of the objects have some type of mark. Considering the estimate that only one-fifth of silverware in New Spain was marked, it is evident that the museum has intentionally gathered pieces that are not only of high quality but also bear the imprint of this added value.

CAT. 75 **Unknown artist, *Presentation Salver***
Mexico, 1674–77. Silver, ⅞ × 9⅝ in. dia. (2.2 × 24.4 cm dia.). Gift of the Collection of Frederick and Jan Mayer, 2013.312

CAT. 76 **Unknown artist, *Candlestick***
Mexico, 1727. Silver, 15¾ × 9 in. (40 × 22.9 cm). Gift of the Collection of Frederick and Jan Mayer, 2013.326A-B

CAT. 77 **Unknown artist, *Crown***
Mexico, ca. 1770. Silver, 7⅛ × 6¾ in. dia. (18.1 × 17.1 cm. dia.). Gift of the Robert Appleman family, 1980.318

CAT. 78 **Unknown artist, *Alms Purse***
Mexico, ca. 1780. Gilded silver, gold-thread fabric, silk lining, and tassels, 8⅜ × 5¾ in. (21.3 × 14.6 cm). Gift of the Collection of Frederick and Jan Mayer, 2013.311

CAT. 79 **Unknown artist, *Two-Handled Footless Bowl (tachuela)***
Guatemala, ca. 1780. Silver, 2¾ × 10½ in., 8 in. rim dia. (7 × 26.7 cm, 20.3 cm rim dia.). Gift of the Collection of Frederick and Jan Mayer, 2013.308

CAT. 80 **Unknown artist, *Footed Bowl***
Mexico, 1823–43. Silver, 5 × 11½ in., 9 in. rim dia. (12.7 × 29.2, 22.9 cm rim dia.). Gift of the Collection of Frederick and Jan Mayer, 2013.370

CAT. 81 **Unknown artist, *Basin***
Mexico, 1779–88. Silver, 13 in. dia. (33 cm dia.).
Gift of Robert Appleman, 1973.218

CAT. 82 **Unknown artist, *Ciborium***
San Salvador, ca. 1780. Gilded silver,
10 × 5¼ in. dia. (25.4 × 13.3 cm dia.). Gift of the
Collection of Frederick and Jan Mayer, 2013.309A-B

CAT. 83 **Unknown artist, *Silver Panel from Altar Frontal***
Mexico or the Philippines, ca. 1785. Silver and wood,
33¼ × 29¼ × 2 in. (84.5 × 74.3 × 5.1 cm). Gift of the
Collection of Frederick and Jan Mayer, 2013.301

Ceramic Convergence and Divergence

Philippe Halbert

Casta paintings like those by Spanish immigrant painter Francisco Clapera now in the collection of the Denver Art Museum constitute compelling visual records of the kinds of goods found in colonial households of New Spain. Although it is the relative domestic harmony and industry of a multiracial family that take center stage in Clapera's *De Chino, e India, Genizara*, the artist also took care to depict a variety of ceramics, including blue and white bowls, cups, and plates (CAT. 84). These are displayed on a wooden shelf above a round-bodied jug whose red color matches that of six other round and rectangular serving wares artfully hung on the wall. The inclusion of such items does more than merely set the scene or suggest painterly depth. Rather, it prompts consideration of extant ceramics also at the Denver Art Museum as further evidence of cultural exchange in what is now Mexico before 1800.

Two zoomorphic earthenware vessels, one in the form of a seated monkey and the other a duck, speak to the persistence of ancient traditions that never completely disappeared (CATS. 85 AND 86). Examples of Tonalá ware, named for a Jalisco town near Guadalajara in western Mexico, are hand-built, low-fired, and equipped with long, funnel-like spouts. Tonalá ceramics were largely produced by Indigenous and multiracial potters whose labor and artistry sustained the legacies of Mesoamerican burnished and slipped ceramics. These outwardly whimsical eighteenth-century objects recall effigy vessels and other antecedents like a Tarascan spouted vessel from Michoacán with geometric slip painting (CAT. 87). Probably used to store water, they are enlivened with hand-painted decoration in red, black, and brown clay slips that suggest more naturalistic details in addition to more stylized floral and vegetal motifs. In comparison, a small Tonalá drinking bowl adopts the profile of the Spanish *bernegal*, or wine cup (CAT. 88). Made with two small handles and embellished with colored clay slips, it likely proved equally convenient for consuming chocolate, a distinctly American foodstuff. Also used for drinking, a cylindrical Tonalá beaker with a red slip foregoes any painted ornament and instead relies on a combination of incised lines and stamped geometric shapes (CAT. 90). Such *búcaros de Indias* were prized for their supposedly fragrant clay and exported to Spain, where they were frequently included in still life paintings as symbols of New World exoticism.

Spanish colonial tin-glazed earthenware, or *mayólica*, is also characterized by cultural admixture. Mayólica production flourished in Muslim Spain and is believed to have been introduced there by way of North Africa in the eighth or ninth century. The tradition continued in Spanish cities like Seville and Talavera de la Reina, and glazed pottery was exported to New Spain early on. Founded east of Mexico City in 1531, Puebla de los Ángeles gave rise to a potters' guild in 1653 that enjoyed a century-long golden age.[1] Puebla potters produced utilitarian mayólica items as well as ornamental fixtures, such as tiles, for the home. A square tile featuring a flying bird in cobalt blue is representative of those used to decorate architectural interiors and exteriors alike (CAT. 89). Tin-glazed tiles harkened back to Islamic precedents, and the fantastically attired horseman gracing the center of a large multipurpose basin, or *lebrillo*, made in Puebla may actually be Muslim (CAT. 92). Thrown on a potter's

1 See Robin Farwell Gavin, Donna Pierce, and Alfonzo Pleguezuelo, eds., *Cerámica y Cultura: The Story of Spanish and Mexican Mayólica* (Albuquerque: University of New Mexico Press, 2003).
2 See Dennis Carr, ed., *Made in the Americas: The New World Discovers Asia* (Boston: Museum of Fine Arts, Boston, 2015); and Meha Priyadarshini, *Chinese Porcelain in Colonial Mexico: The Material Worlds of an Early Modern Trade* (Cham, Switzerland: Palgrave Macmillan, 2018).

CAT. 84 **Francisco Clapera, Spanish, 1746–1810, active in Peru and Mexico, *De Chino, e India, Genizara (From Chinese and Indian, Genizara is born)***
Mexico, ca. 1775. Oil paint on canvas, 20⅛ × 15⅛ in. (51.1 × 39.7 cm). Gift of the Collection of Frederick and Jan Mayer, 2011.428.14

wheel, this ceramic form traces its origins to the period of Muslim rule over Spain, and the use of dots to fill the mustachioed rider and his proud steed is characteristic of Islamic art.

Puebla potters' use of cobalt blue pigments also underscores the influence of blue and white porcelain like the Zhangzhou dish recovered from the *San Isidro*, a Spanish ship that sank off the coast of the Philippines in the late sixteenth century (CAT. 91).[2] Although East Asian porcelain was consumed in New Spain, Puebla tin-glazed earthenware, or Talavera *poblana*, offered a less expensive alternative that was often visually comparable to true hard-paste porcelain. Five concentric bands of leafy vines and other foliage are painted onto a lidded jar with two graceful handles using cobalt blue (CAT. 93). A much larger, barrel-shaped container or planter is distinguished by its use of polychrome paints to represent knotted tassels with bows as well as a series of floral motifs and intertwined rope (CAT. 94). If this object is distinguished by a more varied color palette, its shape and scale resemble those of Chinese porcelain stools, while the rendering of the central register of stylized flowers and leaves in a rich red possibly derives from Chinese textiles and metalwork.

Like those in Clapera's casta paintings, the cross-section of objects discussed here transcends neat binaries, whether aesthetic, material, or technological. Instead, they bear witness to a dynamic, truly global ceramic culture that emerged in New Spain beginning in the sixteenth century. Charting a vibrant course of artistic continuity and innovation, each accompanied larger processes of assimilation and acculturation as new identities were quite literally fashioned in clay.

CAT. 85 **Unknown artist, *Duck Vessel***
Tonalá, Jalisco, Mexico, 1700s. Earthenware with clay slip paints, 8¼ × 8 × 11¼ in. (21 × 20.3 × 28.6 cm). Department acquisition funds, 2002.4A-B

CAT. 86 **Unknown Mexican artist, *Monkey Vessel***
Tonalá, Jalisco, Mexico, 1700s. Earthenware with clay slip paints, 13¼ × 4¼ × 7 in. (33.7 × 10.8 × 17.8 cm). Department acquisition funds, 2002.5

CAT. 87 **Unknown artist, *Spouted Vessel for Pouring Chocolate***
Tarascan region, western Mexico, 1200–1500. Earthenware with colored slips, 9¼ × 11 in. (23.5 × 27.9 cm). Department acquisition funds, 1970.310

CAT. 88 **Unknown artist, *Two-Handled Drinking Bowl (bernegal)***
Tonalá, Jalisco, Mexico, 1650–1750. Earthenware with clay slip paints, 3⅛ × 6¾ in. (8 × 17 cm). Purchased with funds from Irma Boltman, Rene Lassabaterre, Joanna Moldow, Oz Zagar, and Alianza de las Americanas, 2017.92

CAT. 89 **Unknown artist, *Tile***
Puebla, Mexico, 1700s. Tin-glazed ceramic, 5⅝× 5⅝ × ⅜ in. (14.3 × 14.3 × 1 cm). Gift of Robert J. Stroessner, 1984.180

CAT. 90 **Unknown artist, *Beaker***
Tonalá, Jalisco, Mexico, 1650–1750. Red earthenware, 4⅛ × 2⅞ in. (10.5 × 7.3 cm). Funds from Carl Patterson in honor of Jorge Rivas, 2018.304

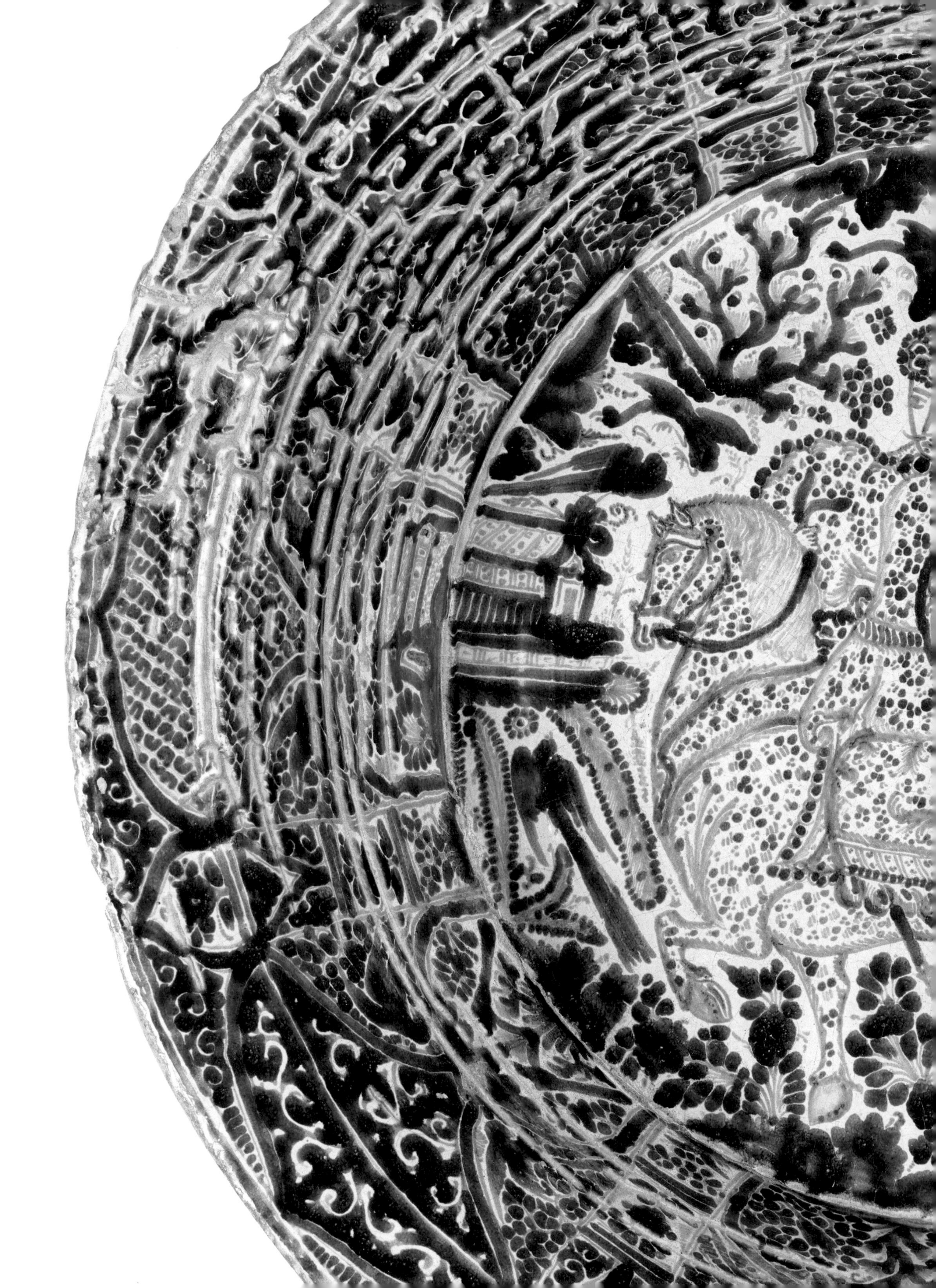

CAT. 91 **Unknown artist, *Dish***
China, 1500s, Ming Dynasty. Porcelain,
2½ × 10¾ in. dia. (6.4 × 27.3 cm dia.).
Gift of Jan and Frederick R. Mayer, 2003.27

CAT. 92 **Unknown artist, *Basin***
Puebla, Mexico, late 1600s. Tin-glazed ceramic, 6 × 26 in. dia. (15.2 × 66 cm dia.). Funds from 2001 Collectors' Choice, 2001.314

CAT. 93 **Unknown artist, *Lidded Jar***
Puebla, Mexico, late 1700s. Tin-glazed ceramic,10⅝ × 7⅞ in. dia. (20.3 × 20 cm dia.). Gift of Robert J. Stroessner, 1984.178A-B

CAT. 94 **Unknown artist, *Barrel-Shaped Jardinière***
Puebla, Mexico, 1700s. Tin-glazed ceramic, 28 × 18 in. dia. (71.1 × 45.7 cm dia.). Funds from the Carl Patterson bequest, 2021.112

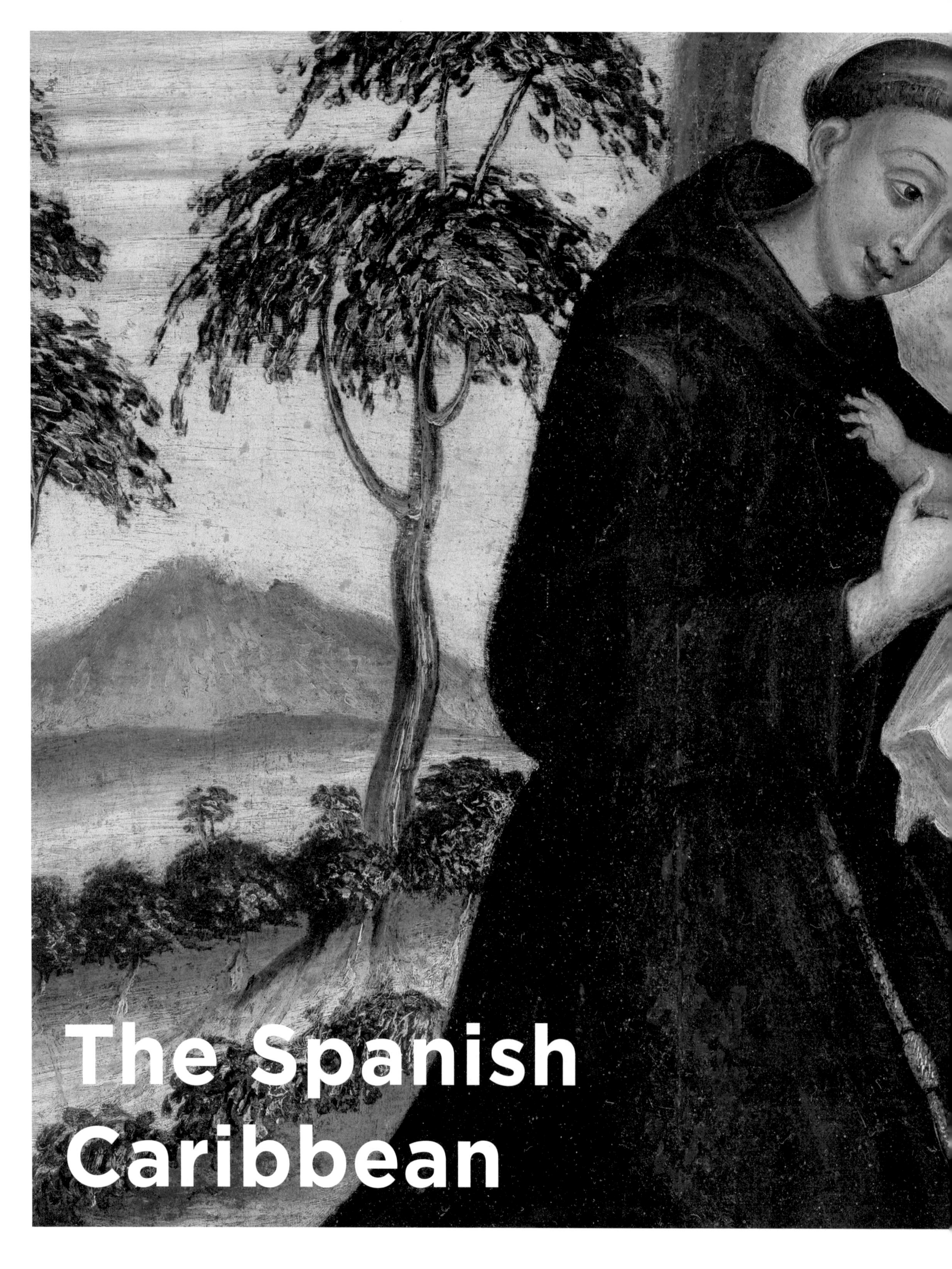

The Spanish Caribbean

Venezuelan Painting and the Caribbean

Janeth Rodríguez Nóbrega

Thanks to the generosity of Patricia Phelps de Cisneros, the Denver Art Museum possesses the best collection of Venezuelan painting outside of Venezuela, featuring the works of the most prominent artists active in the province of Caracas from the end of the seventeenth to the beginning of the nineteenth centuries. Examining this legacy allows us to approach a geographic area such as the Caribbean, usually neglected in the historiography of Latin American art[1] despite the fact that it is a singular space of encounter between people and objects, commerce and contraband, forms and ideas stemming from different regions of Europe, the Americas, Africa, and Asia.

The first Europeans who explored the Venezuelan territory soon discovered that the local nature was not abundant in mineral wealth but in fertile land suitable for agricultural production. They did not find the mythical El Dorado, nor an empire similar to the Inca or the Mexica ones, but they did encounter small tribes of great linguistic and cultural diversity, which were quickly subjugated. In this uninviting environment, the practice of painting began in the hands of colonists who had some knowledge of the trade but who did not find sufficient demand in the initial settlements to develop a competitive art market. Paintings and carvings of European manufacture occasionally arrived at the local ports to satisfy the devotional and representative needs of the population. Only when the first cities were consolidated did the demand for images for domestic consumption and for the altars of churches and convents grow. In the mid-seventeenth century, more specialized workshops were established, staffed by Spanish and Creole artists who began to forge family ties with each other. In this reduced market, it was not necessary to set up a guild to supervise the workshops, a situation that encouraged an informal artistic practice without guild ordinances or examinations to evaluate the artists' training.

Toward the end of the seventeenth century, an anonymous master painter active in El Tocuyo, a town founded in 1545 in the central-western region of Venezuela, stands out. The routes of interregional commerce converged in this town, where Franciscan and Dominican missionaries built their first monasteries, which may suggest that this master was a painter-friar. The few works attributed to this anonymous painter are dated between 1682 and 1702.[2] His paintings are characterized by a palette of intense, warm, and earthy colors made with local materials. His figures are monumental, set against ochre backgrounds, and drawn with the help of schematic and repetitive formulas (CAT. 95). Despite their imperfections, they served as inspiration for local artisans until well into the nineteenth century, encouraging a regional style, but they also had an impact on a Caracas artist of the first half of the eighteenth century.

The painter Fernando Álvarez Carneiro, a descendant of a white family of few means, was born in the port of La Guaira.[3] He settled in the city of Caracas, where he painted for the Franciscan and Dominican monasteries. Through this relationship with the two most important religious orders, he was commissioned on three occasions to paint in the parish church of La Concepción and the Hospital de San Juan Bautista, both in El Tocuyo.[4] These

1 See Jorge Rivas in *De oficio pintor. Arte colonial venezolano. Colección Patricia Phelps de Cisneros* (Santiago de los Caballeros: Centro León; Caracas: Fundación Cisneros, 2007). This catalog of the eponymous exhibition was the first to offer a broad presentation of colonial Venezuelan art outside of this country.

2 Alfredo Boulton, the historian and critic of Venezuelan art, baptized this artist as the "Pintor del Tocuyo" (painter of Tocuyo). The Venezuelan researcher Carlos F. Duarte suggested the name of Francisco de la Cruz, based on the monogram found on the back of this painting, a suggestion rejected by Boulton, since he did not find any documents corroborating this. See Alfredo Boulton, *El pintor del Tocuyo* (Caracas: Ediciones Macanao, 1985), 20–21.

3 Fernando Álvarez Carneiro's production had been catalogued by Alfredo Boulton under the name of "Painter of San Francisco," on account of a series of works with the same formal language preserved in the church of San Francisco in Caracas. The discovery of a representation of Saint Thomas Aquinas, signed and dated with his name, in the collection of the Museo Nacional de Bellas Artes in Cuba, permitted the identification of Álvarez Carneiro's works and the corroboration of information derived from various documents.

4 Alfredo Boulton, *Historia de la pintura en Venezuela*, vol. I, Época colonial (Caracas: Ernesto Armitano, 1975), 90.

5 Don José Antonio Gelabert y Garcés arrived in Havana in 1748 from Santo Domingo (present-day Dominican Republic) to occupy the post of official in the Court of Auditors in Cuba. There he was portrayed by the painter Valentín Arcila in 1770. This is the only Cuban portrait from the eighteenth century preserved in a public museum in the United States, thanks to a donation by Frederick and Jan Mayer.

CAT. 95 **Painter from El Tocuyo, Venezuelan, active 1682–1702, *Saint Michael the Archangel with Saints Francis Xavier and Francis of Assisi***
El Tocuyo, Venezuela, 1682. Oil paint on canvas, 34 × 23¼ in. (86.4 × 59.1 cm). Gift of Patricia Phelps de Cisneros in honor of Carlos Duarte, 2019.74

contracts not only assured him a stable income but also the opportunity to contemplate the works of the anonymous master, from whom he adopted the earthy palette, the drawing of the haloes, and the clouds of rocky consistency. His *Holy Trinity* is a testimony of this contact, although we do not know if this was due to his own taste or at the request of his clients (CAT. 97).

Meanwhile, in Caracas, other painters competed for commissions. One of them was Francisco José de Lerma y Villegas, a *pardo libre*. The term *pardo* was used to identify the mixed castes resulting from the multiracial children of white, Black, and Indigenous populations. Despite his caste, Lerma was a prestigious artist during the first half of the eighteenth century. His work is dominated by figures with elongated forms and faces with sharply profiled noses, inspired by old Italian and Flemish prints, but with vibrant and luminous colors (CAT. 96).

The oeuvre of José Lorenzo Zurita stands out around the same time. He was possibly a descendant of one of the enslaved Africans freed by the priest Lorenzo Zurita in 1692. His good relations with the ecclesiastical authorities and with members of the Caracas elite, whom he portrayed on several occasions, ensured him constant commissions and a fortune upon his death. His work *Saint Joseph with the Christ Child* shows the reinterpretation of the Andalusian painting school, fashioned with a rather limited palette (CAT. 98).

By the second half of the eighteenth century, the Caracas art market was dominated by free multiracial artists, working in most of the artisan trades. An example is the extensive Landaeta family, whose members engaged in painting, sculpture, silversmithing, and music. Prominent among these is the master Antonio José Landaeta, who signed an *Immaculate Conception* that shows a clearer and more pastel-toned palette (CAT. 100). This work reinterprets the Rococo forms of the paintings that arrived in Caracas from the Canary Islands, New Spain, and Puerto Rico, through trade and in the luggage of Spanish officials and missionaries who circulated in the Caribbean, such as the Catalan José Antonio Gelabert y Garcés, whose portrait by the Cuban Valentín Arcila is in the museum's collection (CAT. 99).[5]

CAT. 96 **Francisco José de Lerma y Villegas, Venezuelan, active 1719–1753, *Saint Anthony***
Caracas, Venezuela, 1740s. Oil paint on wood panel, 19⅛ × 24¾ in. (48.6 × 62.9 cm). Gift of Patricia Phelps de Cisneros in honor of Fernando J. Cisneros, 2019.68

From the end of the seventeenth century, artisans from the Canary Islands increasingly migrated to Caracas to try their luck. This archipelago was on the shipping route to the American continent, and it became a port of call for the Spanish fleets. A product of these migrations is the painter, gilder, and sculptor Juan Pedro López, a Caracas-born descendant of Canary islanders, who became the most outstanding artist of the second half of the eighteenth century, sharing the limelight with the Landaeta family (CAT. 101).[6] The pictorial language of López, imitated by other Caracas artists, combines diverse sources: It begins with a dark palette, characteristic of Andalusian painting, which gradually brightens with more vivid, pastel-like colors and softer forms, which seem to be inspired by the paintings from New Spain that frequently arrived in Caracas through the local cocoa trade with the ports of Campeche and Veracruz.

Most Venezuelan paintings are not signed. In very few cases, we find a signature on the painted surface or on the back of the canvas. An exception is the portrait of *Don José Bernardo de Asteguieta y Díaz de Sarralde* (CAT. 102), a judge of the Royal Court of Manila who was transferred in 1788 to the Court of Caracas, where he acted as the general judge of deceased persons' estates. In Caracas, he was portrayed by the painter Rafael Ochoa, a free Black artist active between 1787 and 1809, who not only signed the piece with careful calligraphy but who also displayed his racial pride: "Rafael Ochoa, de calidad negro: lo hizo en Caracas Año 1793" (Rafael Ochoa, of Black caste: he painted it in Caracas in 1793). This is the first known inscription in which a local artist emphasized his race. The very existence of the work indicates that elites, both Spanish and Creole, commissioned pieces regardless of the skin color of the artists. Little is known about Rafael Ochoa; we know that he worked for the Archconfraternity Our Lady of the Rosary, the most important one in the Dominican convent of San Jacinto, acted as an appraiser in wills, and donated some chandeliers to the church of San Mauricio, where the multiracial population of the city worshipped.[7]

Caracas artists tried to follow the dominant styles of contemporary painting in Andalusia, the Canary Islands, and New Spain, adapting it to the representative needs of their market. Most of them produced simple compositions in small formats, with very few figures with inexpressive faces pictured against neutral backgrounds or with few spatial references. Their secular and ecclesiastical clientele demanded a conventional iconography, repeating the images of Christ, the Virgin, and the saints related to the religious orders present in the territory. The local Church did not have to face the challenges of evangelizing Indigenous groups with an elaborate material culture, so the ecclesiastical art did not require exuberant artistic production to overcome existing traditions. For this reason, complex narrative scenes with numerous figures, characteristic of the Baroque, were avoided, even in large format paintings for churches and convents.

6 Carlos F. Duarte attributes more than two hundred paintings and several sculptures to him. See Duarte, *Juan Pedro López. Maestro de pintor, escultor y dorador. 1724-1787* (Caracas: Galería de Arte Nacional, 1996).

7 See Carlos F. Duarte, *Diccionario biográfico documental. Pintores, escultores y doradores en Venezuela. Período hispánico y comienzos del período republicano* (Caracas: Galería de Arte Nacional, 2000), 213.

CAT. 97 **Fernando Álvarez Carneiro, Venezuelan, 1670–1744, *The Holy Trinity***
Venezuela, ca. 1730. Oil paint on canvas, 63⅜ × 40⅝ in. (160.8 × 103 cm). Gift of Patricia Phelps de Cisneros in honor of Carolina Cisneros Phelps, 2019.65

CAT. 98 **José Lorenzo Zurita, Venezuelan, active 1727–1753, *Saint Joseph with the Christ Child***
Caracas, Venezuela, 1740s. Oil paint on canvas, 41 × 34⅞ in. (104.1 × 88.6 cm). Gift of Patricia Phelps de Cisneros in honor of Archduchess Maria Beatrice and Count Riprand of Arco, 2019.75

CAT. 99 **Valentín Arcila, Cuban, active 1700s, *Portrait of José Antonio Gelabert y Garcés***
Pinar del Rio, Cuba, 1770. Oil paint on canvas, 39 × 31 in. (99.1 × 78.7 cm). Gift of Frederick and Jan Mayer, 2009.436

CAT. 100 **Antonio José Landaeta, Venezuelan, active 1748–1799, *Immaculate Conception***
Caracas, Venezuela, ca. 1795. Oil paint on canvas, 29¾ × 18¾ in. (75.6 × 47.6 cm). Gift of Patricia Phelps de Cisneros, 2019.71

S. MATEO.

CAT. 101 **Juan Pedro López, Venezuelan, 1724–1787, *Saint Matthew***
Caracas, Venezuela, ca. 1770. Oil paint on canvas, 54½ × 37¾ in. (138.4 × 95.9 cm). Gift of Patricia Phelps de Cisneros in honor of Mateo R. Barnetche, 2019.72

CAT. 102 **Rafael Ochoa, Venezuelan, active 1787–1809, *Portrait of Don José Bernardo de Asteguieta y Díaz de Sarralde***
Caracas, Venezuela, 1793. Oil paint on canvas, 39½ × 31⅞ in. (100.3 × 80.8 cm). Gift of Carl Patterson in honor of Christoph Heinrich, 2017.96

Venezuela: Furniture at the Crossroads of the Spanish Empire

Jorge F. Rivas Pérez

With the settlement of Hispaniola, or La Española, island in the 1490s, Spain occupied extensive territory in the Caribbean Sea, encompassing the Greater Antilles and the northern coast of South America, which includes vast stretches of coastal areas in present-day Colombia and Venezuela. Because of its geographical location, no part of the Americas was more cosmopolitan or more closely tied to Spain (and the rest of Europe, by extension), the Canary Islands, and Africa than the Caribbean. It was a central hub for both transatlantic and regional trade as well as cultural exchange. The arts from the region showcase a complexity and variety stemming from this privileged position.

Venezuela, in particular, benefited from this rich Caribbean cultural dialogue that included Europe, Mexico, Puerto Rico, and Cuba (CAT. 103). The newest European fashions in the arts arrived first in the Caribbean. Early modern trade in the Spanish Caribbean also regularly included extra-official exchange practices—like smuggling and contraband—with British, Dutch, and French merchants. Such practices were often the origin of coveted luxury items such as clocks (CAT. 107), small case furniture, fine pottery, and textiles.

Furniture from the second half of the 1700s in Venezuela shows the strong influence of Spanish, English, and Dutch visual repertoires (CATS. 105 AND 106), frequently reinterpreted in original ways like the broken cabriole legs found in some tables and chairs (CATS. 104, 109, AND 111). Additionally, immigration from the Canary Islands between the late 1600s and early 1700s significantly shaped artistic developments in Venezuela during the eighteenth century. Brothers Juan Francisco and Gregorio de León Quintana, born to Canary Islands parents, and the master Domingo Gutiérrez, born and trained in La Laguna, Tenerife, were all key cabinetmakers of the period.[1]

Domingo Gutiérrez (1709–1793)

Starting in the 1730s, Gutiérrez emerged as the leading cabinetmaker in Caracas. He produced a wide range of domestic furnishings including chairs, tables, and small case furniture (CATS. 110 AND 108). However, he became famous for his numerous commissions for the Catholic church, which ranged from large altarpieces to furniture such as the chairs for the solium of the Caracas Cathedral, painted and gilded by Juan Pedro López (CAT. 114), with whom Gutiérrez often worked. Gutiérrez's superb carving technique and sophisticated compositions blended intricate rocaille, foliage, and flowers with architectural motifs—often displayed on curved surfaces, such as in the 1766 altarpiece for the Third Order in the church of Saint Francis in Caracas—gained him widespread acclaim. No matter the dimensions of a piece, Gutierrez's sense of balance and proportion distinguish his work from his contemporaries; such refinement is evident, for example, in the small, curved tabernacle with sgraffito decoration made for Don José María de Tovar y Tovar in Caracas (CAT. 112). His ornamental repertoires transcended media; silversmiths such as Domingo Tomás Núñez produced works that

1 On Gutiérrez, see Carlos F. Duarte, *Domingo Gutiérrez: El maestro del rococó en Venezuela* (Caracas: Ediciones Equinoccio, Universidad Simón Bolívar, 1977).

2 Jorge F. Rivas Pérez, "Transforming Status: The Genesis of the New World Butaca," in *Festivals and Daily Life in the Arts of Colonial Latin America: Papers from the 2012 Mayer Center Symposium at the Denver Art Museum*, ed. Donna Pierce (Denver: Denver Art Museum, 2014), 111–28.

3 Jorge F. Rivas Pérez, *El Repertorio Clásico en el Mobiliario Venezolano, Siglos XVIII y XIX* (Caracas: Fundación Cisneros, 2008), 11.

4 See Carlos F. Duarte, "El mobiliario de la época republicana en Venezuela", *Armitano Arte* 1 (December 1982): 11–42.

CAT. 103 **Unknown artist,**
Chest of Drawers for a Sacristy
Cuba, 1750–90. Mahogany, Spanish cedar, brass, and iron, 45¼ × 64¾ × 31⅛ in. (114.9 × 164.5 × 79.1 cm). Gift of Patricia Phelps de Cisneros, 2019.64

clearly show the influence of Gutiérrez (CAT. 113). Gutiérrez was not alone in pioneering rococo styles. From the 1760s to the 1780s, many Caracas cabinetmakers produced finely carved furniture embellished with rocaille, leaves, flowers, and small animals. A particularly fine *butaca* armchair from the 1760s exemplifies the creativity and the fusion of cultures that proliferated in the period (CAT. 115). Butacas originated in the 1600s in Venezuela from Ancient American ritual seat forms later modified with Spanish design elements (FIG. 1). The original form was carved from a single piece of wood. Later butacas were assembled from multiple pieces. In the 1700s, the type continued to evolve, incorporating European decorative features.[2] This example includes fine rocaille details and cabriole legs adorned with a dog's head and a bird.

Changing Tastes

Although some cabinetmakers continued to produce rococo furniture, such as José Ramón Cardozo (CAT. 116), tastes shifted in the late 1700s. European designs from the 1760s and 1770s, popular in Venezuela, displayed a renewed public interest in classical Greek and Roman design influence. Restrained rectilinear shapes, tapered legs, and simple but elegant forms prevailed (CAT. 118). From the late 1780s and well into the 1810s, it was fashionable to use wood veneer, marquetry, and wood inlay, and motifs such as Greek fret, guilloche, palmettes, columns, garlands, ribbons, ovals, and plaques with classical subjects, all connected to the current taste for ornament borrowed from classical antiquity (CAT. 117).

Renowned in his lifetime for his elegant furniture and exquisite craftsmanship, Serafín Antonio Almeida was born in 1752 in Guatire.[3] His personal style was characterized by elegant proportions, balance, symmetry, and refined ornamental motifs in the classical taste (CAT. 119). Active in Caracas from the 1780s, Almeida was the

CAT. 104 **Unknown artist, *Table***
Venezuela, ca. 1775. Spanish cedar, 32½ × 44⅛ × 22⅛ in. (82.6 × 112.1 × 56 cm). Gift of Patricia Phelps de Cisneros, 2017.126

dominant figure in his trade and produced notable works for the church, including the new choir for the cathedral commissioned in 1799. He remained active until the late 1810s and died in Caracas in 1822.

The taste for classical repertoires continued in the aftermath of Venezuela's independence in the 1820s. In addition to local cabinetmakers, immigrants from northern Europe and the United States contributed to the development of visual styles suitable for the new republic, which often continued to refer to Greek and Roman antiquity. Baltimore cabinetmaker Joseph P. Whiting settled in Caracas in 1825 and produced a wide range of classically inspired furniture for the home (CAT. 120), often embellished with golden stencils.[4] Thanks to its location on the Caribbean, Venezuela continued to play a pivotal role in an extensive international cultural network that flourished during the second half of the eighteenth century.

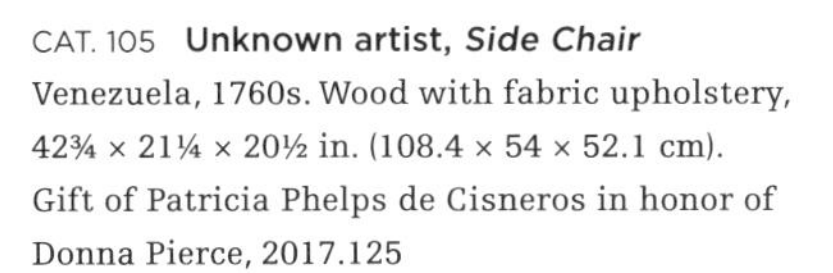

CAT. 105 **Unknown artist, *Side Chair***
Venezuela, 1760s. Wood with fabric upholstery, 42¾ × 21¼ × 20½ in. (108.4 × 54 × 52.1 cm). Gift of Patricia Phelps de Cisneros in honor of Donna Pierce, 2017.125

CAT. 106 **Unknown artist, Side Chair**
Venezuela, mid-1700s. Mahogany with fabric upholstery, 40½ × 21½ × 19½ in. (102.9 × 54.7 × 49.5 cm). Gift of Patricia Phelps de Cisneros, 2017.127

CAT. 107 **Robert Ward, English, active 1751–1775, *Bracket Clock***
London, 1751–75. Bronze, gilded bronze, oil paint, mahogany, and glass, 22½ × 15⅜ × 8¾ in. (57 × 39.1 × 22.1 cm). Gift of Patricia Phelps de Cisneros, 2018.615A-D

CAT. 108 **Attributed to Domingo Gutiérrez, Venezuelan, 1709–1793, *Table***
Caracas, Venezuela, ca. 1775. Cedar wood, 31½ × 48⅛ × 22⅛ in. (80 × 122.1 × 56 cm). Gift of Patricia Phelps de Cisneros in honor of Alicia and Agostinho Figueria de Chaves, 2017.129

CAT. 109 **Unknown artist, *Side Table***
Venezuela, late 1700s. Spanish cedar and mahogany, 29⅜ × 36½ × 18 in. (74.5 × 92.3 × 45.6 cm). Gift of Patricia Phelps de Cisneros, 2017.124

CAT. 110 **Attributed to Domingo Gutiérrez, Venezuelan, 1709–1793, *Corner Table***
Caracas, Venezuela, 1770s. Mahogany, 31¾ × 39⅜ × 27⅝ in. (80.6 × 100 × 70.2 cm). Gift of Patricia Phelps de Cisneros, 2019.66

CAT. 111 **Unknown artist, *Table***
Venezuela, 1770s. Mahogany, Spanish cedar, and brass hardware, 32⅜ × 45¼ × 27½ in. (82.1 × 114.9 × 69.9 cm). Gift of Patricia Phelps de Cisneros in honor of Currie and Thomas A. Barron, 2017.117

CAT. 112 **Domingo Gutiérrez, Venezuelan, 1709–1793, *Tabernacle***
Caracas, Venezuela, 1770s. Gilded wood, closed 20½ × 13 × 4 in. (52.1 × 33 × 10.2 cm). Gift of Patricia Phelps de Cisneros, 2019.70

CAT. 113 **Domingo Tomás Núñez, Venezuelan, 1709–1793, *Portable Sacrarium***
Caracas, Venezuela, ca. 1790. Silver, 6½ × 5⅞ × 2¾ in. (16.4 × 14.9 × 7 cm). Gift of Patricia Phelps de Cisneros in honor of Gisela and Carlos Padula, 2019.73

CAT. 114 **Domingo Gutiérrez and Juan Pedro López, Venezuelan, 1709–1793; Venezuelan, 1724–1787, *Armchair for the Solium of the Caracas Cathedral***
Caracas, Venezuela, 1766. Gilded and painted Spanish cedar and fabric upholstery, 45¾ × 23⅝ × 19½ in. (116 × 60 × 49.5 cm). Gift of Patricia Phelps de Cisneros in honor of Gustavo A. Cisneros, 2019.69

FIG. 1 Unknown Arawak artist, *Duho (stool)*, Dominican Republic, 1292–1399. Carved wood with gold inlay; 8⅝ × 17¾ × 6½ in. (22 × 44 × 16.5 cm).

CAT. 115 **Unknown artist, *Butaca Armchair***
Venezuela, 1770s. Mahogany with fabric upholstery, 45¼ × 28⅜ × 17 in. (114.9 × 72.1 × 43 cm). Gift of Patricia Phelps de Cisneros in honor of Jorge Rivas, 2017.128

CAT. 116 **Jose Ramón Cardozo, Venezuelan, active ca. 1775–1798, *Armchair for the Choir of Caracas Cathedral***
Caracas, Venezuela, 1797. Mahogany with velvet upholstery, 53⅜ × 31⅛ × 25⅝ in. (135.6 × 79.1 × 64.9 cm). Gift of Patricia Phelps de Cisneros in honor of Adriana Cisneros de Griffin, 2019.67

CAT. 117 **Unknown artist, *Linen Press Wardrobe***
Cumaná, Venezuela, 1799. Spanish cedar, hardwood veneer, and silver hardware, 6 ft. 6⅝ in. × 49½ in. × 21⅛ in. (199.1 × 125.6 × 53.5 cm). Gift of Patricia Phelps de Cisneros in honor of Guillermo Cisneros Phelps, 2017.120A-B

CAT. 118 **Unknown artist, Side Table**
Venezuela, late 1700s. Mahogany and brass hardware, 28¾ × 32⅛ × 17 in. (73 × 81.4 × 43 cm). Gift of Patricia Phelps de Cisneros, 2017.119

CAT. 119 **Serafín Antonio Almeida, Venezuelan, 1752–1822, *Butaca Armchair***
Caracas, Venezuela, 1795–1800. Spanish cedar veneered in gateado and carreto woods with fabric upholstery, 49 × 30⅜ × 31½ in. (124.5 × 77 × 80 cm). Gift of Patricia Phelps de Cisneros in honor of Rafael Romero, 2017.121

CAT. 120 **Joseph P. Whiting, American, 1800–1849, active in Caracas, 1824–1845, *Side Chair***
Caracas, Venezuela, ca. 1824–45. Mahogany upholstered in horsehair fabric, 33¼ × 18⅛ × 20⅛ in. (84.5 × 46 × 51 cm). Gift of Patricia Phelps de Cisneros, 2017.130

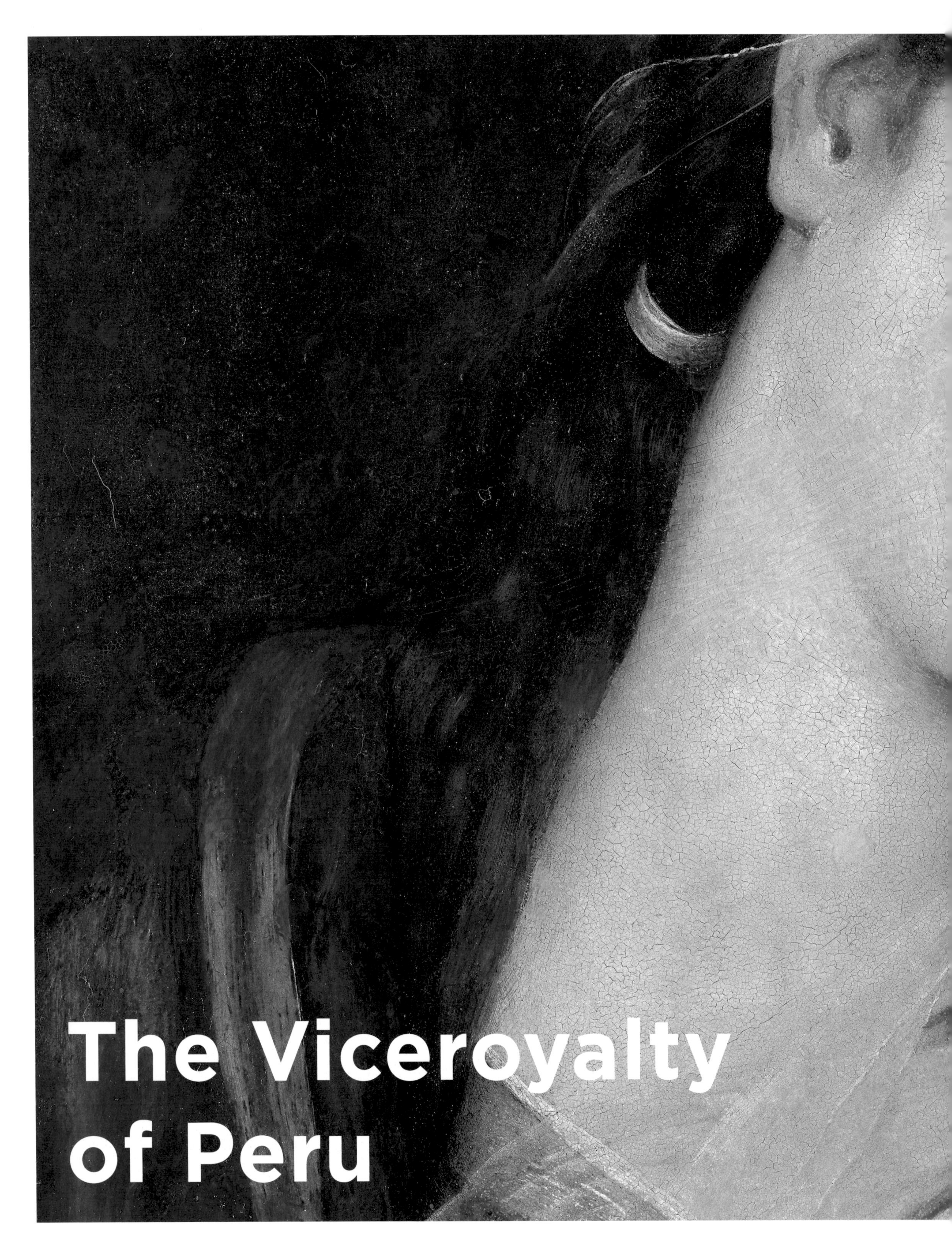

The Viceroyalty of Peru

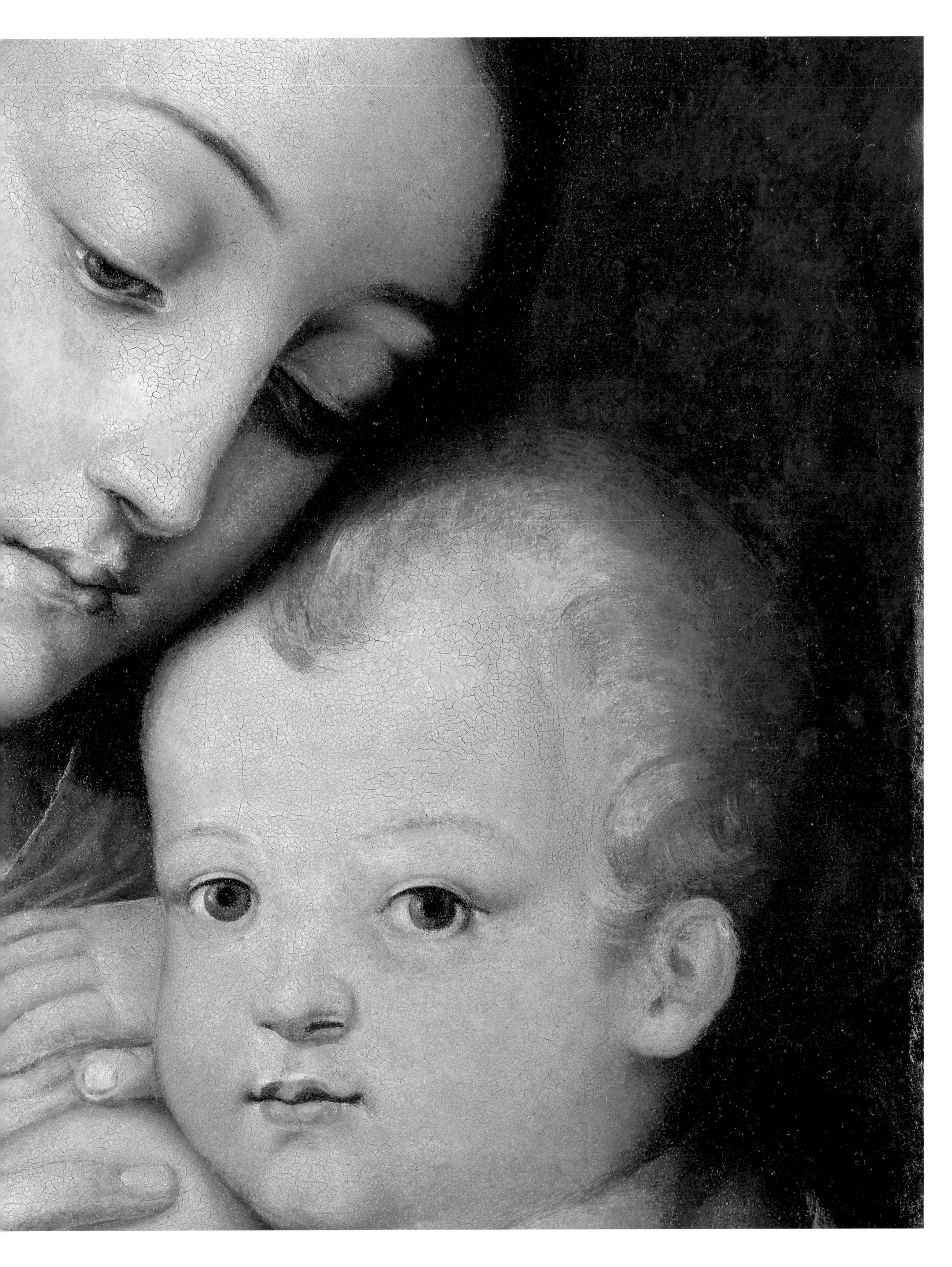

From New Granada to Denver: Particularities and Pluralities of a Painting Collection

Olga Isabel Acosta Luna

When observing the approximately thirty paintings preserved in the Denver Art Museum whose origin has been identified and attributed to the region of New Granada[1] and Great Colombia between the seventeenth and nineteenth centuries, certain features stand out that invite one to consider these works as a collection that makes visible the logics of production and artistic thinking prevalent in this geographic area from the colonial period up to the present day, often unknown outside of Columbia. These paintings, perhaps the largest collection of New-Granadan paintings existing outside Colombia, were traditionally attributed to the brushes of artists active in seventeenth-century Santafé (present-day Bogotá), such as Gregorio Vásquez de Arce y Ceballos (1638–1711) and his brother Juan Bautista (1630–1677), or Gaspar de Figueroa (1594–1658) and Baltasar Vargas de Figueroa (1629–1667), but some of these attributions have been reconsidered for this volume (CATS. 121–26). Such attributions are a twentieth-century global historiographical evaluation of Latin American art production during the centuries of Spanish domination. That is, the effort to identify Vásquez, Figueroas, Medoros, and Gutiérrez everywhere, inside and outside of Columbia, attests—if somewhat timidly—to the fact that the recognition of these artists has allowed New-Granadan works to be accepted into the art historical canon and, consequently, to be regarded as artworks.[2]

Having partly overcome the fear of anonymity and having recognized in this anonymity the diversity and particularities of a pluralistic production, the art history of Colombia and Latin America is today facing an interesting revision of eighteenth- and nineteenth-century historiographies. They were replicated in the twentieth century within the framework of the invention of "civilized" republics, which in the case of Colombia was founded in *criollismo* (the celebration of local culture)—its family lineages and defining ideals. Consequently, the defense of a Roman and Andalusian origin for New-Granadan painting, echoed in Spain and in the rest of the Americas, represents a contradictory and violent claim that echoes delirious intentions to exclude plurality. Consequently, in the last two decades, understanding how the history of Latin American art has been constructed has become an enriching priority.[3]

For this reason, I would like to suggest a brief reading of the Denver Art Museum's collection of New-Granadan painting, focusing on different aspects in some of the works from what is usually considered. These signs allow us to think of them as a group lacking a common and uniform origin, most of them assembled by the collector Daniel C. Stapleton during his stay in Colombia and Ecuador between 1895 and 1914 and donated to the museum in 1990 by the Renchard family.[4] The collection demonstrates diverse pictorial and geographic connections and traditions beyond the established canonical authorships and dates.

In light of this reflection, a painting dated 1866 with an unusual subject,

1 The terms *New Granada* and *New Granadan* are used here to refer to the New Kingdom of Granada (1538–1717) as well as to its successor, the Viceroyalty of New Granada (1717–1819).

2 During the work on the publication of this article, I have proposed several revisions of attributions and of authorships for New-Granadan works that have been accepted by the Denver Art Museum.

3 Among others, see Laura Liliana Vargas Murcia, *Del pincel al papel: Fuentes para el estudio de la pintura en el Nuevo Reino de Granada* (Bogotá: ICANH, 2014); Jaime H. Borja Gómez, *Los ingenios del pincel. Geografía de la pintura y cultura visual en América colonial* (Bogotá: Ediciones Uniandes, 2021), https://losingeniosdelpincel.uniandes.edu.co; Olga Isabel Acosta Luna, "¿En el museo o en la iglesia? En busca de un discurso propio para el arte colonial neogranadino, 1920-1942" *H-ART* 0 (2017): 46–67, doi: http://dx.doi.org/10.25025/hart00.2017.04; Museo Colonial, *Catálogo de pintura Museo Colonial* (Bogotá: Ministerio de Cultura, 2016).

4 I am grateful to Jorge F. Rivas Pérez for the generous information he provided to me. On Stapleton's collection see Jorge F. Rivas Pérez, "Daniel Casey Stapleton. Del convento al museo: El coleccionismo norteamericano en Sudamérica a la vuelta del siglo veinte," lecture presented online at the international conference *El hecho religioso en América Latina. Práctica, poder y religiosidad, siglos XVI-XX* (April 12–16, 2021). See also Michael Brown, "D. C. Stapleton: Collecting Spanish Colonial Art in Colombia and Ecuador from the Gilded Age to the First World War," in *The Arts of South America, 1492–1850. Papers from the 2008 Mayer Center Symposium at the Denver Art Museum*, ed. Donna Pierce (Denver: Denver Art Museum, 2010), 168–224.

CAT. 121 **Attributed to Gregorio Vásquez de Arce y Ceballos, Colombian, 1638–1711, Penitent Mary Magdalene**
Bogota, Colombia, 1600s. Oil paint on wood panel, 13 × 11 in. (33 × 27.9 cm). Gift of the Stapleton Foundation of Latin American Colonial Art, made possible by the Renchard family, 1990.355

CAT. 122 **Unknown artist,**
Vision of Saint Thomas Aquinas
Colombia, ca. 1695. Oil paint on wood panel, 20¾ × 14½ in. (52.7 × 36.8 cm). Gift of the Stapleton Foundation of Latin American Colonial Art, made possible by the Renchard family, 1990.361

CAT. 123 **Unknown artist,**
María orante y dolorosa (Praying and Sorrowful Virgin Mary)
Colombia, ca. 1675. Oil paint on wood panel, 19½ × 13⅝ in. (49.5 × 34.6 cm). Gift of the Stapleton Foundation of Latin American Colonial Art, made possible by the Renchard family, 1990.518

Saint Anthony Abbot (CAT. 127), is a striking work that hints at Stapleton's interest in religious art beyond the colonial tradition. It was painted by Francisco Torres Medina, son of Ramón Torres Méndez (1809–1885),[5] a well-known painter in nineteenth-century Bogotá. In his *Saint Anthony Abbot*, Torres Medina followed the path of his father by breaking with colonial tradition and proposing more universal models of religiosity. The years Stapleton spent in Colombia and Ecuador were years in which, with the exception of Torres Méndez's work, religious art was still being produced following the iconography established during the colonial period. During that time, the Church and the State were renewing their vows after the secularization attempts during the nineteenth century, which led to the expropriation and expulsion of religious communities from Colombia in the 1860s. Although the patrimony of colonial art in the churches and convents of the expelled communities had been drastically dismembered, a large body of religious works began to circulate in civilian spaces, a situation that may have helped Stapleton in the formation of his collection.[6]

The taste for religious painting in this collection also reveals an interest in certain devotional iconographies datable to a broad period between 1739 and 1830, defined by a variable territory where the administrations of New Granada and Quito were brought together under one viceroyalty until their definitive separation from Great Colombia. This means that the varied pictorial works produced in Quito, Popayán, Tunja, and Santafé during the seventeenth century were created in a single administrative and political territory. The praying and sorrowful Virgin Marys in the collection are an example of this variety. A common motif generally linked to the iconography developed by Sassoferrato, in the past attributed to Vasquez and his family, is displayed in the *María orante y dolorosa* (Praying and Sorrowful Virgin Mary) (CAT. 123). Her suffering is captured

5 Efraín Sánchez Cabra, *Ramón Torres Méndez. Pintor de la Nueva Granada 1809-1885* (Bogotá: Fondo Cultural Cafetero, 1987), 34–36.
6 *Estado del arte. Pintura en tiempos de desamortización* (Bogotá: Instituto Caro y Cuervo, 2017), https://www.caroycuervo.gov.co/museos/guia-de-estudio-estado-del-arte-pintura-en-tiempos-de-desamortizacion-museos/#m; *El museo-taller. Reflexiones sobre algunas pinturas y sus*

CAT. 124 **Unknown artist, The Virgin and Saint Joseph Adoring the Sleeping Christ Child with Saint Francis of Assisi**
Colombia, 1600s. Oil paint on canvas, 22 × 14¼ in. (55.9 × 36.2 cm). Gift of the Stapleton Foundation of Latin American Colonial Art, made possible by the Renchard family, 1990.329

here almost in an indexical manner, without recourse to explicit attributes of Christ's martyrdom, as is done in the early nineteenth-century *Virgin Mary* commissioned in Popayán "for the devotion of Don José María Lemos y Hurtado" (CAT. 128), a companion piece to a painting of *Saint Joseph* (CAT. 129). Here the Virgin Mary evokes the pain and death of her son, holding in her hand the crown of thorns, an attribute also present in the canvas of the *Virgin of Sorrows* identified as from Quito (CAT. 130). There Mary expresses her pain through the attributes of the Passion of Christ, inscribed in a composition dominated by the saturated coloring, reminding us of the spectacular polychromy, the flesh tones, the gilding, and the false appliqués of Quito sculptures from the same time, an evocation also present in *Christ Child Surrounded by the Instruments of the Passion* (CAT. 131).

Two paintings of *Virgin of Monguí* and a portable altarpiece of the *Virgin of Chiquinquirá* in particular, all from the eighteenth century, are the works that best illustrate the characteristic phenomena that stand out in New-Granadan pictorial production as well as the circulation that local devotional images may have enjoyed beyond their original geographical limits (CATS. 132–34). These pieces copy the clothing and jewelry added or painted on the figures of the Virgin and Child in the original canvases, reflecting the widespread devotion to particular Marian images located in Indigenous villages in the former province of Tunja. Today, the original canvases of the Virgin of Monguí (FIG. 1) and of Chiquinquirá are still venerated and occupy the principal position in their respective basilicas in Monguí and Chiquinquirá.

The canvases that depict the Virgin of Monguí allude, as a general motif, to the rest during the flight of the Virgin Mary, Saint Joseph, and the Child to Egypt, narrated in the Gospel of Pseudo-Matthew.[7] This text served to develop a widespread iconography in the Catholic Andean world that reinforced the Christian discourse around the nuclear family and the unity between mother, father, and children, allowing concerns and scenes of the region's everyday life to be depicted in these compositions.[8] As in other Andean examples, in this case the *Rest on the Flight into Egypt*, formerly attributed to Gaspar de Figueroa and Baltasar Vargas de Figueroa (CAT. 125), depicts Joseph taking care of his family and Mary not only stopping to rest on her journey but also resuming her sewing, which she has left in a basket at her feet while she breastfeeds Jesus.

For its part, the image of the Virgin of Chiquinquira is derived from a *Sacra conversazione* between the Virgin Mary with the Child and St. Anthony of Padua and St. Andrew the Apostle.[9] This has

pintores desatendidos (Bogotá: Instituto Caro y Cuervo, 2020), https://www.caroycuervo.gov.co/museos/el-museo-taller-primera-edicion/#m.

7 The Gospel of Pseudo-Matthew 20, 1–2, in *Los evangelios apócrifos*, ed. Aurelio de Santos Otero (Madrid: Biblioteca de Autores Cristianos, 1993): 210–11.

8 Juan Pablo Cruz, "La pintura de la Sagrada Familia. Un manual de relaciones familiares en el mundo de la Santafé del siglo XVII," *Memoria y sociedad* 18, nr. 36 (January–June 2014): 100–17, doi: 10.11144/Javeriana.MYS18-36.psfm.

9 Olga Isabel Acosta Luna, *Milagrosas imágenes marianas en el Nuevo Reino de Granada* (Madrid/ Frankfurt: Iberoamericana/ Vervuert, 2011), 219–23.

been the most recognized and copied New-Granadan miraculous image since the late sixteenth century and up to the present day, inside as well as outside Colombia. The fame of this painting owes much to its role as the venerable Virgin of the Indigenous population of Chiquinquirá, expressed in the legendary narrations about the painting's materiality. The original canvas is a cotton blanket *más ancha que larga* typical of the region and painted in tempera without any ground, which caused the image to blur. Because of this blurring, legend has it that after the entreaties of a devout woman, and in the presence of a child and a baptized Indigenous woman, the canvas miraculously repaired itself in December 1586 and came to be venerated.[10] The small portable altar in the Stapleton collection has a painted version on wood as its central image, probably derived from the engraving made by Ioannes Pérez in 1735 (FIG. 2). Saint Francis of Assisi and Saint Jerome are depicted on the doors of the small altar. This is not surprising, for although the Virgin of Chiquinquirá is a representation of the Virgin of the Rosary worshipped by the Dominicans since the seventeenth century, other religious orders and secular clergy were also devoted to this image.

Since its origin, the variable legend about the miraculous power of the Virgin of Monguí also connected the Virgin's importance to the local Indigenous population. The legend says that during their visit to Philip II in Spain in 1557, the Muisca chiefs Sogamoso and Monguí offered the monarch "precious stones, the golden idols, and rare animals of varied and fiery feathers."[11] In gratitude, the king gave two paintings to the illustrious visitors: the Holy Family for chief Sogamoso and a Saint Martin of Tours for Chief Monguí. Upon returning to their places of origin, the chiefs noticed that each had the wrong painting. Sogamoso tried by various means to recover the canvas of the Holy Family. But it was all in vain because in the morning the paintings again appeared in the wrong places. This phenomenon was finally interpreted by the chief and his people as the will of the painting of the Virgin (on the canvas of the Holy Family) to stay in Monguí and as a demonstration of its miraculous capacity.[12] In another telling, tradition proposes that it was Charles V who painted this canvas,[13] and the palette of colors used by the "monarch painter" is also part of the legend that materially and formally justifies the work. In 1763, the priest Basilio Vicente de Oviedo explained that, according to tradition, the reason for the difference in skin tones between St. Joseph and his family was that the monarch, knowing "that the Indians of this Kingdom were brown, painted the Patriarch Saint Joseph as olive-skinned".[14]

We have briefly reviewed part of the Denver Art Museum's collection of New-Granadan paintings in an attempt to suggest possible logics that led an individual to assemble this collection. A haphazard and eclectic exercise in collecting, initiated by Stapleton and taken up by the museum, offers new geographies and evaluations of New-Granadan art based on dispersed objects, now reunited and converted into a corpus. These fragments of the colonial past, by sharing the same rooms and storerooms, highlight the plurality of colonial painting, which is often lacking in local collections that have remained intact over time.

10 Olga Isabel Acosta Luna, "La Virgen de Chiquinquirá. Reflexiones sobre una "imagen tan desblanquecida, y sin facciones" *Materia Americana*, ed. Gabriela Siracusano and Agustina Rodríguez (Buenos Aires: Eduntref, 2020), 399–401.

11 Luis Carlos Mantilla, *Franciscanos en Colombia 1700-1830*, vol. III (Bogotá: Ediciones de la Universidad de San Buenaventura, 2000), 306. The author quotes from Basilio Vicente de Oviedo, *Cualidades y riquezas del Nuevo Reino de Granada. Manuscrito del siglo XVIII* (Bogotá: Imprenta Nacional, 1930). Available online at: http://www.cervantesvirtual.com/obra-visor/cualidades-y-riquezas-del-nuevo-reino-de-granada-manuscrito-del-siglo-xviii/html/b443b182-a415-11e1-b1fb-00163ebf5e63.html.

12 Ibid., 301.

13 According to Lucas Fernández de Piedrahita, Charles V was the painter of the *Virgin of Monguí*. See Lucas Fernández de Piedrahita, *Historia General de las Conquistas del Nuevo Reino de Granada* Part I, Book VI, Chapter V (Bogotá: Imprenta de Medardo Rivas, 1881), 156. According to Basilio Vicente de Oviedo, it was an English painting acquired by Philip II after the death of his wife Mary Tudor. See Oviedo, *Cualidades y riquezas*, 123.

14 Oviedo, *Cualidades y riquezas*, 123. One should note that Oviedo mentions the fact in order to debunk it, claiming that Saint Joseph's skin tone is due to him being "painted in the shade."

CAT. 125 **Unknown artist, *Rest on the Flight into Egypt***
Colombia, 1600s. Oil paint on canvas, 51½ × 42¾ in. (130.81 × 108.59 cm). Gift of the Stapleton Foundation of Latin American Colonial Art, made possible by the Renchard family, 1990.321

CAT. 126 **Unknown artist, *Saint Michael the Archangel***
Colombia, 1600s. Oil paint and gold on wood panel,
16¾ × 13½ in. (42.5 × 34.3 cm). Gift of the Stapleton
Foundation of Latin American Colonial Art, made
possible by the Renchard family, 1990.334

CAT. 127 **Francisco Torres Medina, Colombian, ca. 1841–1906, *Saint Anthony Abbot***
Colombia, 1866. Oil paint on canvas, 19¼ × 16¼ in. (48.9 × 41.3 cm). Gift of the Stapleton Foundation of Latin American Colonial Art, made possible by the Renchard family, 1990.351

CAT. 128 **Unknown artist, *Virgin of Sorrows***
Colombia, early 1800s. Oil paint on canvas,
17 × 13¾ in. (43.2 × 34.9 cm). Gift of the Stapleton
Foundation of Latin American Colonial Art, made
possible by the Renchard family, 1990.363

CAT. 129 **Unknown artist, *Saint Joseph***
Colombia, early 1800s. Oil paint on canvas, 17 × 14 in. (43.2 × 35.6 cm). Gift of the Stapleton Foundation of Latin American Colonial Art, made possible by the Renchard family, 1990.354

CAT. 130 **Unknown artist, *Virgin of Sorrows***
Ecuador, late 1700s. Oil paint on canvas with silver lace trim, 25¼ × 19½ in. (64.1 × 49.5 cm). Gift of the Stapleton Foundation of Latin American Colonial Art, made possible by the Renchard family, 1990.327

CAT. 131 **Unknown artist, *Christ Child Surrounded by the Instruments of the Passion***
Ecuador, 1700s. Oil paint on tin, 9¾ × 13 in. (24.8 × 33 cm). Gift of the Stapleton Foundation of Latin American Colonial Art, made possible by the Renchard family, 1990.335

CAT. 132 **Unknown artist, *Virgin of Monguí***
Colombia, late 1700s. Oil paint and gold leaf on canvas, 25 × 22¼ in. (63.5 × 56.5 cm). Gift of the Stapleton Foundation of Latin American Colonial Art, made possible by the Renchard family, 1990.341

CAT. 133 **Unknown artist, *Virgin of Monguí***
Colombia, 1727. Oil paint on wood panel with applied metallic sequins, 5⅞ × 4 in. (14.9 × 10.2 cm). Gift of the Stapleton Foundation of Latin American Colonial Art, made possible by the Renchard family, 1990.529

CAT. 134 **Unknown artist, *Portable Altar with the Virgin of Chiquinquirá and Saints Francis and Jerome***
Colombia, 1700s. Oil paint and gold leaf on wood, 11¼ × 25¾ × 11¼ in. (28.6 × 65.4 cm). Gift of the Stapleton Foundation of Latin American Colonial Art, made possible by the Renchard family, 1990.340

FIG. 1 Unknown artist, *Virgin of Monguí*, Colombia, second half of the 1700s. Oil paint on canvas. Main altar of the Basilica of Our Lady of Monguí, Monguí, Colombia. Courtesy of Olga Isabel Acosta.

FIG. 2 Unidentified embroiderer, *Our Lady of the Rosary of Chiquinquirá*, ca. 1735. Illuminated and embroidered engraving by Ioannes Pérez. Museo Colonial, Bogotá, Colombia, 4780B. Photo source Álvarez White 1986, 59.

Painting in the Andes

Ricardo Kusunoki Rodríguez

The introduction of Western visual languages and their gradual transformation constitute a key chapter in the cultural rupture that followed the Spanish conquest of the Andes. In a great part of the region, the Inca employed a style of art that was essentially symbolic and geometric. Neither the few figurative elements in the Inca visual repertoire nor the prehispanic traditions of naturalist representation had any connection with the visual codes that characterized European painting. For this reason, the Native population looked upon the first Western images that arrived with a certain fascination, even though these styles were already out-of-date by erudite European tastes.

The present-day scarcity of paintings from this early period reveals that the material culture of the conquest was soon replaced by an art of greater sophistication. This complexity was encouraged by an increasing circulation of people, paintings, prints, and many other objects. These changes coincided with the intensification of the missionary process in the last third of the sixteenth century. While images played a decisive role in explaining the dogmas of Catholicism, they also ensured that Andean societies assumed a globally shared visual universe as their own.

The Denver Art Museum preserves a crucial work of Andean viceregal painting, the *Virgen de Belén* (*Virgin of Bethlehem*) or *Virgen de la Leche* (*Madonna Lactans*, CAT. 135), a work by Mateo Pérez de Alesio. Like Bernardo Bitti (1548–1610) and Angelino Medoro (1567–1631), this artist is a decisive figure in the emergence of the principal pictorial traditions, or schools, in the region. Born in Puglia, Italy, Pérez de Alesio had achieved notoriety after executing, around 1572, a mural in the Sistine Chapel commissioned by Pope Pius V. Preceded by this fame, he passed through Seville before moving to Lima in 1587. It is probable that here he designed the prototype of the *Virgen de Belén*, based on models created in Rome by the painter Scipione Pulzone.[1] At least four versions are known, all on copper plates and of similar size, although certain differences in style suggest the participation of followers. The Denver version is very close to the one that, according to tradition, was the favorite image of Saint Rose of Lima and that today is located in the sanctuary built over her former home.

The cosmopolitan refinement of the work explains why the artist was considered the local archetype of the court painter promoted by elite European culture. At the same time, the absence of his signature in all the versions and the serial logic that gave them meaning suggest instead the everyday labor of viceregal painters. In fact, the European ideal of an "intellectual" artistic practice experienced a sporadic development in the Andes, where very different dynamics firmly took root, generally related to the devotional function of the images.

An example of this is a *Holy Family with Angels and Saint John* (CAT. 136). When it was painted in Cuzco at the end of the seventeenth century, the city had become the main artistic center of the Peruvian viceroyalty, thanks to the work of numerous Indigenous masters, who established a sustained dialogue with Flemish art. Like many works from the region, it is likely that the painting was designed after a Flemish print.[2] In any case, the impact of that school is also present in the idealized forest landscape that serves as a backdrop to the

1 On the model of the *Virgen de la Leche* and its impact on viceregal painting, see Francisco Stastny, *El manierismo en la pintura colonial latinoamericana* (Lima: Universidad Nacional Mayor de San Marcos, 1981); Luis Eduardo Wuffarden, "Virgen de la Leche o de Belén," in *La colección Petrus y Verónica Fernandini. El arte de la pintura en los Andes*, ed. Ricardo Kusunoki (Lima: Museo de Arte de Lima, 2015): 30–45.

2 On the influence of Flemish prints as models in Cuzco, see Francisco Stastny, "La presencia de Rubens en la pintura colonial," *Revista Peruana de Cultura*, nr. 4 (Lima, January 1965): 5–35; Aaron Hyman, *Rubens in Repeat: The Logic of the Copy in Colonial Latin America* (Los Angeles: Getty Research Institute, 2021).

3 On the highpoint of the Cuzco tradition see José de Mesa and Teresa Gisbert, *Historia de la pintura cuzqueña* (Lima: Fundación Wiese, 1982); Luis Eduardo Wuffarden, "Surgimiento y auge de las escuelas regionales, 1670-1750," in Luisa Elena Alcalá and Jonathan Brown, *Pintura en Hispanoamérica 1550-1820* (Madrid: Ediciones El Viso, 2014), 307–63; Marta Penhos, "Pintura de la región andina: Algunas reflexiones en torno a la vida de las formas y sus significados," in *Pintura de los reinos. Identidades compartidas. Territorios del mundo hispánico, siglos XVI-XVIII*, ed. Juana Gutiérrez, vol. III (Mexico City: Fondo Cultural Banamex, 2008), 820–77; Ricardo Kusunoki, "Esplendor y ocaso de los maestros cuzqueños (1700-1850)," in *Pintura cuzqueña*, ed. Luis Eduardo Wuffarden and Ricardo Kusunoki (Lima: Museo de Arte de Lima, 2016), 39–57.

4 See Ramón Mujica Pinilla, *Ángeles apócrifos en la América virreinal* (Lima: Fondo de Cultura Económica), 1992.

5 See Janeth Rodríguez Nóbrega, "El oro en la pintura de los reinos de la monarquía española," in Gutiérrez, *Pintura de los reinos*. vol. IV, 1314–75.

CAT. 135 **Mateo Pérez de Alesio, Italian, active in Peru, ca. 1547–1606, *Virgen de la Leche (Madonna Lactans)***
Peru, ca. 1600. Oil paint on copper, 21⅞ × 16¼ in. (55.6 × 41.3 cm). Purchased with funds from Frederick and Jan Mayer, Alianza de las Artes Americanas, Carl Patterson, David and Boo Butler, Spanish Colonial Acquisitions and Deaccession Funds including by exchange the Stapleton Foundation of Latin American Colonial Art, made possible by the Renchard family, 2016.213

action, as well as in the way each element of the scene is depicted. Although the prestige of the northern models influenced artists of very diverse traditions, few places showed such an attachment to these reference points as Cuzco. Yet this was no relationship of dependence. The Cuzco painters recombined elements from the Flemish tradition and infused them with a very different expressive function. They thus created a highly idealized and unnaturalistic pictorial language, which lends the sacred images a supernatural and, at the same time, an attractive quality.

Cuzco became the center of creative processes that encompassed broad areas of the southern Andes and also gave rise to new iconographies.[3] For example, angels acquired a particular courtly grace when they wore costumes composed of high skirts, lace sleeves, and open laced boots, or assumed an appearance similar to that of the harquebusiers of the viceregal guards (CAT. 137).[4] Along the same lines, religious painting incorporated frequent allusions to immediate reality, without contradicting an artificial and barely veristic ideal of beauty. Thus, a small portable panel shows Saint Francis Xavier as a preacher (CAT. 138), alluding to the missionary labor he carried out in India, Japan, and China, but with a formula often found in Latin American painting: His Asian audience has been replaced by one of Amazonian Indigenous people. Moreover, their faces and the detailed depiction of their clothes show that such figures were drawn from life.

This particular way of understanding religious painting assumes a more radical formulation in the striking images of the *Virgin of Immaculate Conception with Franciscan Saints* and *Saint*

Joseph and the Christ Child (CATS. 139 AND 140). In both, the elements taken from European models have assumed their own tone, to the point of losing connection with their original references. A new ideal of refinement is evident in the gilding that covers various elements of the composition. Although it has sometimes been related to Gothic painting, the use of gold in Andean colonial images was not an archaic trait. Rather, it was the culmination of a local taste conscious of its specificity, in which the brilliance of the images was not only associated with the sacred but also with the ostentation that characterized the viceregal elites.[5]

The success of Cuzco painting in the Andean region did not prevent the concurrent development of other distinct traditions, although they often appealed to the same audience. The comparisons become evident in images such as the "true portraits" of sculptures with miraculous reputations. By disseminating Andean cults such as that of the Virgin of Copacabana or the Cristo de los Temblores (Christ of the Tremors), those paintings helped to consolidate a shared sense of belonging among different sectors of viceregal society.[6] The genre fulfilled a similar function for those who sought to maintain their identification with very distant places of personal or familial origin. This is the case of *Virgin of the Victory of Málaga* and the *Christ of Grace of Las Navas del Marqués*, which must have been commissioned by Spaniards residing in the Peruvian viceroyalty (CATS. 141 AND 142).

The supernatural charge emanating from the image of the Virgin, made by an anonymous master from Cuzco, contrasts with the realistic intentions of the author of the second canvas, the Upper Peruvian Melchor Pérez de Holguín.[7] Active for nearly four decades in Potosí, a city whose wealth was proverbial throughout the world, Pérez de Holguín seems to have worked primarily for an elite clientele. He sought to embody for them the archetype of the noble painter as disseminated by Spanish artistic treatises, portraying himself in several of his compositions. The Denver Art Museum also has a *Saint Joseph Holding the Christ Child* by the same master (CAT. 143), a devotional image whose sentimental and anecdotal tone is characteristic of his late work.

Like Cuzco or Potosí, Lima was one of the main artistic centers of the Andean region. It had the advantage of being the capital of the viceroyalty of Peru, which until 1717 encompassed most of the Spanish dominions in South America. By then, the city's predominance had stimulated both its architectural development and its transformation into a center of consumption of objects of diverse origins. Lima's painters had to compete with the circulation of Cuzco canvases until, in the middle of the eighteenth century, a pictorial tradition was established around the viceregal court.[8]

One of the main actors in this resurgence was Pedro Díaz,[9] whose refined devotional images often reworked models of Italian or French Neoclassicism, as is the case of the *Virgin and Child* (CAT. 144), based on a composition by Jacopo Amigoni (ca. 1685–1752) (FIG. 1). The most notable part of his oeuvre, however, was in the field of portraiture. In all probability, he is the author of the portraits of the spouses Simón de Lavalle and María del Carmen Cortés Santelizes y Cartavio (CATS. 145 AND 146), parents of José Antonio de Lavalle y Cortés,

6 Ramón Mujica, "Semiótica de la imagen sagrada: La teúrgia del signo en clave americana," in *Orígenes y devociones virreinales de la imaginería peruana*, ed. Ramón Mujica (Lima: Universidad Ricardo Pala, Instituto Cultural Peruano Norteamericano, 2008), 163–77.

7 José de Mesa and Teresa Gisbert, *Holguín y la pintura altoperuana del virreinato* (La Paz: Biblioteca Paceña, 1956).

8 On the Lima pictorial tradition, see Ricardo Estabridis, "Cristóbal Lozano, paradigma de la pintura limeña del siglo XVIII," in *Barroco Iberoamericano. Territorio, Arte y Espacio y Sociedad*, ed. Ana Maria Aranda (Sevilla: Universidad Pablo de Olavide, 2001), 298–316; Luis Eduardo Wuffarden, "Ilustración versus tradiciones locales, 1750-1825," in Alcalá and Brown, *Pintura en Hispanoamérica 1550-1820*, 365–401; Ricardo Kusunoki, "'La reina de las artes': Pintura y cultura letrada en Lima (1750-1800)," *Illapa Mana Tukukuq*, nr. 7 (Lima, 2010): 51–61.

9 See the biographical article on Díaz by Anthony Holguín, "Un retrato de Santa Rosa de Lima firmado por el pintor Pedro Díaz," *Illapa Mana Tukukuq*, nr. 16 (Lima, 2019): 46–55.

10 See Alba Choque, "Pinturas del virreinato del Perú en el MUBAM. Retratos del comerciante José Antonio Lavalle, conde de Premio Real, y Mariana Zugasti," in *Pinceles y gubias del barroco hispanoamericano*, ed. María de los Ángeles Fernández Valle, Carme López Calderón, and Inmaculada Rodríguez Moya (Sevilla: Andavira Editora, EnredArs, 2019), 229–42.

CAT. 136 **Unknown artist, *Holy Family with Angels and Saint John***
Cuzco, Peru, late 1600s. Oil paint on canvas, 53¼ × 48½ in. (135.3 × 123.2 cm). Gift of Mr. and Mrs. Frank Jager, 1978.119

first Count of Premio Real. The works were executed shortly after José Antonio received the title in 1782, when the couple had already passed away, which explains the impersonal appearance of their faces. In fact, the pair of canvases was part of a set that also included portraits of the first Count and his wife from Lima, Mariana de Zugasti, now in the Museum of Fine Arts of Murcia.[10] More than a demonstration of filial love, the function of the paintings was to certify the foundational moment of the new noble lineage: the union that positioned it between both worlds. While the Creole mother symbolizes belonging to local power networks, built up over more than two centuries, the Spanish father represents the direct link with the sources of all noble legitimacy, especially due to his Biscayan and unquestionably noble origin.

Toward the end of the viceroyalty, Díaz's works reflected the impact of new styles that contributed to accentuating the traditional cultural counterpoint between Lima and the Andean south. While the capital reaffirmed its role as the main site of reception of cosmopolitan novelties, Cuzco and Upper Peru remained faithful to the artistic languages they had forged. After independence, this same dynamic would lead to the disappearance of all traces of Lima's old court painting, while the old colonial traditions of the Andean south would serve as the basis for the emergence of the so-called popular arts.

CAT. 137 **Attributed to Leonardo Flores, Bolivian, active 1665–1683,** ***Angel with Veronica's Veil***
Bolivia, ca. 1660–1665. Oil paint on canvas, 61⅛ × 35¼ in. (155.3 × 89.5 cm). Gift of Dr. Belinda Straight, 1984.717

CAT. 138 **Unknown artist,** ***Saint Francis Xavier with Indians and Mission***
Southern Andes, ca. 1700. Oil paint on wood panel, 12½ × 9 in. (31.8 × 22.9 cm). Gift of Robert J. Stroessner, 1991.1165

CAT. 139 **Diego Quispe Tito, Peruvian, 1611–1681,** ***Virgin of Immaculate Conception with Franciscan Saints***
Cuzco, Peru, ca. 1675. Oil paint on canvas, 64 × 48 in. (162.6 × 121.9 cm). Gift of John Critcher Freyer for the Frank Barrows Freyer Collection at the Denver Art Museum, 1969.344

CAT. 140 **Unknown artist,**
Saint Joseph and the Christ Child
Cuzco, Peru, ca. 1700–30. Oil paint and gold leaf on canvas, 31¼ × 26½ in. (79.4 × 67.3 cm). Gift of Engracia Freyer Dougherty for the Frank Barrows Freyer Collection at the Denver Art Museum, 1969.354

CAT. 141 **Unknown artist,**
Virgin of the Victory of Málaga
Cuzco, Peru, late 1600s or 1700s. Oil paint and gold leaf on canvas, 59 × 43¾ in. (149.9 × 111.1 cm). Gift of John C. Freyer for the Frank Barrows Freyer Collection at the Denver Art Museum, 1969.345

NRA S.ra LAVITORIa DMALAGA

VERDADERO RE,T.O,
DEL SS,MO, XP,O,
D, GRACIA EN LA VI,
LLA D, LAS NAVAS
DE UNA ZENCA
DE ZEBADA SE
BOLBIO TRIGO POR
PEDIRLO UNA DE
VOTA A SU MAGES
TAD

CAT. 142 **Melchor Pérez de Holguín, Bolivian, ca. 1665–1732, *Christ of Grace of Las Navas del Marqués***
Potosí, Bolivia, 1701–20. Oil paint on canvas, framed 67¾ × 53 in. (172.1 × 134.6 cm). New World Department/Deaccessions Fund, 1997.147

CAT. 143 **Melchor Pérez de Holguín, Bolivian, ca. 1665–1732, *Saint Joseph Holding the Christ Child***
Potosí, Bolivia, ca. 1710. Oil paint and gold leaf on canvas, 22¾ × 17¾ in. (57.8 × 45.1 cm). Bequest of Robert J. Stroessner, 1992.67

FIG. 1 Joseph (Giuseppe) Wagner (after Jacopo Amigoni), *Non dormitabit neque dormiet qui custodit*, after 1739. Etching.

CAT. 144 **Pedro Díaz, Peruvian, active 1770–1815, *Virgin and Child***
Lima, Peru, 1770–80. Oil paint on canvas, 28½ × 26½ in. (72.4 × 67.3 cm). Gift of Carl Patterson, 2016.53

CAT. 145 **Attributed to Pedro Díaz, Peruvian, active 1770–1815,** ***Portrait of María del Carmen Cortés Santelizes y Cartavio***

Lima, Peru, after 1782. Oil paint on canvas, 31 × 25 in. (78.7 × 63.5 cm). Funds from Jan & Frederick R. Mayer, Carl & Marilynn Thoma, Jim & Marybeth Vogelzang, and Lorraine & Harley Higbie, 2000.250.2

CAT. 146 **Attributed to Pedro Díaz, Peruvian, active 1770–1815, *Portrait of Simón de la Valle y Cuadra***
Lima, Peru, after 1782. Oil paint on canvas, 30½ × 25 in. (77.5 × 63.5 cm). Funds from Jan & Frederick R. Mayer, Carl & Marilynn Thoma, Jim & Marybeth Vogelzang, and Lorraine & Harley Higbie, 2000.250.1

The Nativity Scene in the Andes: New Iconography and New Materials

Carmen Fernández-Salvador

The nativity scene, as the representation of the birth of Christ in the stable in Bethlehem is known, achieved enormous popularity in Europe and Spanish America during the eighteenth century. The Neapolitan nativity scene, characterized by elaborate stagings, was imported by Charles III to Spain, from which it rapidly spread throughout Latin America.[1] In the Andes, it was usually located in monasteries, especially in nuns' convents, although it was also displayed in domestic spaces. What is special about the nativity scene is that, by combining religious figures and scenes with secular and everyday elements, it allowed Latin American artists to introduce local references, thus reinventing the codes of European art. Through their iconography and materiality, nativity scenes expressed concerns related to the construction of prestige and social order.

The central axis of the nativity scene, known as the *misterio* (mystery), is composed of the Virgin, Saint Joseph, and the Child Jesus. They are accompanied by the ass and ox, as well as shepherds and the Magi. Sometimes, the nativity scene consisted only of the central scene, which was displayed in boxes or small portable altarpieces. A variant of these portable nativity scenes assumes the form of a spherical diptych, carved in ivory by artisans from Quito, such as the piece in the Victoria and Albert Museum (FIG. 1).[2] In this diptych, which shows the nativity in one half and the flight to Egypt in the other, the polychromy is typical of eighteenth-century Quito sculpture. Often, however, the birth of Jesus was accompanied by secondary scenes that, threaded together, wove a more complex narrative, including the dream of Saint Joseph, the flight to Egypt, or the massacre of the innocents. Elaborate stage sets that imitated local architecture were usually built for these secondary scenes. This is the case in the nativity scene belonging to the Convento del Carmen Bajo in Quito, which depicts the façades of Quito houses, often decorated with Solomonic columns very similar to those that adorn the altarpieces of colonial churches.

In addition to religious scenes, other scenes were strictly secular and focused on the representation of local types, some mundane and others curious. In these sculptures, the attention to detail in clothing suggests a concern for distinguishing and ordering the different socio-racial groups that inhabited Spanish American cities. On the one hand, these figures responded to the interest in travelers' accounts that classified Latin American society by its costumes and customs. On the other hand, they expressed the fear of the dominant groups in regard to the growing and impoverished masses. The Andean region was marked by popular protest during the second half of the eighteenth century.[3] In Quito, an example of this was the so-called rebellion of the barrios, in addition to the innumerable Indigenous uprisings in rural areas. In spite of the threat that subordinate groups represented to the colonial order, the nativity scenes portrayed the urban masses and the

1 See, for example, Francisco Manuel Valiñas López, *La estrella del camino. Apuntes para el estudio del belén barroco quiteño* (Quito: Instituto Metropolitano de Patrimonio, 2011); Adrián Contreras Guerrero, *Escultura en Colombia: Focos productores y circulación de obras (siglos XVI-XVIII)* (Granada: Universidad de Granada, 2019), 199–210; Ángel Peña Martín, "El gusto por el belén napolitano en la corte española", in *Simposio reflexiones sobre el gusto*, eds. Ernesto Arce, Alberto Castán, Concha Lomba, and Juan Carlos Lozano (Zaragoza: Institución Fernando el Católico, 2012), 257–76.

2 Marjorie Trusted, "Propaganda and Luxury: Small-Scale Baroque Sculptures in Viceregal America and the Philippines," in *Asia and Spanish America: Trans-Pacific Artistic and Cultural Exchange, 1500–1850*, ed. Donna Pierce and Ronald Otsuka (Denver: Denver Art Museum, 2009), 160–62.

3 See, for example, Martin Minchom, *El pueblo de Quito 1690-1810: Demografía, dinámica sociorracial y protesta popular* (Quito: Fondo de Salvamento, 2007), 221–60. For a similar discussion of painting of local customs see Rosemarie Terán Najas, "Facetas de la historia del siglo XIX, a propósito de las estampas y relaciones de viajeros," in *Imágenes de identidad: Acuarelas quiteñas del siglo XIX*, ed. Alfonso Ortiz Crespo (Quito: FONSAL, 2005), 63–82.

4 Alexandra Kennedy, "Arte y artistas quiteños de exportación," in *Arte de la Real Audiencia de Quito, siglos XVII-XIX*, ed. Alexandra Kennedy (Madrid: Nerea, 2002), 185–203.

5 Leslie Todd, "Reconciling Colonial Contradictions: The Multiple Roles of Sculpture in Eighteenth-Century Quito" (PhD diss., University of Florida, 2019), 55–60.

FIG. 1 Unknown artist, *The Nativity and the Flight into Egypt*, Quito, Ecuador, ca. 1750–1800. Ivory with silver mounts; 2⅛ in. dia. (6.5 cm dia.). © Victoria and Albert Museum, London.

Indigenous people of the rural areas in a picturesque manner, as stereotypical, docile, and peaceful figures.

An example of the interest in the picturesque is the figure of an Indigenous woman, probably a market vendor, with inviting gestures and a laughing expression (CAT. 147). The viewer's attention is drawn to the meticulous representation of her clothing, of the woven and embroidered designs that transform the woman into an object of contemplation. In contrast, the figure of a child with his trunk, barefoot and dressed in humble clothes (CAT. 148), reminds us of the poverty that plagued many of the ordinary inhabitants of Quito. Nevertheless, like the Indigenous woman, the child displays a calm attitude, with a hint of resignation in his expressive gaze.

Among the Indigenous figures from the peripheral rural areas depicted in the Quito nativity scenes are the *yumbos*. In the eighteenth century, this term defined the inhabitants of the cloud forest to the northwest of Quito and the strip of jungle to its east. As can be seen in other works from the period, the yumbos appeared as exotic figures, often wearing little clothing, with painted faces and colorful feather headdresses, and laden with the fruits they brought to sell in the city's markets.

The main figures of the nativity scenes were often made from traditional materials and with traditional decorative techniques. Like other Quito sculptures of the period, the two figures of Saint Joseph and the Virgin Mary (CAT. 149) are carved in wood and polychromed. But unlike the characteristic seventeenth-century decoration, in which part of the paint layer was removed to reveal the underlying gold leaf, eighteenth-century Quito artists applied gilding directly to the painted surface, creating floral designs. For the faces, they used lead masks, in which they inserted glass eyes, which lends greater realism to the figures. The hands are removable and must have been carved separately. In the three figures of the Magi (CAT. 150), likewise carved in wood, the horses' saddles are decorated with colorful fabrics that recall the use of glued-on fabric, frequently used by Quito sculptors to simulate the folds of the garments.

In their different strategies of manufacture and decoration, these sculptures reveal the complex work of the colonial sculpture workshops, marked by the collaboration between

CAT. 147 **Unknown artist,**
Peasant Woman
Ecuador, 1700s. Painted wood,
7 × 5 × 3½ in. (17.8 × 12.7 × 8.9 cm).
Gift of the Stapleton Foundation of Latin American Colonial Art, made possible by the Renchard family, 1990.509

CAT. 148 **Unknown artist,**
Boy with Small Trunk
Ecuador, 1700s. Painted wood,
6¾ × 3½ × 4¾ in. (17.1 × 8.9 × 12.1 cm).
Gift of the Stapleton Foundation of Latin American Colonial Art, made possible by the Renchard family, 1990.588

sculptors, gilders, and painters. In eighteenth-century Quito, this process became more efficient in order to satisfy the growing demand for sculptures not only for the local market but also for buyers in cities such as Popayán, Bogotá, Medellín, and even Santiago de Chile. Thus, the hands which were carved separately suggest the marked specialization of the artisans tasked with producing parts for a single work in a serialized and standardized manner. The lead mask and the glued fabric, on the other hand, are examples of what Alexandra Kennedy describes as the "shortcuts" of Quito artisans employed to ensure the rapid and efficient manufacture of the sculptures.[4]

It is also important to explore the symbolic value of the materials used. Painters of sculpture in Quito used plaster and white lead pigment for the faces of the sacred figures. In order to achieve the glossy flesh tones characteristic of eighteenth-century Quito sculpture, the surface was rubbed with a sheep's bladder. As Leslie Todd has pointed out, this was intended to emphasize the whiteness of the skin, in contrast to the artists' own darker skin colors, and highlights the racial hierarchy that characterized the colonial social order.[5] Other materials were likewise consciously chosen as symbols of social prestige.

Occasionally, the face of a sculpture was made from wood or ivory. The removable hands of Saint Joseph and the Virgin Mary could also be made of ivory, as can be seen in the sculptural ensemble of the Metropolitan Museum (FIG. 2). Ivory used by the local artisans arrived in the galleon that connected Manila with Acapulco, although objects already carved in Asia were also imported. Being an exotic material, it was especially valued by artists and collectors of the era.

Although nativity scenes from Quito are undeniably important, similar scenes were also made in Peru, often with local materials. An example of this is a figure of the baby Jesus made of an alabaster-like stone (CAT. 151). This material, extracted from the quarries of Huamanga (present-day Ayacucho), was appreciated for its texture and luminosity. Despite its resemblance to alabaster, once soaked in water it became soft and easy to carve with a knife.[6] Like the Christ Child, the kneeling bull in the nativity scene, also made of this material, was decorated with polychromy (CAT. 152).

6 Johanna Hecht, "Vision of Death of Saint Francis Xavier," in *Converging Cultures: Art and Identity in Spanish America*, ed. Diana Fane (New York: Brooklyn Museum of Art, 1996), 247.
7 Alexandra Kennedy, "Mujeres en los claustros: Artistas, mecenas y coleccionistas," in Kennedy, *Arte de la Real Audiencia de Quito*, 109–127.

The figures of the nativity scenes could be made by professional artisans but also by amateur carvers. As Alexandra Kennedy has pointed out, it is possible that the nuns in the cloisters of Quito carved and decorated the small sculptures.[7] The nativity scene was open to experimentation and in a continuous process of renovation. The nuns, like other collectors, added objects, constructed stagings, and transformed the figures, which they dressed in elaborate costumes and adorned with jewelry and hair.

The nativity scenes not only encouraged the devotion of the faithful but also constructed fictions about colonial and nineteenth-century society. The possibility of interpreting local circumstances and experimenting with new materials allowed Latin American artists to innovate, departing from the tradition of European nativity scenes.

CAT. 149 **Unknown artist, *Virgin Mary and Saint Joseph***
Ecuador, 1700s. Painted wood with glass inlay, each approx. 9¼ × 5⅝ × 4 in. (23.5 × 14.3 × 10.2 cm). Gift of the Stapleton Foundation of Latin American Colonial Art, made possible by the Renchard family, 1990.498 and 1990.496

CAT. 150 **Unknown artist, *Three Kings on Horseback (Balthasar, Caspar, Melchior)***
Ecuador, 1700s. Paint, silver, gold leaf, and barniz de Pasto on wood with fabric, dimensions variable. Gift of the Stapleton Foundation of Latin American Colonial Art, made possible by the Renchard family, 1990.547–552

CAT. 151 **Unknown artist, *Baby Jesus***
Peru, 1700s. Painted alabaster, 3 × 3¼ × 7¾ in. (7.6 × 8.3 × 19.7 cm). Gift of Frank Barrows Freyer II for the Frank Barrows Freyer Collection at the Denver Art Museum, 1969.361.1

FIG. 2 *Nativity*, Ecuador and Philippines, 1700s or possibly later. Polychromed and gilded wood; ivory touched up with polychromy (face and shoulders); 7¾ in. The Metropolitan Museum of Art: Gift of Loretta Hines Howard, 1964, 64.164.172.

CAT. 152 **Unknown artist, *Kneeling Bull***
Peru, 1700s. Painted alabaster, 3 × 1¼ × 4½ in. (7.6 × 3.2 × 11.4 cm). Gift of Engracia Freyer Dougherty for the Frank Barrows Freyer Collection at the Denver Art Museum, 1972.259

Furniture in the Andes

Jorge F. Rivas Pérez

For millennia, the rich and diverse geography of the Andes, extending south from the Caribbean in Venezuela to Cape Horn in Chile, shaped the development of local cultures and their histories. When the Spanish conquered mainland South America in the first half of the 1500s, they encountered complex societies with rich cultural traditions. The powerful and artistically sophisticated Inca empire encompassed almost the entire range of the Andes, and its culture greatly influenced the region. Within a few decades, the influx of European settlers dramatically transformed the local communities and their traditions. The remarkable cultural interchange that followed brought Europe, the Americas, and, beginning in the 1560s, Asia together through a dynamic exchange of goods, artistic practices, and ideas, originating unique societies along the Andes. The origins of Spanish-style furniture making in the Andes can be traced back to the mid-1500s when Spanish cabinetmakers settled in the region and established guilds.[1] The development of furniture making in the region presents a special case within the Americas because some communities had limited contact with the colonial metropolis and remained to some degree impervious to stylistic changes and fashions.

The rise of urbanism and commercial exchange significantly influenced furniture production in the region, partly because colonial upper classes frequently engaged in extravagant wealth display, often defying sumptuary laws forbidding such excesses. Luxury goods and fine furniture adorned domestic interiors and symbolized good taste and a cosmopolitan lifestyle. Local craftspeople counted on a demanding clientele eager to outfit their dwellings and public buildings in the latest styles. In addition to locally made furniture, costly imports from Spain and other localities of the vast Spanish Empire (CATS. 153 AND 154) made their way into homes, churches, public buildings, and the workshops of local artists (CAT. 155). Costly inlaid case furniture was very popular in the Viceroyalty of Peru in the 1600s and 1700s and was proudly displayed in the *estrado* (ladies' sitting room) of upper-class houses (FIG. 1).[2] Several locations became renowned for this type of furniture, including Quito (CAT. 156), some towns around Cuzco, and in other communities in the Andean highlands (CATS. 157 AND 158).[3]

Initially, cabinetmakers adhered to traditional Spanish furniture types. For example, from the 1600s until the mid-1700s, inventories customarily listed Spanish-style leather armchairs (*sillas de brazos*) that were locally made (*de la tierra*). Records sometimes listed plain leather or hide; however, in upscale settings, documents showed the extensive use of leather, sometimes embroidered with gold and silver threads (CAT. 159) and other times embossed and polychromed (CAT. 160). However, one of the most distinctive aspects of Andean furniture is the impact of prehispanic craft traditions and visual vocabularies. The creation of new and original furniture traditions with their specific decorative repertoires, distinguished from both Iberian and prehispanic precedents, took several centuries and many generations of cabinetmakers to evolve and flourish. For example, the barniz de Pasto, a lacquer-like technique produced in present-day

1 Jorge Rivas, "Observations on the Origin, Development, and Manufacture of Latin American Furniture," in *The Arts in Latin America, 1492–1820.*, ed. Joseph J. Rishel and Suzanne Stratton-Pruitt (Philadelphia: Philadelphia Museum of Art, 2006), 477.

2 María del Pilar López Pérez, *En torno al estrado: cajas de uso cotidiano en Santafé de Bogotá , siglos XVI al XVIII: arcas, arcaces, arquillas, arquetas, arcones, baúles, cajillas, cajones, cofres, petacas, escritorios y papeleras* (Bogotá: Museo Nacional de Colombia, 1996).

3 Jorge Rivas, "American Luxury" in *Arte Colonial: Colección Museo de Arte de Lima*, ed. Ricardo Kusunoki and Luis Eduardo Wuffarden (Lima: Asociación Museo de Arte de Lima, 2016), 77.

CAT. 153 **Unknown artist, *Writing Desk Decorated with Scenes from Ovid's Metamorphoses Moralized***
Spain, ca. 1600. Wood with ivory and metal, 11½ × 21¾ × 9¾ in. (29.2 × 55.2 × 24.8 cm). Gift of the Stapleton Foundation of Latin American Colonial Art, made possible by the Renchard family, 1990.314

Colombia and Ecuador, was based on a similar technique used to decorate ceremonial Inca wood cups, called *keros* (CAT. 162), and other small objects. Beginning in approximately 1600, it was used in a wide range of objects and small furniture in present-day Colombia and Ecuador (CAT. 162 AND SANABRAIS, CAT. 192).[4] Barniz de Pasto artisans employed a hybrid style of decoration that mixed Indigenous, European, and Asian motifs, an early example of globalization.

Certain localities earned great notoriety for their production of unique furniture and objects. For example, Cuzco, the former capital of the Inca empire, was known for its richly carved and gilded woodwork (CATS. 163 AND 164), a celebrated style that surged in the second half of the 1600s. Huamanga (now Ayacucho, Peru) was one of the main centers of the viceregal leather industry.[5] Huamanga's leather-bound chests and boxes (CAT. 165) derived from the famous Andalusian *cordobanes* (embossed polychromed leather). Pieces usually showcase a rich relief decoration featuring an extensive repertoire of motifs, which combine European designs with Andean plants and animals. Woodcarving was one of the specialties of the Audiencia de Quito (Royal Audience of Quito), ranging from elaborate altarpieces to exquisitely carved small pieces (CAT. 166).

As in other regions of the Americas, Catholic missions played an important role in introducing European crafts and artistic styles to Indigenous populations. Jesuits active in the 1600s and 1700s in South America introduced the local communities to a wide spectrum of artistic practices at their missions throughout southern Bolivia, northern Argentina, and Paraguay. For example, woodworking proliferated in the missions of Moxos and Chiquitos (present-day Bolivia); there, Indigenous artisans produced carved furniture and objects that blend European and Asian ornamental repertoires with local motifs that usually include local flora and fauna imagery that were exported across South America (CAT. 167).[6] In addition to small carved objects and case furniture, other missions produced painted furniture, such as the pieces from the Franciscan missions in Paraguay (CAT. 168).

Starting in the mid-1700s, tastes shifted across the Andean region as consumers searched for cosmopolitanism.

4 Mitchell Codding, "The Lacquer Arts of Latin America," in *Made in the Americas: The New World Discovers Asia*, ed. Dennis Carr (Boston: MFA Publications, 2015), 85–86; Maria del Pilar Lopez Perez, "El Barniz de Pasto. Encuentro entre tradiciones locales y foráneas que han dado identidad a la región Andina del Sur de Colombia," in *Patrimonio cultural e identidad*, ed. Paz Cabello Carro (Madrid: Ministerio de Cultura, 2007), 225–34.

5 Jorge Rivas, "Decorative Arts of the Local Baroque," in Kusunoki and Wuffarden, *Arte Colonial*, 201–2.

6 Rivas, "Local Baroque," 212; David Block, *Mission Culture on the Upper Amazon: Native Tradition, Jesuit Enterprise and Secular Policy in Moxos, 1660–1880* (Lincoln: University of Nebraska Press, 1994), 68.

CAT. 154 **Unknown artist, *Writing Desk***
Nuremberg, Germany, 1575–1600. Wood with gilded metal, 25 × 38 × 17½ in. (63.5 × 96.5 × 44.5 cm). Gift of the Stapleton Foundation of Latin American Colonial Art, made possible by the Renchard family, 1990.306

Cabinetmakers freely embraced and reinterpreted the latest European furniture trends, particularly in larger cities like Lima, Cuzco, Quito, and Bogotá. Spanish, British, and, to a lesser degree, French furniture styles from the 1700s often found their way into homes and public buildings (FIG. 2). The furniture from this period normally showed the sinuous features associated with the Rococo style: cabriole legs and carved ornamentation featuring rocaille, vegetation, and organically shaped elements (CAT. 169).[7] Painted and gilded furniture became immensely popular in the 1700s, and cabinetmakers developed distinct carving styles and ornamental repertoires that today we associate with specific cities and makers (CATS. 171 AND 172). The interiors from the second half of the 1700s are remarkable for the use of lavish sets of matching seat furniture which included at least a pair of settees (CAT. 173) for women and many chairs for men. Still in the late 1790s, women would sit cross-legged as dictated by decorum and use inherited from Islamic Spain (FIG. 3).

As in Europe and North America, by the late 1700s, repertoires associated with ancient Greece and Rome became fashionable in Spanish America; the Andean region was not an exception. In Lima in the early 1800s, for example, the Basque architect, painter, and sculptor Matías Maestro became a central figure in the reception and appropriation of the Neoclassical repertoires as part of a larger process of modernization and renovation in the arts endorsed by local elites.[8] Although painted and gilded furniture was still fashionable at this time (CAT. 174), the upper classes favored marquetry furniture embellished with classical ornamental repertoires (CAT. 170). The taste for classical repertoires persisted well after independence in the 1820s, when new developments of the style emerged, this time associated with ideas of free republics and nation-building. Across the Andes, the furniture from this period is mostly austere and frequently embellished with inlays or marquetry depicting classical motifs (SEE MAJLUF, CAT. 203) instead of the elaborate gilt-bronze mounts found in European furniture of the time.

7 María Campos Carlés de Peña, *A Surviving Legacy in Spanish America: Seventeenth- and Eighteenth-Century Furniture from the Viceroyalty of Peru* (Madrid: Ediciones El Viso, 2013), 331–81.
8 Rivas, "The Emergence of Neoclassicism," in Kusunoki and Wuffarden, *Arte colonial*, 253–4.

CAT. 155 **Unknown artist, *Lap Desk***
Ecuador, 1700s. Wood with silver, 8 × 23½ × 17¼ in. (20.3 × 59.7 × 43.8 cm). Gift of the Stapleton Foundation of Latin American Colonial Art, made possible by the Renchard family, 1990.318

FIG. 1 *A Spanish Woman of Peru in Waistcoat and Petticoat . . .* , from Amédée François Frézier, *Relation du voyage de la Mer du Sud aux côtes du Chily et du Perou: Fait pendant les années 1712, 1713 & 1714* (Paris, 1716), pl. VI-3. Image courtesy BnF.

CAT. 156 **Unknown artist, *Writing Desk***
Ecuador, 1600s. Wood with gilded iron, closed 25 × 35 × 19 in. (63.5 × 89 × 48.3 cm). Funds from the Stapleton Foundation of Latin American Colonial Art, made possible by the Renchard family by exchange, and funds from Ethel Sayre Berger by exchange, 2019.869

CAT. 157 **Unknown artist, *Chest***
Peru, 1700s. Wood with iron, 31½ × 16½ × 14¼ in. (80 × 42 × 36.2 cm). Gift of the Stapleton Foundation of Latin American Colonial Art, made possible by the Renchard family, 1990.293

CAT. 158 **Unknown artist, *Chest***
Ayacucho, Peru, early 1700s. Spanish cedar with leather and gilded iron, 24½ × 42⅛ × 20⅞ in. (62.1 × 107 × 53 cm). Gift of Patricia Phelps de Cisneros in honor of Natalia Majluf, 2017.123

CAT. 159 **Unknown artist, *Armchair***
Ecuador or Colombia, 1700s. Wood, leather, silver thread, and metal, 42½ × 26 × 25 in. (108 × 66 × 63.5 cm). Gift of the Stapleton Foundation of Latin American Colonial Art, made possible by the Renchard family, 1990.307

CAT. 160 **Unknown artist, *Armchair***
Ecuador or Colombia, 1700s. Painted wood, leather, and brass, 43 × 28 × 22¼ in. (109.2 × 71.1 × 56.5 cm). Gift of the Stapleton Foundation of Latin American Colonial Art, made possible by the Renchard family, 1990.291

CAT. 161 **Unknown artist, *Portable Writing Chest***
Colombia, early 1700s. Barniz de Pasto and silver leaf on wood with glass and bone, 7½ × 13½ × 11½ in. (19.1 × 34.3 × 29.2 cm). Gift of the Stapleton Foundation of Latin American Colonial Art, made possible by the Renchard family, 1990.301

CAT. 162 **Unknown artist, *Kero (ceremonial cup)***
Peru, ca. 1600. Wood with pigmented resin inlay, 8 × 6¾ in. dia. (20.3 × 17.1 cm dia.). Bequest from the Estate of Leon H. Snyder, 1978.288

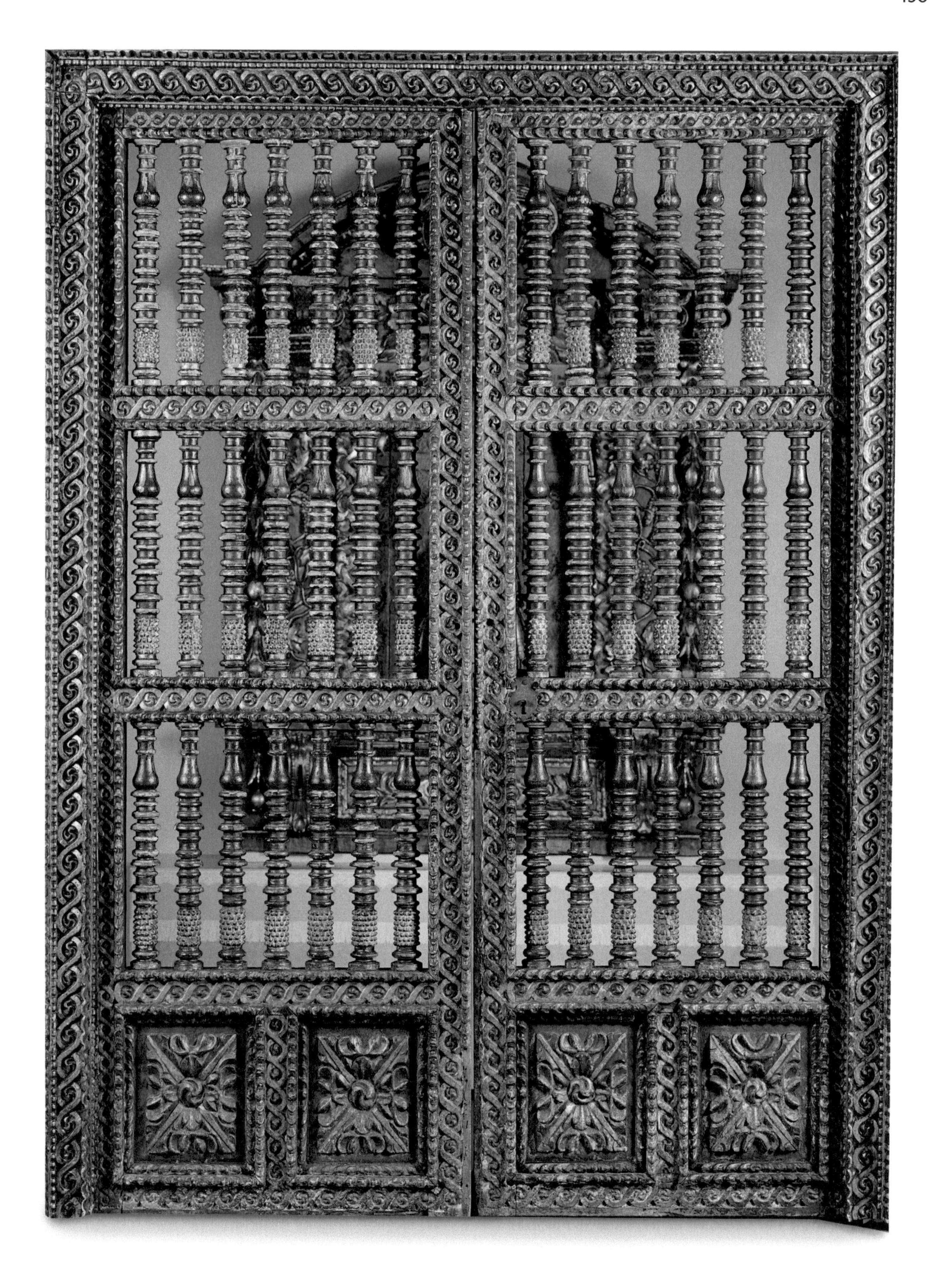

CAT. 163 **Unknown artist, *Pair of Gates***
Cuzco, Peru, 1700s. Paint and gold leaf on wood with iron, each door 8 ft. ½ in. × 35 in. × 4½ in. (245.1 × 88.9 × 11.4 cm). Gift of Mrs. Meritt Gano Jr., 1959.127A-D

CAT. 164 **Unknown artist, *Bed***
Cuzco, Peru, 1700s. Wood and gold leaf, 52¾ in. × 7 ft. 1¾ in. (134 × 217.8 cm). Gift of Engracia M. Dougherty, 1981.181A-F

CAT. 165 **Unknown artist, *Trunk***
Peru, 1700s. Wood with painted leather and gilded iron. 7½ × 15 × 22½ in. (19 × 38.1 × 57.2 cm). Gift of Engracia Freyer Dougherty for the Frank Barrows Freyer Collection at the Denver Art Museum, 1972.262A-B

CAT. 166 **Unknown artist, *Casket***
Ecuador, late 1700s–early 1800s. Wood and iron, 5 × 8½ × 4½ in. (12.7 × 21.6 × 11.4 cm). Gift of Mr. and Mrs. Robert S. Black, 1993.114

CAT. 167 **Unknown artist, *Coca Box (coquera)***
Moxos or Chiquitos, Bolivia, 1700s. Wood, 11 × 7⅞ in. (27.9 × 19.8 cm). Funds from Carl Patterson in honor of Richard A. Haynes, 2017.417A-B

CAT. 168 **Unknown artist, *Armoire***
Paraguay, ca. 1750. Painted wood, closed 71½ × 36¼ in. (181.6 × 92.1 cm). Anonymous gift, 1992.44A-B

FIG. 2 François Robert Ingouf, *Creole Lady from Peru Dressed according to the Custom of Lima*, 1774. Etching and engraving.

CAT. 169 **Unknown artist, *Chair***
Colombia, 1700s. Paint and gold leaf on wood with velvet upholstery, 46 × 28 × 28 in. (116.8 × 71.1 × 71.1 cm). Gift of the Stapleton Foundation of Latin American Colonial Art, made possible by the Renchard family, 1990.287

CAT. 170 **Unknown artist, *Chest of Drawers***
Peru, late 1700s. Wood, 43 × 50¼ × 24¾ in. (109.2 × 127.6 × 62.9 cm). Gift of John C. Freyer for the Frank Barrows Freyer Collection at the Denver Art Museum, 1971.439

CAT. 171 **Unknown artist, *Writing Desk***
Ecuador, mid-1700s. Paint and silver leaf on wood with iron hardware, 18 × 25 × 18½ in. (45.7 × 63.5 × 47 cm). Gift of Mr. and Mrs. Robert S. Black, 1993.113A-I

CAT. 172 **Unknown artist, *Headboard***
Ecuador, late 1700s. Paint and silver leaf on wood, 66 × 61⅝ in. (167.6 × 156.5 cm). Gift of Mrs. Doster Wetherill, 1971.468

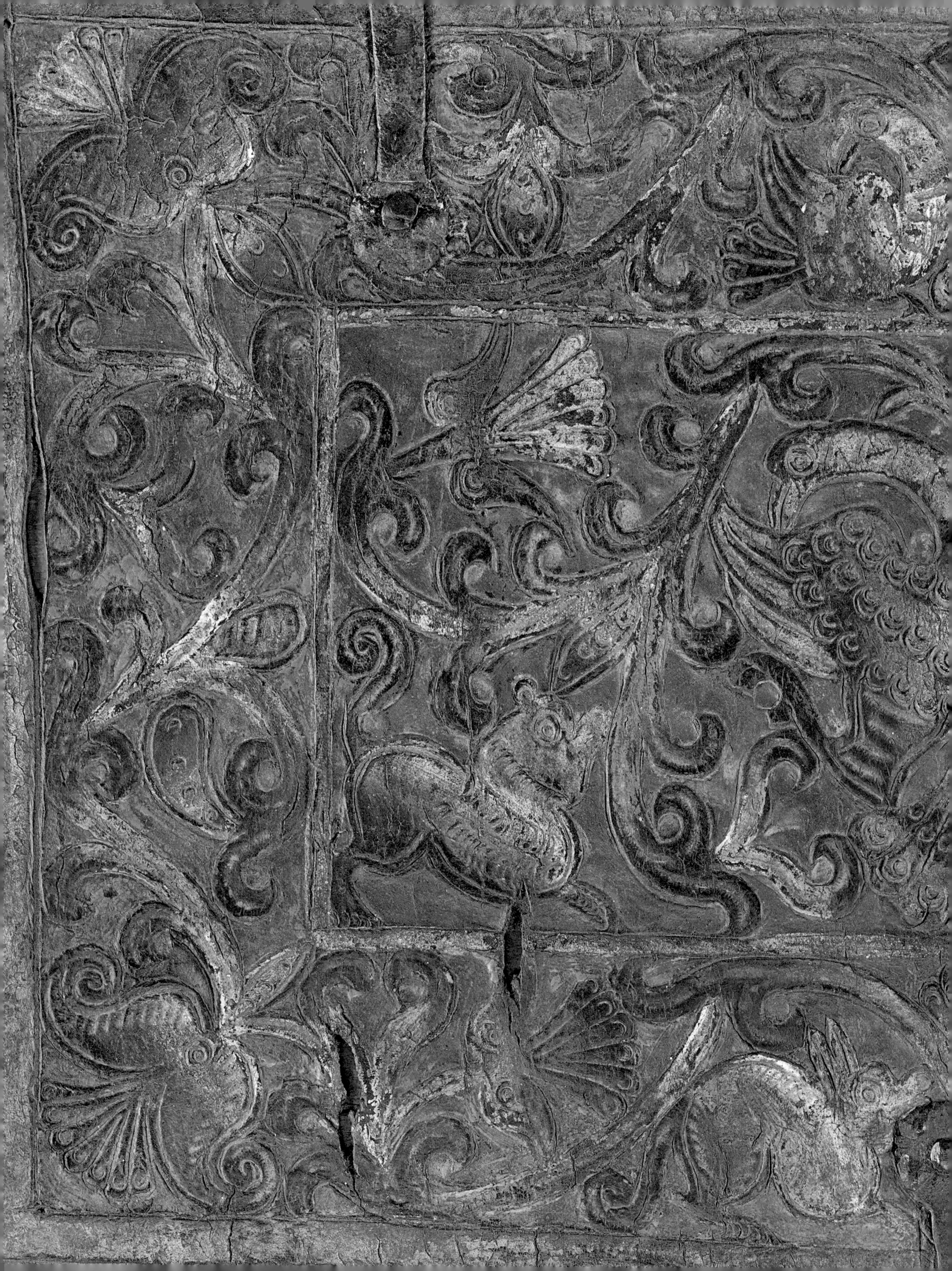

Historia de Chile.
N.°30
UNA TERTULIA EN 1790.
(Santiago.)

CAT. 173 **Unknown artist, *Settee***
Peru, 1760s–70s. Wood with fabric upholstery, 49 × 86 × 25 in. (124.5 × 218.4 × 63.5 cm). Gift of John Critcher Freyer for the Frank Barrows Freyer Collection at the Denver Art Museum, 1969.375.2

FIG. 3 *Historia de Chile. No. 30. Una tertulia en 1790 (History of Chile. No. 30. A gathering in 1790).* Print from Claudio Gay, *Atlas de la historia física y política de Chile* (Paris: En la Imprenta de E. Thunot, 1854) vol. 1, No. 30. Library of Congress Prints and Photographs Division, Washington DC. Via www.loc.gov/item/2003670343/

CAT. 174 **Unknown artist, *Settee***
Cuzco, Peru, ca. 1800–10. Painted and gilded wood with fabric upholstery, 30½ × 83½ × 25¼ in. (77.5 × 212.1 × 64.1 cm). Gift of Frank Barrows Freyer II for the Frank Barrows Freyer Collection at the Denver Art Museum, 1969.377

South American Silversmithing

Luis Eduardo Wuffarden Revilla

During the conquest of South America, the Spanish were amazed at the abundance of precious metals and recognized the technical skill that had been achieved by prehispanic artisans—Quimbaya, Chimu, and Inca—in the field of metallurgy. That is why Pedro de Cieza de León, referring to ancient Peru, wrote in 1553 that "the native Indians of this kingdom were great masters of the arts of working in silver, and of building."[1] The conquerors had by then discovered gold and precious stones in the New Kingdom of Granada, the site of the legendary El Dorado, while in the southern Andes the "rich mountain" of Potosí was discovered—the largest silver deposit in the world. The latter was regarded by writers of the era as a providential discovery for the expansion of the Spanish monarchy and of Christianity in the Americas.[2] Its immense production not only contributed to revolutionizing the world economy but also stimulated the emergence of local traditions of silversmithing, which were tied to the cultural models of the emerging viceregal society.

As was to be expected, the foundation of urban centers gave rise to a growing demand for liturgical and decorative gold and silver pieces for the ecclesiastical buildings that were being erected. At the same time, the sumptuous display of Creole civil and ceremonial life contributed to bolstering the widespread concept of *lujo indiano* (Indigenous opulence). In this sense, it soon became evident that the volume and weight of the works were as or more important than their formal qualities. Another determining factor in the evolution of the medium was the coexistence of two parallel communities: the "republic of Spaniards" and the "republic of Indians," established by the legislation of the viceroy of Peru Francisco de Toledo (governed 1569–1581), which gave rise to very distinct types of objects. In accordance with his organizational policy, Toledo himself ordered the concentration of Indigenous villages, or *aillus*, dedicated to silversmithing in certain areas, with the purpose of exploiting a highly specialized labor force while at the same time incorporating certain Indigenous techniques into Western uses.[3]

It is possible to trace some key facets of this fascinating history of assimilation and invention in the South American silver pieces preserved in the Denver Art Museum's collection. Among the most characteristic Creole types here are vessels in widespread use in Spain since the sixteenth century that took root in the New World and, over time, underwent important transformations. An eloquent example of this is the *bernegal* or *tachuela*, a round drinking bowl with two handles in the form of scrolls. A late seventeenth-century example (CAT. 175) with a sober design embodies this type of form, still quite close to its Spanish models. Subsequently, this basic form gave rise to the smaller Andean *cocchas*, or ritual vessels, with chiseled or embossed decoration on the bottom, as well as locally inspired motifs on the handles, which have remained in use in traditional ceremonies of offering, or "payment," to the earth.

Two large basins bear witness to the importance acquired by this type of object as an element of ostentation, both in the civil and ecclesiastical spheres. The first, dated to the seventeenth century, is distinguished by its elliptical and concave central container,

1 Pedro de Cieza de León, *Crónica del Perú* (Lima: Pontificia Universidad Católica del Perú, 1984), 229. Quote taken from *The Travels of Pedro de Cieza de Leon…*, trans. Clements R. Markham, (London: T. Richards, 1864), Chapter 114, 403.

2 According to the anonymous chronicler of Yucay, "for such great goods such as these [evangelization] no returnee sends from Peru to Spain anything but the fruit of what he extracts from this rich and powerful mountain." For his part, friar Reginaldo de Lizárraga described this mine as "the wealth of the world, terror of the Turk, of the heretic, silence of the barbarous nations." See *El anónimo de Yucay frente a Bartolomé de las Casas* (Cuzco: Centro de Estudios Regionales Andinos Bartolomé de las Casas, 1995), 161, and Reginaldo de Lizárraga, *Descripción del Perú, Tucumán, Río de la Plata y Chile* (Madrid: Dastin, 2002), 220.

3 On the Indigenous silversmiths, see Luisa María Vetter Parodi, *Plateros indígenas en el virreinato del Perú: siglos XVI y XVII* (Lima: Fondo Editorial de la Universidad Nacional Mayor de San Marcos, 2008).

4 Raveneau de Lussan, *Journal du voyage fait a la Mer du Sud avec les flibustiers de l'Amerique* (Paris: Jacques Le Fevre, 1705), 335.

5 On the tupos, their nomenclature, and their evolution see Luisa María Vetter Parodi and Paloma Carcedo de Mufarech, *El tupo: símbolo ancestral de identidad femenina* (Lima: Gráfica Biblos, 2009).

CAT. 175 **Unknown artist,**
Two-Handled Footless Bowl
Colombia or Ecuador, late 1600s.
Silver, 2 × 7 in. dia. (5 × 17.8 cm dia.).
Gift of the Stapleton Foundation of Latin American Art, made possible by the Renchard family, 1990.398

while its broad outer contour unfolds a play of curves and counter-curves of great refinement (CAT. 176). Its smooth surface contrasts with that of a later platter made for religious use and of Upper Peruvian origin (today Bolivia) (CAT. 178). It is rectangular and takes the shape of a trough in the center; its voluminous reliefs, achieved by means of embossing, depict foliage, scrolls, and figures of flying angels. It displays a variegated ornamental design, clearly linked to the *mestizo* taste characteristic of the religious architecture of the Andean south and the Altiplano between approximately 1680 and 1780.

Other pieces of a more utilitarian nature recall the intensive use of silver, even in objects that in Europe were usually made from other metals. In this regard, the French buccaneer Raveneau de Lussan noted with astonishment that in Peru "the abundance of this rich metal is so great that most of the things we make in France from steel, copper, or iron are here made from silver."[4] This is the case of a basin used by a barber or surgeon for bloodletting (CAT. 177), with a fine Rococo design in the form of a scallop shell. It testifies to the stylistic change produced in the last third of the eighteenth century, when the aesthetic currents associated with the Enlightenment burst forth with force, particularly in the major cities of the viceroyalty. A pot from a similar period for potpourri, or for domestic interior perfumery (CAT. 179), combines the purity of its design with the Baroque style of the typical Andean handles and the animal figurine that crowns the openwork lid. Its form is inspired by contemporary European vessels that served similar functions but were originally made of porcelain or earthenware.

It is interesting to note the same stylistic changes in the evolution of private devotional objects, which achieved a renewed popularity in relation to the concept of "enlightened piety." This type of object is represented in this collection by paintings on metal in an overelaborate style, whose sumptuous frames emphasized the opulence of their owners. The frame of *La Dolorosa* (VIRGIN OF SORROWS, CAT. 180) offers a local reworking of Rococo intermingled with earlier traditions, while that of *San Juan Evangelista* (SAINT JOHN THE EVANGELIST, CAT. 181) sports a Neoclassical design based on ribbons and garlands, echoing the aesthetic leadership of Matías Maestro (1766–1835), whose influence radiated from Lima to the southern Andes and left its mark on practically all the decorative arts. Another silver frame (CAT. 182), surrounding

CAT. 176 **Unknown artist, *Basin***
Colombia, 1600s. Silver, 3 × 19 × 12¾ in. dia. (7.6 × 48.3 × 32.4 cm). Gift of the Stapleton Foundation of Latin American Colonial Art, made possible by the Renchard family, 1990.480

a Mexican painting of the Virgin of Guadalupe, dates from an earlier period and comes from Popayán, in New Granada. Its undulating profile alternates rocaille motifs with openwork areas that reveal great technical sophistication. In each of these cases, the resulting stylistic hybridity reiterates, once again, the ability of local artisans to creatively interpret European models.

In the northern territories of Quito and Bogotá, which later in the eighteenth century constituted the viceroyalty of New Granada, a type of colorful jewelry is prominent, which frequently combines gold with emeralds, pearls, and other stones to add volume to high-quality mounts. This region is the source for some small jewels of meticulous and elaborate workmanship, such as a cross that probably sat upon the crown of a religious sculpture (SEE RIVAS PÉREZ, CAT. 9). Its sophisticated workmanship and brilliant color is also found in other pieces for civilian use, such as the chatelaine pick (CAT. 183) used on a garment frequently worn by the Creole upper classes and an imposing tiara of Rococo design (CAT. 184), whose openwork foliage frames jewels that surpass their Old World prototypes in luxury.

Within the silver adornments and jewels that were part of the ethnic apparel among the Native elites, the *tupus*, or *tupos* (*ttipqui* in Quechua), represent a unique case of formal disjunction.[5] This generic name encompasses several types of ornamental metal pins used by Indigenous women to hold their *lliclla*, or mantle. They are composed of a sharp shank, which fulfilled the actual utilitarian function, and a decorative head, usually of considerable size, which could assume varied forms. These accessories had been made of silver ever since pre-Inca times, probably due to the ancestral symbolic association of the white metal with the tears of the moon, or *quilla*, and, therefore, with the veneration of a lunar divinity that, in turn, was identified with the feminine side of the cosmos.

After the Spanish conquest, the tupo managed to adapt to the new political circumstances. Its use continued to identify the women of Indigenous nobility and reached its peak during the so-called Inca Renaissance

CAT. 177 **Unknown artist, *Barber's Basin***
Peru, mid-1700s. Silver, 15¾ × 11½ in. (40 × 29.2 cm). Gift of the Robert Appleman family, 1980.313

during the eighteenth century. After the defeat of the rebel chieftain Túpac Amaru in 1781, the tupos again underwent important changes, which accelerated with the advent of the republic. The pieces gathered here belong to this latter period, most of which correspond to the type known as *cuchara* (SPOON, CAT. 184). Their late-colonial precedents were tolerated by the Spanish authorities since they were considered free of the feared Inca symbolism. These pieces concentrate their ornamentation on the concave part, often decorated with a burin. Their extensive decorative repertoire suggests a Romanticist inspiration, including everything from birds, vegetal motifs, and mermaids to representations of the sun and moon (SEE MAJLUF, CAT. 202).

In contrast, the varayok cane has an indisputable Hispanic origin, which Native peoples transformed by endowing it with vernacular content (CAT. 185). They are cone-shaped sticks made of hardwood, covered with silver cladding at both ends, in addition to silver bands that encircle them along their entire length and an accumulation of chains, crosses, and adornments displaying great variety of sacred and profane motifs. Their moment of greatest splendor was a consequence of the gradual resurgence of Indigenous peoples and communities during the republic, as they were symbols of ancestral authority. This explains the symbolic importance invested in this type of object by the twentieth-century Indigenous intellectuals, who were able to intuit in them a cultural continuity that traversed the various periods of Andean history.

CAT. 178 **Unknown artist, *Platter***
Bolivia, ca. 1725–50. Silver, 3 × 13¾ × 21 in.
(7.6 × 34.9 × 53.3 cm). Gift of the Robert Appleman
family, 1986.456

CAT. 179 **Unknown artist, *Potpourri Vase***
Peru or Bolivia, 1700s. Silver, 10 × 8½ in. dia.
(25.4 × 21.6 cm dia.). Gift of the Stapleton Foundation of Latin American Colonial Art, made possible by the Renchard family, 1990.482

CAT. 180 **Unknown artist, *Virgin of Sorrows***
Cuzco, Peru, late 1700s–early 1800s. Oil paint on metal with silver frame, framed 19½ × 14⅜ × 2 in. (49.5 × 36.5 × 5 cm). Gift of Freyer family, 2018.611

CAT. 181 **Unknown artist, *Saint John the Evangelist***
Peru, late 1700s or early 1800s. Oil paint and gold leaf on copper with silver frame, framed 8 × 6 × ⅜ in. (20.3 × 15.2 × 1 cm). Gift of John Critcher Freyer for the Frank Barrows Freyer Collection, 1971.432

CAT. 182 **Nicolás Enríquez, Mexican, 1704–ca. 1790, *Virgin of Guadalupe***
Mexico, ca. 1740. Oil paint on copper with silver frame, framed 52¾ × 35¾ × 1⅝ in. (134 × 90.8 × 4.1 cm). Gift of the Collection of Frederick and Jan Mayer, 2013.303

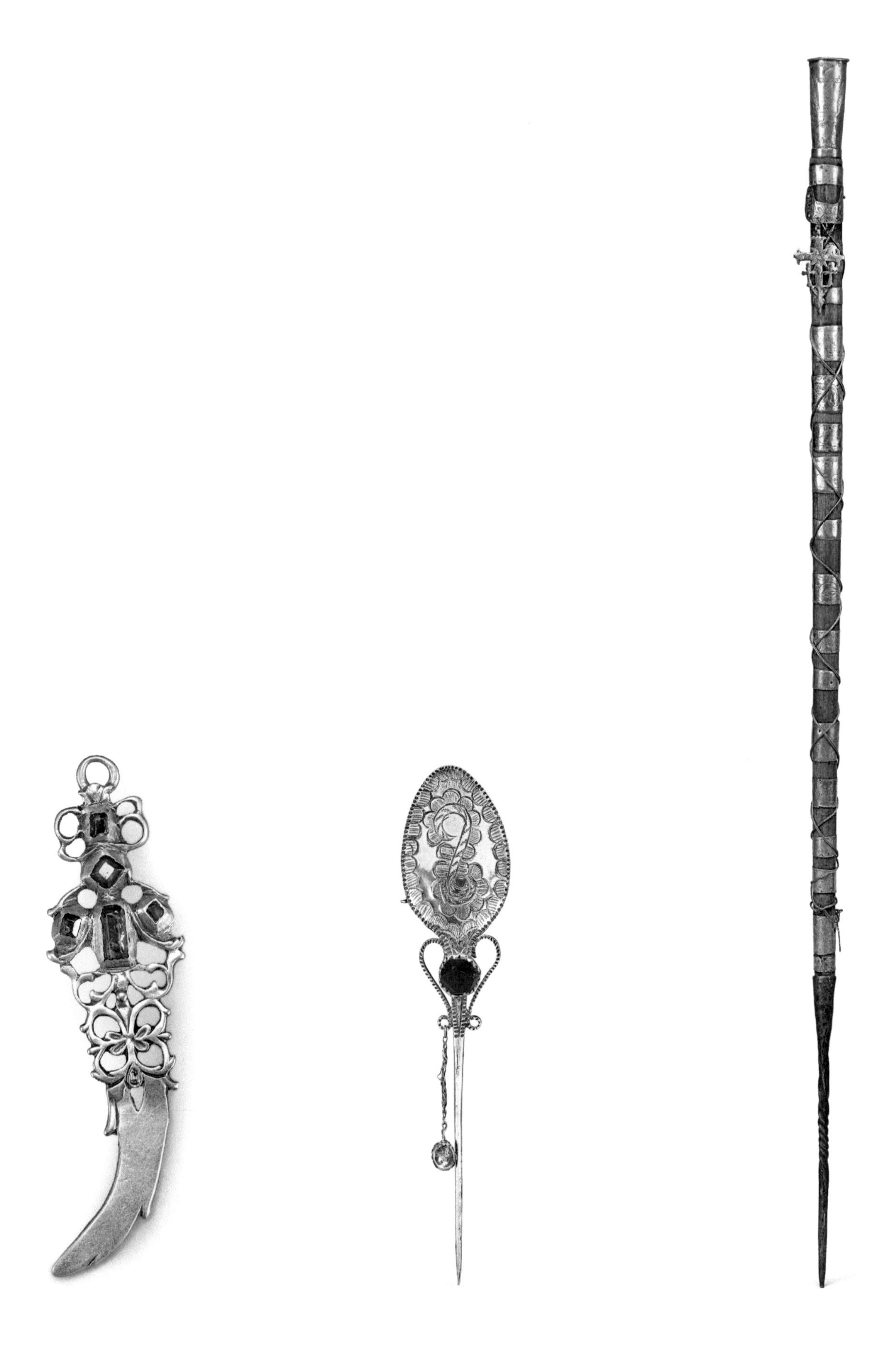

CAT. 183 **Unknown artist, *Chatelaine Pick***
Colombia or Ecuador, ca. 1650. Gold and emeralds, 2½ × ½ in. (6.4 × 1.3 cm). Gift of the Stapleton Foundation of Latin American Colonial Art, made possible by the Renchard family, 1990.525

CAT. 184 **Unknown artist, *Mantle Pin (ttipqui)***
Peru, 1800s. Silver alloy and glass, 7½ × 1¾ in. (19.1 × 4.4 cm). Gift of Mrs. Harry K. Runnette, 1966.193

CAT. 185 **Unknown artist, *Varayok Staff***
Peru, late 1800s. Wood and metal, 49½ × 1½ in. (125.7 × 3.8 cm). Estate of Leon H. Snyder, 1978.273A-B

CAT. 186 **Unknown artist, *Tiara***
Colombia or Ecuador, ca. 1730. Gilded silver with emeralds, pearls, and glass, 2½ × 5½ × 3¾ in. (6.4 × 14 × 9.5 cm). Bequest of Robert J. Stroessner, 1992.74

Epilogue

Asia and Spanish America

Sofía Sanabrais

1 In 2006, the Mayer Center at the Denver Art Museum presented "Asia and Spanish America: Trans-Pacific Artistic and Cultural Exchange," the first symposium of its kind to present this research in a public forum.

2 For a larger historical discussion see Sofía Sanabrais, "Desired and Sought by the Rest of the World: Asian Art in the Hispanic World," in *Art and Empire: The Golden Age of Spain*, ed. Michael A. Brown (San Diego: The San Diego Museum of Art, 2019).

3 For the 1560 inventory of Charles V, that included among many items, porcelain made in China that displayed his royal insignia, see Pedro de Madrazo, "Über Kronungsinsignien und Staatsgewänder Maximilian I. und Karl V. und ihr Schicksal im Spanien," *Jahrbuch der kunsthistorischen Sammlungen des allerhöchsten Kaiserhauses*, IX (1889), 45–51.

4 See Juan Grau y Monfalcón, *Memorial informativo al rey nuestro señor en su real, y supreme consejo de las India: pro la insigne, y siempre leal ciudad de Manila, cabeza de las islas Philipinas: sobre las pretensions de aquella ciudad, é islas, y sus vecinos, y moradores, y comercio con la Nueva España*, Madrid, 1637. Published in E. H. Blair and J. A. Robertson, *The Philippine Islands, 1493–1898*, vol. 22 (Cleveland, OH: The Arthur H. Clark Company, 1903–09), 93–4.

5 For more on Hispano-oriental and Luso-Indian ivory sculpture see Beatriz Sánchez Navarro de Pintado, *Marfiles cristianos del oriente en México* (Mexico City: Fomento Cultural Banamex, A.C., 1986).

6 See Mitchell Codding, "The Decorative Arts in Latin America, 1492–1820," in *The Arts in Latin America, 1492–1820*, ed. Joseph J. Rishell and Suzanne L. Stratton. (Philadelphia: Philadelphia Museum of Art, 2006), 98–121.

7 See Sofía Sanabrais, "From *Byōbu* to *Biombo*: The Transformation of the

As early as the sixteenth century, the convergence of the worlds of religion, commerce, and diplomacy connected Asia and Spanish America and transformed the material culture of the early modern world. The cross-cultural exchange of artistic traditions that revealed the impact of Asian material culture on the art of Spanish America can be seen in the remarkable collection of the Denver Art Museum, a pioneer in the collecting, research, and exhibition of this art.[1]

By the sixteenth century, European expansion to Asia in search of spices was well underway and the quest for the evangelization of the non-Christian world soon followed. The Portuguese and Spanish took control of existing commercial centers and established new ones in places like Manila, Nagasaki, Goa, and Macao. China's demand for silver from the mines of American cities like Potosí and Zacatecas facilitated the exchange of Asian luxury goods. The results of this expansion far exceeded the mere exchange of commodities—it signaled a new era in global trade as objects from Japan, China, and India flooded marketplaces, introducing entirely new material and visual vocabulary of artistic influence.[2]

The Hapsburg rulers of Spain began collecting objects from Asia as early as the reign of the Emperor Charles V.[3] Spain's colonization of the Philippines in 1565 and the subsequent establishment of the Manila galleon trade facilitated Philip II's access to Asian goods. Spanish America was profoundly affected by the influx of luxury goods from Asia brought on the galleons that made annual trips from Manila to Acapulco in the viceroyalty of New Spain from 1565 to 1815.

The vogue for Asian things in Mexico, and subsequent local attempts to recreate certain styles and techniques, predated by a century that of chinoiserie and *Japonisme* in Europe. The high esteem in which such objects were regarded was expressed in an elaborate 1637 memorial to King Philip IV of Spain and the Council of the Indies by the Procurator General of the Islands, Juan Grau y Monfalcón: "In Asia and the regions of the Orient," he wrote, "God created some things so precious in the estimation of man, and so peculiar to those provinces that, as they are only found or manufactured therein, they are desired and sought by the rest of the world."[4]

Exotic raw materials like mother-of-pearl, ivory, and tortoise shell were imported to the Americas and aroused wonder among artists and collectors. Ivory tusks from elephants were valued in India and in the Philippines prior to colonization and, as a raw material, were charged with notions of spiritual and temporal goodness, purity, and virtue.[5] The Philippines was one of the greatest producers of Christian images in ivory, and Native and Chinese artists created many of the delicately carved sculptures exported to the Americas. Ivory was ideal for rendering human figures more realistic through the application of layers of paint. Artists drew on conventional Christian imagery and incorporated the stylized treatment of hair as seen in the *Christ Child* (CAT. 187) and in the drapery of the *Immaculate Conception* (CAT. 188), recalling East and South Asian sculptural traditions.

Since ivory could not be sourced in the Americas, artists found native substitutes. In Mexico and Peru, artists replaced ivory with local alabaster (known as *huamanga* in Peru). The

CAT. 187 **Unknown artist, *Standing Christ Child (Salvator Mundi)***
Philippines, 1600s. Ivory, 17 × 6 × 3½ in. (43.2 × 14.2 × 8.9 cm). Bequest of Robert J. Stroessner, 1992.61

translucent, white, soft material was easy to carve and paint. This finely carved, double-sided image of *Saint Michael and the Virgin and Child with Saints Dominic and John the Baptist* (SEE NEFF, CAT. 57) by Diego de Reinoso, an exquisite example of Asian influences on Spanish American art, reveals that the snail-like clouds surrounding St. Michael resemble Indian carving techniques seen in sculptural models.

Shell, specifically mother-of-pearl, was valued for its lustrous surface and applied in pieces as a veneer over wooden surfaces. In Japan, it was frequently used as inlay on portable lacquer altars that were exported to the Americas. This image of *St. Ignatius Loyola* (CAT. 189) by the Mexican artist Agustín del Pino is a fine an example of an *enconchado*, a Spanish American innovation that derived its name from the Spanish word for shell, *concha*. In these paintings, small fragments of shell and mother-of-pearl were inlaid onto the surface of a wooden support in a mosaic-like manner. Enhanced by the shimmering fragments, devotional images like *St. Ignatius Loyala* sparkled when viewed by candlelight. In *Christ Teaching in the Temple* (CAT. 190), the luminous nature of the concha on the garments of each figure added a level of preciousness to the work of art. The colonial enconchado tradition can trace its sources of influence to Japan, Korea, and India in works of art fabricated for both secular and religious use.

While the primary trade route of the Manila galleons was directed toward Acapulco, several voyages took place between Manila and the Peruvian port of Callao. Asian commodities flooded the market to satisfy the insatiable appetites of wealthy Peruvian consumers made rich from the silver mines. The northern Andes region (present-day Colombia, Venezuela, and Ecuador) also received their fair share of Asian goods. Luxury household furnishings were exported to the New World and had a lasting impact on local art production, especially lacquerwork.

Captivated by the incredible beauty and luminosity of Japanese lacquers, artists utilized *mopa mopa*, a native resin that mimicked the smoothness of Asian lacquer. Mopa mopa is a translucent pale green, natural resin used in the region of Pasto, Colombia, before the arrival of the Spaniards. It is the main ingredient in lacquer wares known as barniz de Pasto (Pasto varnish) produced in Peru, Colombia, and Ecuador.[6] This chest (CAT. 192) is a remarkable example of the barniz de Pasto tradition. The silver fittings on this chest and the decorative landscape with

Japanese Folding Screen in Colonial Mexico," *Art History* 38, no. 4 (Fall 2015): 778–91.

8 For an introduction to the Spanish domestic interior, see Jorge F. Rivas Pérez, "Spanish Magnificence: Cosmopolitan Luxuries at Home in the Golden Age," in *Art and Empire: The Golden Age of Spain*, ed. Michael A. Brown (San Diego: The San Diego Museum of Art, 2019), 111–41.

CAT. 188 **Unknown artist,**
The Immaculate Conception
Goa, India, 1700s. Ivory, paint, and wood, height 12 in. (30.5 cm). Gift of Olive Bigelow, 1971.473

CAT. 189 **Agustín del Pino, Mexican, active 1700–1720s,**
Saint Ignatius Loyola
Mexico, ca. 1700. Oil paint and mother-of-pearl on wood panel (*enconchado*), 33½ × 23½ in. (85.1 × 59.7 cm). Gift of the Collection of Frederick and Jan Mayer, 2013.302

fanciful flora and fauna point to a well-discerning patron. The silver handles attached to the sides and the reinforced straps on its bottom suggest it was likely intended for transport.

Mexican lacquer is also represented in the museum's collection. This chest (CAT. 191) from Olinalá is a typical example of the bright and colorful lacquer work for which the region is known. The sgraffito, or scratched, designs on the silver-pigmented borders of the surface were a common feature of lacquer chests. Chests with elaborate silver locks kept valuables safe.

At the center of this trade with Asia was a new format that transformed secular painting: the Japanese folding screen. Folding screens came to the Americas through the Manila galleon trade and by Japanese embassies that brought them to Mexico as gifts.[7] Local artists adapted the new format, known as *biombo*, after *byōbu* (the Japanese word for screen). Its versatility contributed to its adaptation to daily life; it was freestanding, portable, and multipaneled and was ideal for painting. Biombos were an indispensable element in domestic interiors. Colonial archival records often identify them as *biombos de cama*, which reinforced intimacy surrounding the bed, and as *rodaestrados* when they delineated the space surrounding the *estrado*, a raised platform in the *salón del estrado*, or sitting room, of both Spanish and New Spanish residences.[8]

In the seventeenth century, biombos often depicted historical subjects, like this one showing the conquest of Mexico on the front and Mexico City on the back (FIG. 1). Typically screens at this time were dominated by multitudes of figures, creating dynamic compositions. By the eighteenth century, however, scenes of daily life began to replace literary and historical subject matter, as in this charming ten-panel screen, *Garden Party on the Terrace of Country Home*, illustrating a group of partygoers (CAT. 193). With the change in subject matter, there is also a shift from small-scale to nearly life-size figures that dominate the composition. Party goers and card players arranged across the screen appear to highlight the progression of the strict social hierarchy of New Spanish society.

This brief examination of the influence of Asia on the arts of Spanish America reveals that through the lens of art, it is possible to see how the introduction of new materials and formats, as well as the global desire for objects across oceans, transformed the material culture of the Spanish American world.

AD
MAIOREM
DEI
GLORIAM

CAT. 190 **Unknown artist, *Christ Teaching in the Temple***
Mexico, 1600s. Oil paint with shell inlay on wood panel, 11¼ × 14½ in. (28.6 × 36.8 cm). Gift of Robert J. Stroessner, 1991.1160

CAT. 191 **Unknown artist, *Maque Chest***
Olinalá, Guerrero, Mexico, ca. 1770s. *Maque* (lacquer) on wood and silver, 7¼ × 11 × 6 in. (18.4 × 27.9 × 15.2 cm). Gift of Charles G. Patterson III, 2021.423

CAT. 192 **Unknown artist, *Chest***
Colombia, 1700s. Barniz de Pasto and silver leaf on wood with silver, 15¼ × 22½ × 10¼ in. (38.7 × 57.2 × 26 cm). Gift of the Collection of Frederick and Jan Mayer, 2015.545

CAT. 193 **Unknown artist, *Garden Party on the Terrace of a Country Home***
Mexico, ca. 1720–30. Oil paint on canvas with gold, 7 ft. 3⅛ in. × 18 ft. 4 in. (221.1 × 559 cm). Gift of the Collection of Frederick and Jan Mayer, 2009.759

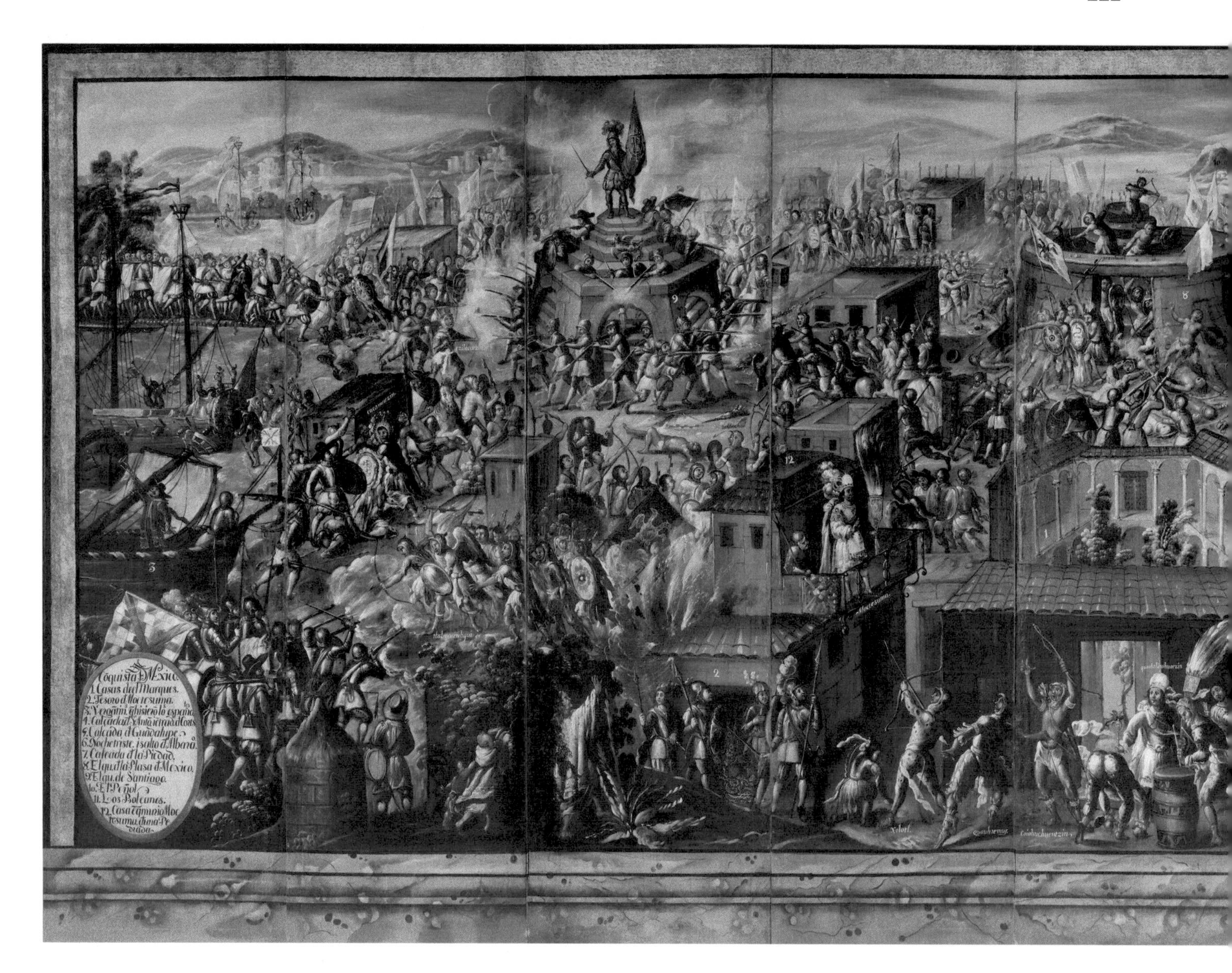
Cōquista D. Mexico.
1. Casas del Marques.
2. Tesoro d. Moctesuma.
5. Calcada d. Guadalupe.
6. Noche triste. i salto d. Albarado.
7. Calcada d. la Piedad.
8. El qu. d. la Plasa d. Mexico.
9. El qu. de Santiago.
10. El Peñol.
11. Los Bolcanes.

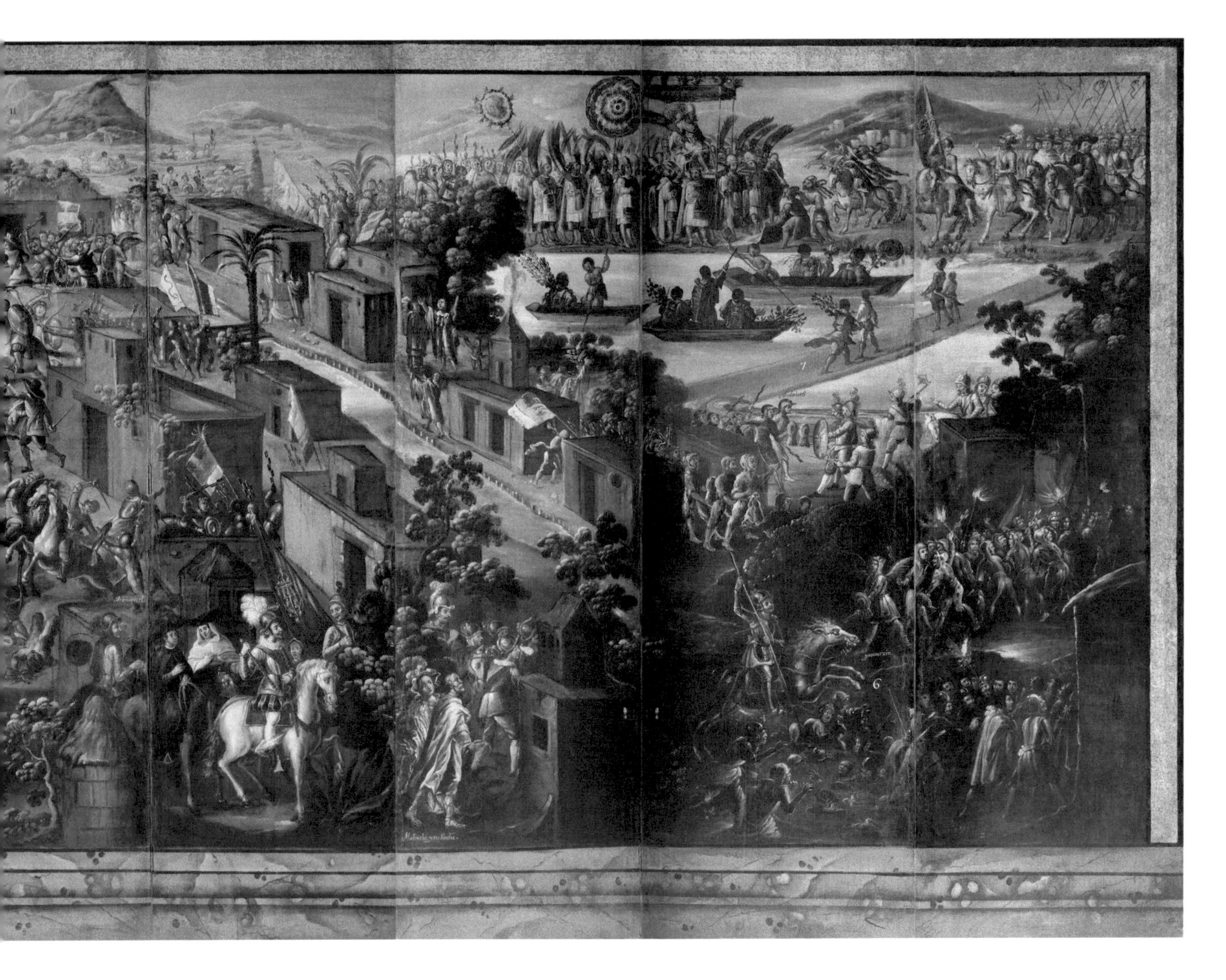

FIG. 1 Unknown artist, *Folding Screen with the Conquest of Mexico* (front), Mexico, late 1600s. Oil paint on canvas, ten-panel folding screen; overall 6 ft. 10⅝ in. × 18 ft. 4 in. (210 × 560 cm). Colección Museo Soumaya. Fundación Carlos Slim A. C. / Ciudad de México, México.

New Mexico's Unmistakable *Santos*: Artistic Bricolage and the Formation of Style

James M. Córdova

A distinctive style of *santos* (painted and sculpted religious art) emerged in New Mexico in the decades leading up to 1800, identifiable on its own terms and rooted in a culturally dynamic environment. Featuring stylized images of the saints, geometric and natural motifs, and a colorful but limited palette of local and imported paints, these striking works met the local demand for sacred art during New Mexico's Spanish colonial, Mexican, and American territorial periods. As part of a larger web of artistic production, they selectively drew upon local and foreign works including European and Mexican graphic prints, Mexican colonial ceramics, local Indigenous paintings and ceramics, and other santos.

Franciscan friars first introduced Christian images in New Mexico in the early seventeenth century.[1] Many of these works were imported from Mexico and Spain along the Camino Real, a road that connected northern New Mexico to Mexico City and to an extensive global trade network.[2] In some cases, the friars or Indigenous artists with whom they worked made religious images. Because much was destroyed in the 1680 Pueblo Revolt against the Spanish, today little is known about the religious art of this early era. But by the late eighteenth century, Spanish and Mexican religious art, along with locally produced santos, populated New Mexico's religious institutions and private homes.[3]

Santos can be categorized into painted wooden panels (*retablos*) (CATS. 194 AND 195), gesso relief panels (CAT. 196), and painted sculptures in the round (*bultos*) carved mostly out of cottonwood root (CATS. 197 AND 198). Altar screens (*retablos mayores* and *colaterales*) (CAT. 199) combine retablos and sometimes bultos within architectural frameworks and were usually made for churches and private chapels. The artists who produced santos identified themselves as sculptors (*escultores*) and painters (*pintores*) although the term *santero* is commonly used today.[4]

Painted animal hides (CAT. 200 AND FIG. 1) are among the earliest devotional objects made in New Mexico. By the 1630s, a workshop of Native artists in Santa Fe, the Spanish capital, manufactured them for export to central Mexico.[5] They employed the Indigenous method of brain tanning and painting directly on hide surfaces so that the pigments saturated the material like a stain.[6] The Denver Art Museum's *Crucifixion with Instruments of the Passion* (CAT. 200) shows us that eighteenth-century hide-painting artists still used the same methods as their predecessors. The strong sense of line, draftsmanship, and naturalism allude to one or several imported printed images that served as models for artists in Spanish America. In the early modern world, graphic prints circulated in international trade networks to which New Mexico belonged. Yet despite their impact on Spanish colonial art, local artists did not simply copy them. This is evident in some New Mexican hide paintings that selectively deviate from their printed sources and, in some cases, may reference Indigenous Pueblo motifs and Mexican Talavera ceramics.[7]

1 E. Boyd, *Popular Arts of Spanish New Mexico* (Santa Fe: Museum of New Mexico Press, 1974), 96–97, 118; William Wroth, *Christian Images in Hispanic New Mexico: The Taylor Museum Collection of Santos* (Colorado Springs: The Taylor Museum of the Fine Arts Center, 1982), 37–38; Marie Romero Cash, *Santos: Enduring Images of Northern New Mexican Village Churches* (Boulder: University Press of Boulder, 1999), 9–10, 54–55.

2 James E. Ivey "'*Ultimo Poblado del Mundo*' (The Last Place on Earth): Evidence for Imported Retablos in the Churches of Seventeenth-Century New Mexico," in *El Camino Real de Tierra Adentro*, vol. 2, compiled by Gabrielle G. Palmer and Stephen L. Fosberg, Cultural Resources Series 13 (Santa Fe: Bureau of Land Management, 1999), 177–195.

3 Robin Farwell Gavin, "Creating a New Mexico Style," in *Converging Streams: Art of the Hispanic and Native American Southwest*, eds. William Wroth and Robin Farwell Gavin (Santa Fe: Museum of Spanish Colonial Art, 2010), 39, 49; Marianne Stoller, "The Early *Santeros* of New Mexico: A Problem in Ethnic Identity and Artistic Tradition," in *Transforming Images: New Mexican* Santos *in-between Worlds*, eds. Claire Farago and Donna Pierce (University Park: Pennsylvania State University Press, 2006), 117–33.

4 José Antonio Esquibel and Charles M. Carrillo, *A Tapestry of Kinship: The Web of Influence of Escultores and Carpinteros in the Parish of Santa Fe, 1790–1850* (Los Ranchos de Albuquerque: LPD Press, 2004), 5.

5 For more on New Mexican hide paintings, see Boyd, *Popular Arts*, 118–43.

6 Donna Pierce, "Hide Painting in New Mexico: New Archival Evidence," in Farago and Pierce, *Transforming Images*, 139.

Hispano-Pueblo bricolage appears in some santos, namely in specific abstracted designs such as the stepped-terrace *remate* that crowns the museum's *Virgin of Seven Sorrows* gesso relief (CAT. 196). Bricolage is also apparent in the two-dimensional rendering of human figures in retablos (CATS. 194, 195, AND 199) and landscape or nature-based images that are analogous to motifs in blue-on-white *loza* ceramics imported from central Mexico as well as local Pueblo kiva murals and rock art (FIG. 2).[8] Retablos, Pueblo pottery, and kiva murals share certain compositional features including two-dimensional banding and framing; the rotation, mirroring, inversion, and repetition of images or design motifs; and a two-dimensional, planar surface that lacks the illusionary pictorial depth of a third dimension.[9] Despite these similarities, cross-cultural bricolage in New Mexico's santos does not indicate fusion of Hispano and Pueblo symbols and their meanings, but rather it points to a shared graphic system and aesthetic borne of centuries of Hispano-Pueblo relations. This allowed for a range of understandings and uses of santos that depended on the viewer's cultural frame of reference. Furthermore, this range did not necessarily violate the Christian message and devotional value of the santos, but in many cases, it would have supplemented them in a manner that spoke to New Mexico's diverse cultural makeup.

Altar screens were the largest and most extravagant kind of devotional art in New Mexico (CAT. 199). The earliest ones were imported from central Mexico, but the first locally made pieces date to the late eighteenth century when Bernardo Miera y Pacheco, a Spanish immigrant and polymath, made altarpieces for several Pueblo churches as well as Santa Fe's military chapel.[10] The anonymous Laguna Santero and Pedro Fresquís—perhaps New Mexico's first locally born santero—produced altar screens for Hispano and Pueblo churches and provided local models for the following generation of santeros. This same period in New Mexico witnessed strong relations between Pueblo and Hispano communities, the end of violent Comanche raids, an economic and demographic boom, and the rise of local sodalities (religious brotherhoods and sisterhoods composed of laypersons).[11] Additionally, newly founded Hispano and Genízaro towns required santos for

CAT. 194 **José Rafael Aragón, American, ca. 1795–1862, *Our Lady of Guadalupe***
Chamisal, New Mexico, ca. 1830. Water-based paint on wood panel, 9 × 6¾ in. (22.9 × 17.1 cm). Funds contributed by The R. H. and Esther F. Goodrich Foundation, 1981.138

7 Donahue-Wallace, Kelly, "Hide Paintings, Print Sources, and the Early Expression of a New Mexican Colonial Identity," in Farago and Pierce, *Transforming Images*, 156–57.
8 Claire Farago, "Transforming Images: Managing the Interstices with a Measure of Creativity," in Farago and Pierce, *Transforming Images*, 165; Gavin, "Creating a New Mexico Style," 45.
9 Farago, "Managing the Interstices," in Farago and Pierce, *Transforming Images*, 170–77; for an alternative

CAT. 195 **Pedro Antonio Fresquís American, 1749–1831, *Saint Veronica's Veil***
Truchas, New Mexico, late 1700s or early 1800s. Water-based paint on wood panel, 19½ × 14 × ⅞ in. (49.4 × 35.6 × 2.2 cm). Gift of Anne Evans Collection, 1936.3

their churches, chapels, and chapter houses, while older religious structures in Santa Fe also fed the demand.[12]

By about 1800, a new generation of santeros emerged in and around Santa Fe. Since there were no official artist guilds or art schools in New Mexico, local workshops where masters taught apprentices perpetuated the art form. Additionally, several santeros formed kinship ties with each other and with professional carpenters through *compadrazgo*, social and sacramental relations established in godfatherhood/godmotherhood and when sponsoring a couple at marriage.[13] In this context, the second wave of New Mexican–born santeros came into being. They include the brothers José Aragón and José Rafael Aragón, as well as Anastacio Casados and Manuel Benavides.[14] Like some of their predecessors, they partially based their work on imported images and local artwork, which now included the first generation of local made santos. In addition to their own art production, these santeros repaired some of the older santos, thereby gaining invaluable knowledge of the local style, materials, and artistic techniques.[15] In this manner, they not only perpetuated New Mexico's santo tradition, but in the process, they also refined it with their own contributions.

Church and government officials along with merchants, influential private residents, and the local devout composed santeros' client base. Additionally, the Hermandad de la Sangre de Cristo, known today as the Hermandad de Nuestro Padre Jesús Nazareno, or

analysis of the compositional characteristics of New Mexican santos premised on medieval and early modern European models of painting, see Thomas J. Steele SJ, *Santos and Saints: The Religious Folk Art of Hispanic New Mexico*, 4th ed. (Santa Fe: Ancient City Press, 1994), 18–39.

10 Donna Pierce and Robin Farwell Gavin, "The Altar Screens of Bernardo Miera y Pacheco," in *The Art and Legacy of Bernardo Miera y Pacheco: New Spain's Explorer, Cartographer, and Artist*, ed. Josef Díaz (Santa Fe: Museum of New Mexico Press, 2013), 63–102.

11 Ross Frank, *From Settler to Citizen: New Mexican Economic Development and the Creation of Vecino Society, 1750–1820* (Berkeley: University of California Press, 2000), 70, 122–50, 182.

12 Genízaros were detribalized Indigenous captives in New Mexico who spoke Spanish and were practicing Catholics. See Frances Leon Swadesh, *Los Primeros Pobladores: Hispanic Americans of the Ute Frontier* (South Bend: University of Notre Dame Press, 1974), 31–52; see also José Esquibel, "The Formative Era for New Mexico's Colonial Population," in Farago and Pierce, *Transforming Images*, 64–79; Paul Kraemer, "The Dynamic Ethnicity of the People of Spanish Colonial New Mexico in the Eighteenth Century," in Farago and Pierce, *Transforming Images*, 80–98; and Estevan Rael Gálvez, "Coyote Convergence: Introduction through Interrogation," in Wroth and Gavin, *Converging Streams*, 13–24.

13 Esquibel and Carrillo, *Tapestry of Kinship*, 16.

14 Until Esquibel and Carrillo identified Benavides by name, he was widely referred to in the literature as the anonymous "Santo Niño Santero." Esquibel and Carrillo, *Tapestry of Kinship*, 5–9.

CAT. 196 **Circle of Laguna Santero, *The Virgin of Seven Sorrows***
New Mexico, late 1700s or early 1800s. Water-based paint and gesso on wood panel, 22½ × 14 in. (57.2 × 35.6 cm). Gift of Anne Evans Collection, 1936.12

more commonly known as "the Penitentes," significantly added to this demand.[16] This influential sodality of laymen used santos in their religious pageants and ceremonies held in their chapter houses, called *moradas*.[17] By 1900, they still commissioned the dwindling number of santeros who were now competing with American manufacturers that supplied inexpensive and mass-produced religious images to New Mexico. Despite this, the artform experienced several revivals, one in the 1920s and another in the latter half of that century that has persisted to the present day. Today we recognize that the unmistakable style of New Mexico's santos is due to the selective appropriations of local and foreign artistic sources, which santeros reconfigured in new and creative ways while also adding their own contributions—a strategy contemporary santeros still practice.

15 Charles M. Carrillo, "A Saintmaker's Palette (Appendix E)," in E. Boyd, *Saints and Saint Makers of New Mexico*, rev. ed., ed. Robin Farwell Gavin (Santa Fe: Western Edge Press, 1998), 99–104; Rutherford J. Gettens and Evan H. Turner, "The Materials and Methods of Some Religious Paintings of Early Nineteenth-Century New Mexico," *El Palacio* 58 (1951): 3–16.

16 Boyd, *Popular Arts*, 440–83; Marta Weigle, *Brothers of Light, Brothers of Blood: The Penitentes of the Southwest* (Albuquerque: University of New Mexico Press, 1976); Thomas J. Steele SJ and Rowena A. Rivera, *Penitente Self-Government: Brotherhoods and Councils, 1797–1947* (Santa Fe: Ancient City Press, 1985).

17 William Wroth, *Images of Penance, Images of Mercy: Southwestern* Santos *in the Late Nineteenth Century* (Norman: University of Oklahoma Press, 1991).

CAT. 197 **José Rafael Aragón, American, ca. 1795–1862, *Our Lady of Mount Carmel***
Santa Fe or Córdova, New Mexico, ca. 1830. Painted wood, 29 × 10¾ in. dia. (73.7 × 27.3 cm dia.). Funds from Walt Disney Imagineering, 1989.3A-C

CAT. 198 **José Benito Ortega, American, 1858–1941, *Saint Isidore the Farmer***
Mora County, New Mexico, ca. 1880. Painted wood, 24¼ × 23 in. (61.6 × 58.4 cm). Purchase for the Anne Evans Collection at the Denver Art Museum, 1949.16

CAT. 199 **Antonio Molleno, American, active ca. 1815–1845, *Altar Screen***
New Mexico, ca. 1825. Water-based paint on wood panel, each panel approx. 23½ × 10½ in. (59.7 × 26.7 cm), overall height 77 in. (195.6 cm). Gift of Anne Evans Collection, 1936.16

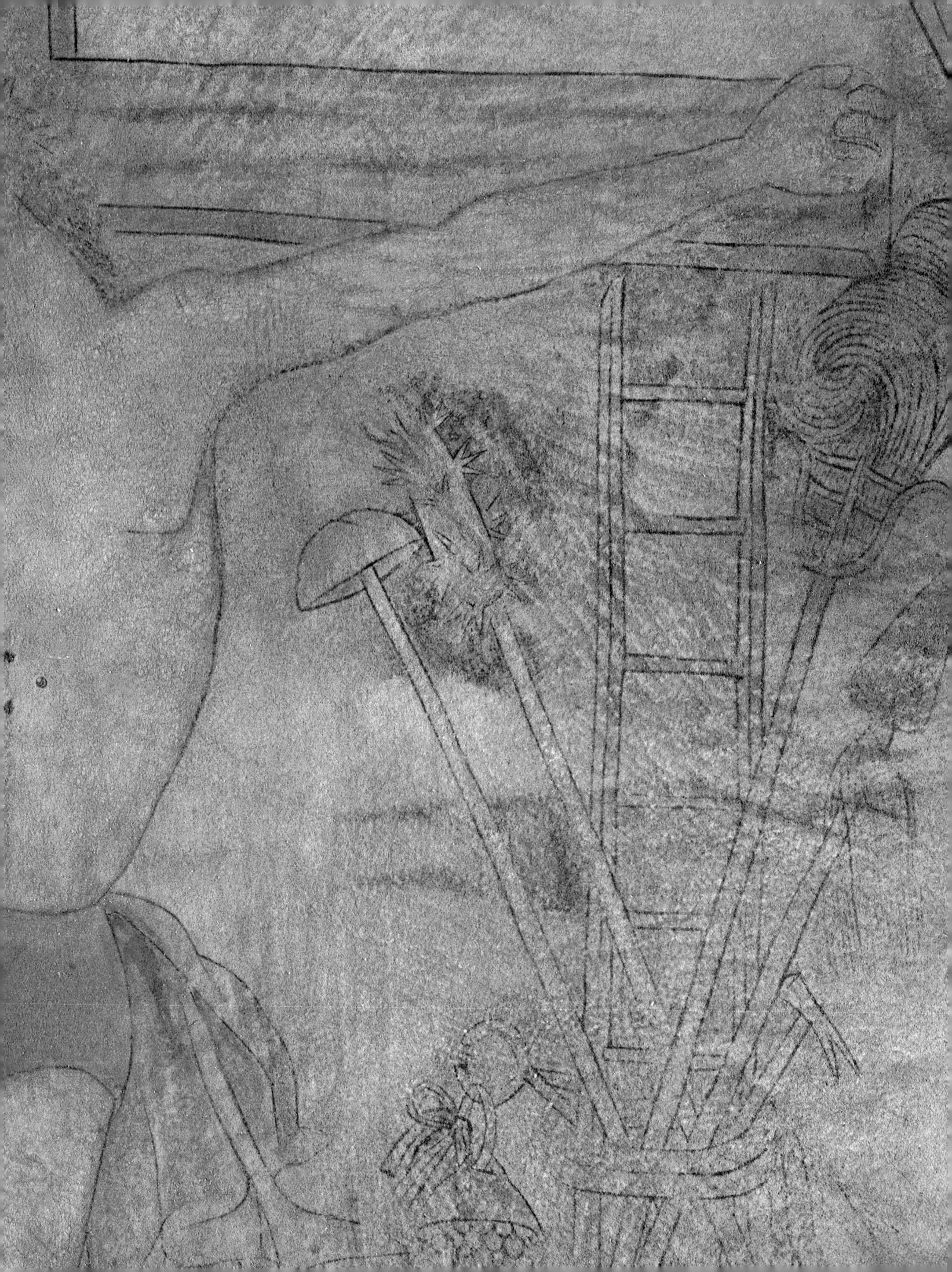

INRI

CAT. 200 **Unknown artist, *Crucifixion with Instruments of the Passion***
New Mexico, 1700s. Painted buffalo hide, 55½ × 48 in. (141 × 121.9 cm). Gift of Mrs. Frederic H. Douglas, 1956.111

FIG. 1 *Nuestra Señora de la Asunción de la Iglesia de Santa María la Redonda de Ciudad de México (Our Lady of the Assumption of the Church of Santa María la Redonda in Mexico City)*, northern New Mexico, 1700s. Natural pigments on hide, 33½ × 26¾ in. (85.1 × 67.9 cm). Museum of International Folk Art, Gift of the Fred Harvey Collection of the International Folk Art Foundation, FA.1979.64.119. Photo by Kate Macuen.

FIG. 2 Pedro Antonio Fresquís, *Saint Damascus, Pope and Confessor, ca. 1800. Water-based paint on wood panel. Museum of Spanish Colonial Art, Santa Fe, 1968.012.*

Toward Modernity: Spanish America after Independence

Natalia Majluf

Like all revolutions, the wars of Latin American independence promised a new beginning. The nations founded on this promise looked to a future that was not yet defined, where the only true certainty was the idea of forward movement to what seemed like inevitable progress. For elites across the region, the recent past was something to be left behind and with it the bounds and limits that Spanish imperialism had imposed on commerce, thought, and international exchange. Colonial artistic traditions were part of that past.

Historians have debated the impact of independence. From the perspective of the economy and of society they have argued, with reason, that political revolution did not quite transform the rigid social hierarchies and inequalities of colonial society and that the republican promises that fueled the energies of war remained unfulfilled. From the perspective of cultural history and of the arts, however, the period was one of great changes. Over the course of the nineteenth century, imports displaced the local production of everyday objects, new patterns of patronage decreased the Church's power over artistic creation, and new aesthetic languages managed to displace late-colonial aesthetics, introducing the visual description of landscape, social types, and customs that were rarely portrayed in colonial art (CAT. 201). Considering a longer historical framework, the effectiveness and radicality of those changes make the nineteenth century a moment of profound cultural transformations. Yet it is also true that modernization was uneven and fractured in more centralized countries, where cities gained undue prominence, and commercial circuits often bypassed inland areas. Art production throughout the region reveals these differences.

Cuzco, the ancient capital of the Inca and a major center of pictorial production throughout the eighteenth century, entered a period of decline, cut off from both older commercial circuits and new international patterns of coastal trade. Unlike Lima and other major capitals, it did not witness a flood of imported images and foreign artists, and its painters, sculptors and weavers largely continued colonial forms of artistic production. Change thus came to Cuzco at a gentler pace.

The series of Inca portraits produced sometime in the mid-1800s by an unknown artist shows the complexity of local art's insertion in modernity (CAT. 205). The artist drew on previous pictorial traditions and typologies but reformulated them to fit new demands. Inca paintings had played a crucial political role during the colonial period as part of the complex assertion of the claims of the Indigenous nobility, Creole elites, and other authorities seeking to appeal to the Inca as emblems of political legitimacy.[1] In the aftermath of the late-eighteenth-century rebellions that shook the foundations of colonial power, the paintings became contentious, and their production was explicitly banned. Their meanings, however, were forever changed by republican ideas imposed after independence: As

1 Gustavo Buntinx and Luis Eduardo Wuffarden, "Incas y reyes españoles en la pintura colonial peruana: la estela de Garcilaso," *Márgenes* 4, no. 8 (December 1991): 151–210.

2 Natalia Majluf, "De la rebelión al museo: Genealogías y retratos de los incas, 1780-1900," in *Los incas, reyes del Perú*, ed. Natalia Majluf (Lima: Banco de Crédito del Perú, 2005), 253–319.

3 The Denver Art Museum series was originally in a British collection.

4 For an overview of nineteenth-century academies, see Oscar E. Vázquez, ed., *Academies and Schools of Art in Latin America* (New York and London: Routledge, 2020).

5 On Gutiérrez, see *Discursos de la piel. Felipe Santiago Gutiérrez (1824-1904)* (Mexico City: Museo Nacional de Arte, 2017), 132–41.

6 For Gutiérrez's comments on Ribera's work in Rome in 1868, as well as for the copy he made of the painter's Saint Bartholomew during his visit to the Prado in November 1870, see Fausto Ramírez's entry on the Saint Bartholomew in Esther Acevedo, Arturo Camacho, Fausto Ramírez, and Angélica Velázquez Guadarrama, *Catálogo comentado del acervo del Museo Nacional de Arte. Pintura. Siglo XIX. Tomo I* (Mexico City: Instituto de Investigaciones Estéticas, Museo Nacional de Arte, 2002), 277–83. For references to Spanish art in nineteenth-century Colombia, see also Olga Isabel Acosta Luna, "Felipe Santiago Gutierrez y los comienzos de la Academia en Colombia," in *Diego, Frida y otros revolucionarios* (Bogotá: Museo Nacional de Colombia, 2009), 72.

7 According to the museum's records, the painting was collected by Daniel Casey Stapleton (1858–1920) while living in Colombia and Ecuador (1895–1914). On Gutiérrez's work in

specific laws took away the privileges of Inca nobles and democratic ideals displaced monarchical succession, the significance of this revived pictorial tradition was also altered. Though formally similar to previous series of Inca kings, the new portraits did not convey political agency but served as objects of prestige for those wishing to associate with an idealized imperial past or as historical documents ultimately destined to serve as testament of the Inca in schoolbooks and museums.[2] Like many similar series, the Denver portraits appear to have been created as part of an emerging market for local antiquities that developed in Cuzco and Lima to satisfy the interest of travelers and antiquarians.[3] Though framed by modern demands, these paintings reflect forms of image-making that were as firmly grounded in colonial traditions as they were distant from the advances that new aesthetic ideals were making throughout the region.

In contrast, Felipe Santiago Gutiérrez's exacting portrayal of an older man traces the inroads of the modern system of the arts, especially in large urban centers like Rio de Janeiro and Mexico City, where formal teaching institutions early contributed to advancing academic ideals (CAT. 204).[4] Gutiérrez (1824–1904) trained in the Mexican Academy of San Carlos, and his career as painter, teacher, and critic exemplifies the pursuit of artistic modernity, undertaken with passion and determination during extended travels through Mexico, Europe, and the Americas.[5] Gutiérrez made the oil study, which appears to have been painted from nature, in the early 1870s, most likely as part of his studies at the San Fernando Academy of Fine Arts in Madrid, where he briefly worked under Federico de Madrazo y Kuntz and Carlos Luis de Ribera. Studies of elderly models were then becoming a staple of academic workshops, as the growing taste for

CAT. 201 **Pedro Antonio Gualdi, Italian, 1808–1857; active in Mexico, 1838–1851, *The Cathedral of Mexico City***
Mexico, 1850. Oil paint on canvas, framed 31⅞ × 42 × 2⅝ in. (81 × 106.7 × 6.7 cm). Gift of the Collection of Frederick and Jan Mayer, 2013.335

establishing formal art training in Bogotá, see Olga Isabel Acosta Luna, "Forming the National School of Fine Art in Colombia. Local Desires and External Influences," in *Academies and Schools of Art in Latin America*, ed. Vázquez, 65–78.

CAT. 202 **Unknown artist,**
Mantle Pin (ttipqui)
Peru, 1800s. Silver-plated copper, height 9½ in. (24.1 cm). Gift of Mrs. LeRoy Schwartz, 1954.156

CAT. 203 **Unknown artist,**
Chest of Drawers
Ecuador, ca. 1830–40. Wood, metal, and glass, 48½ × 41½ × 23½ in. (123.2 × 105.4 × 59.7 cm). Gift of the Stapleton Foundation of Latin American Colonial Art, made possible by the Renchard family, 1990.538

naturalism—informed by the advances of new visual technologies—brought Baroque realism into aesthetic focus. Gutiérrez's painting clearly evokes his admiration for the Spanish pictorial tradition and especially for Jusepe de Ribera (Lo Spagnoletto), whose works he had admired in Italy, emulated in his academic studies in Rome, and devoutly copied in Madrid.[6] The painting, made on paper, was no doubt part of the belongings he brought to Colombia on one of the many trips he undertook to collaborate in the establishment of an art academy, an objective partially achieved with a private academy he directed in 1873 and which, beginning in 1881, bore his name.[7] Author of a pictorial treatise, active critic, and promoter of the fine arts in the many cities he visited, Gutiérrez's trajectory exemplifies the cosmopolitan outlook and the almost missionary drive of nineteenth-century painters in their quest to establish a modern system of the arts.

That ideal, however, remained largely unrealized. In most places, its materialization through institutions, public exhibitions, and critical debate was partial and limited, and though new aesthetic languages and formats spread rapidly, their reach was often mediated by older traditions. Formal innovation sometimes transformed traditional typologies in genres like cabinetry, jewelry and *tupu* pins (CATS. 202 AND 203 AND WUFFARDEN, CAT. 184). In other cases, visual languages did not adapt as quickly to new fashions in genres like portraiture, which achieved a previously unknown popularity in the hands of artists who trained in colonial workshops or who operated outside of academic strictures. These artists produced some of the most striking images in Latin America's transition to modernity (CAT. 208). In many places forms of production maintained older patterns of consumption, distribution, and aesthetic form, as in ceramics and weaving, although modifications would also gradually affect their production (CATS. 206 AND 207). In the long nineteenth century, as the region saw the end of one political regime and the beginning of a new one and as the vast territories previously dominated by Spain entered the circuits of global capitalism and trade, few things were to remain unchanged.

CAT. 204 **Felipe Santiago Gutiérrez, Mexican, 1824–1904, *Portrait of an Old Man***
Colombia, 1873–75. Oil paint on paper laid on canvas, 29½ × 25 in. (74.8 × 63.5 cm). Gift of the Stapleton Foundation of Latin American Colonial Art, made possible by the Renchard family, 1990.559

MANCCO CCAPAC, INCA I.º D. PERU.

MAMA OCLLO HUACCO, I.ª CCOYA D. PER.º

SINCHI ROCCA II. INCA.

LLOQQUE YUPANQUI, III. INCA.

VIRACOCHA, VIII. INCA.

PACHACUTEC, IX. INCA.

INCA YUPANQUI X. INCA.

TUPAC YUPANQUI, XI. INCA.

CAT. 205 **After Marco Chillitupa Chávez, Cuzco, Peru, active ca. 1820–1840, *Set of Portraits of Inca Rulers and Francisco Pizarro, Spanish Conqueror of Peru***
Lima or Cuzco, Peru, 1830–50. Oil paint on canvas, each approx. 25¼ × 19¼ in. (51.4 × 48.8 cm). Gift of Dr. Belinda Straight, 1977.45.1-16

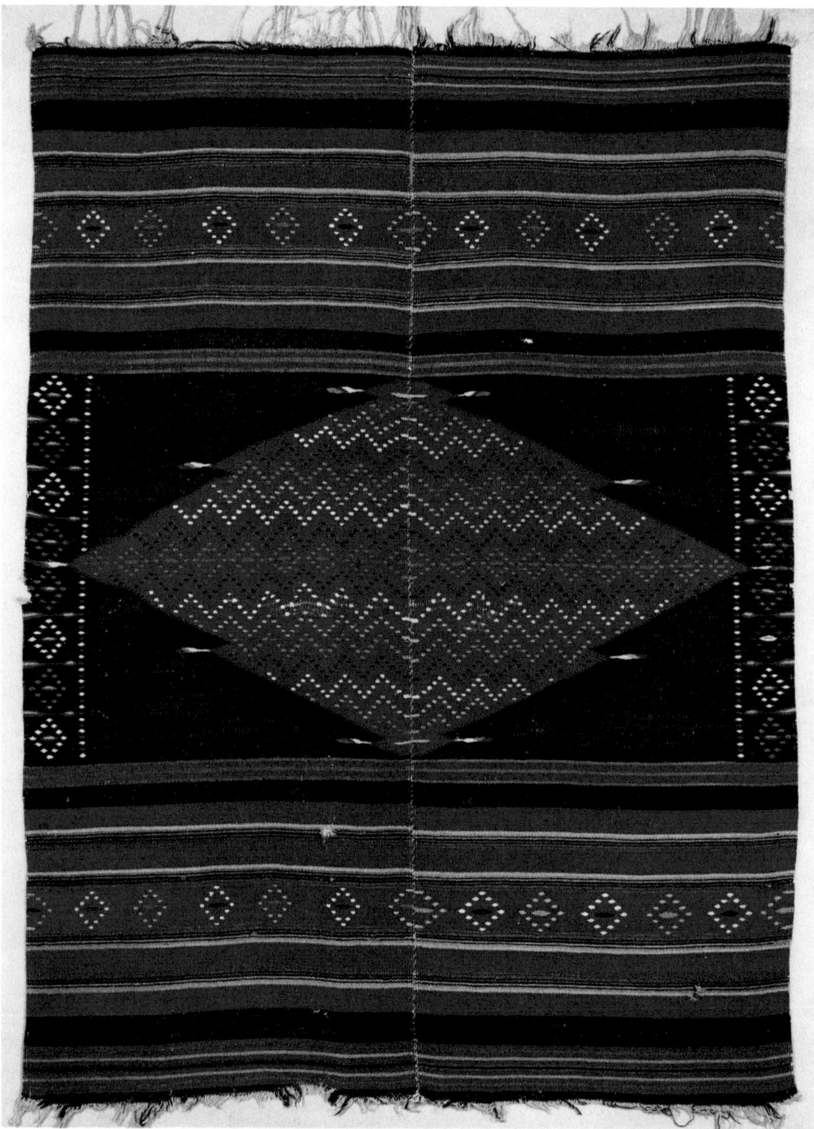

CAT. 206 **Unknown Aymara artist, *Mantle***
Potosi, Bolivia, 1700s. Camelid hair, 40½ × 49 in. (102.9 × 124.5 cm). Neusteter Textile Collection at the Denver Art Museum: Gift of Lael Johnson, 2012.335

CAT. 207 **Unknown artist, *Blanket***
Mexico, late 1800s or early 1900s. Wool, 79 × 60 in. (200.7 × 152.4 cm). Neusteter Textile Collection at the Denver Art Museum: Gift of Mrs. W. A. Butchart, 1945.235

CAT. 208 **Attributed to Luis García Hevia, Colombian, 1816–1887, *Woman with Earring***
Colombia, around 1850. Oil paint on canvas, 31½ × 24¼ in. (80 × 61.6 cm). Gift of Dr. Belinda Straight, 1984.718

Colonial Phantoms in Modern and Contemporary Art in Latin America

Raphael Fonseca

From the names of avenues and monuments to national holidays, the phantom of European colonialism haunts Latin America, including its modern and contemporary art. In this short text, a comparison of two painters—the Mexican José Clemente Orozco and the Brazilian André Griffo—shows how modern and contemporary contexts shape the attitudes toward colonial visual culture. Orozco is one of the most renowned Mexican painters in art history, and Griffo is a young artist who has achieved global prominence. Violence, pain, death, and trauma can be found in works by both artists, and their historical contexts form how they appropriated colonial ideas in contrasting ways.

As a muralist, Orozco, along with his contemporaries Diego Rivera (1886–1957) and David Alfaro Siqueiros (1896–1974), created a modern, dramatic, and expressionistic style to convey Mexico's precolonial past and its future, post-revolutionary possibilities to the public. In *Via Crucis*, Orozco depicts a familiar Christian scene—Jesus Christ carrying the cross on which he will be crucified—that many artists, going back to the Middle Ages, depicted before him (CAT. 209). Though Orozco was interested in the heroes and martyrs of the classical tradition, he charged his modern compositions with drama, using expressive colors and brushstrokes to convey his subjects. Surrounding the central figure of Christ, a group of pious, robed figures kneel and silently accompany Christ, while soldiers and other figures engage in physical violence against him. By concentrating on these extremes, Orozco reflects on the contradictions of good and evil.

By approaching a traditional subject in a modern manner, Orozco leads his viewer—one who experienced the existential, social, and technological changes of the early twentieth century—into a dialogue with the *memento mori* tradition: remember death, remember Christ, and, if possible, change your behavior while still alive. Orozco's painting demonstrates how modern artists experimented with new media and ways of painting while still relying on colonial narratives steeped in traditional Christianity. Like so many other influential Latin American artists, Orozco reflected on death as suggested by Christianity in the midst of modern progress and industrialization. Tradition and modernism, therefore, could go hand in hand.

Contemporary artist André Griffo, born in Barra Mansa, in the state of Rio de Janeiro, also engages Latin America's colonial past to draw attention to history's impact on the present. *Instruções para administração das fazendas 5* (Instructions to the administration of farms 5) belongs to a series of paintings that depict various views of one of the oldest religious buildings in Rio de Janeiro: the Santa Casa da Misericórdia (Holy House of Mercy), a hospital established by the Brotherhood of Mercy in the second half of the 1500s (CAT. 210). It is the oldest hospital in Rio de Janeiro and is still in operation today, offering its services to the public.

CAT. 209 **José Clemente Orozco Mexican, 1883–1949, *Via Crucis (Christ Carrying the Cross)***
Mexico, ca. 1940. Gouache paint on canvas, 33⅝ × 29½ in. (85.4 × 74.9 cm). Gift of Nancy Rogers and Edward D. Pierson in Memory of Mary Vandusen and Charles Bolles Rogers, 1983.241. © 2022 Artists Rights Society (ARS), New York/SOMAAP, Mexico City.

With exacting realism, Griffo depicts a corridor in the hospital and ties the brotherhood's charity to the Black slavery that spread quickly in Brazil with the arrival of the Portuguese, as enslaved men built the hospital. The institution's benefactors, portraits of whom hang on the walls of the corridor, were connected to Black slavery for centuries as religious men, farmers, and representatives of power. On the black-and-white tiled floor, Griffo paints miniature Black men who seem to have rebelled against forced labor to build another reality; they make a hole in the floor and plant a tree similar to a baobab, an ancient tree found in different parts of Africa and often associated with wisdom. With this realistically painted but dreamlike scene, Griffo reminds the viewer of the impurity of the church's charitable acts and the physical violence inflicted during colonization.

Griffo does not look nostalgically on Latin America's colonial past and instead foregrounds how centuries of invasion and extermination affect the lives and social memory of contemporary Latin Americans. He does not depict the violence that occurred in this hospital, but he suggests an exercise in historical revision through his images.

With the persistence of colonial iconographies, including those of Christianity, and more recent decolonial critiques of those iconographies, modern and contemporary Latin American artists like Orozco and Griffo challenge viewers to rethink their positions and assumptions of the past. Even when experimenting with new approaches to traditional media like painting, modern artists like Orozco can be seen continuing the visual tropes of colonial Mexico. Contemporary artists like Griffo, however, seem more interested in deconstructing colonial tropes and proposing to the viewer an autopsy of colonial traumas that haunted—and still haunt—Latin America. The power of a collection like the one at the Denver Art Museum lies in the fact that one can return to older and newer objects, place them alongside each other, and exercise a critical gaze to contemplate the countless untold and complex stories of the Americas—their past, present, and future.

CAT. 210 **André Griffo, Brazilian, born 1979, *Instruções para administração das fazendas 5 (Instructions for the administration of farms 5)***
Brazil, 2021. Oil and acrylic paint on canvas, 63 × 47¼ in. (160 × 120 cm). Gift of Álvaro Piquet Pessôa, 2021.601

Textos en español

Apropiación e invención en las artes de Hispanoamérica

Jorge F. Rivas Pérez

En 2021, el Museo de Arte de Denver volvió a instalar las salas de su colección permanente, lo que nos ha permitido mostrar más piezas que nunca de nuestra colección de arte latinoamericano. A las colecciones existentes de arte colonial, moderno y contemporáneo se les suma una sala dedicada exclusivamente al arte latinoamericano del siglo XIX, que es única en Estados Unidos. (CATS. 7 Y 8). La colección incluye piezas que nunca se han expuesto, lo que nos permite ahora poder contar historias más inclusivas, incorporar expresiones de artistas y miembros de la comunidad, y proporcionar un contexto social e histórico más amplio a nuestros visitantes. Aunque esta publicación no incluye todas las obras destacadas de la colección, la selección que presentamos aquí proporciona una excelente visión general sobre su importancia, profundidad y variedad. Esperamos que este volumen sirva como punto de partida para todas las personas interesadas en explorar las complejas circunstancias históricas que dieron lugar a las artes de América Latina, la extraordinaria originalidad e inventiva de sus artistas y la riqueza de su patrimonio artístico.

Con el fin de ofrecer una mayor claridad, este libro se organiza por regiones y materiales, además, distintos ensayos iluminan el complejo paisaje artístico, con sus porosas fronteras y cuestiones superpuestas, de un vasto territorio que fue gobernado por la Corona española. Los textos, redactados por prestigiosos especialistas de Estados Unidos, América Latina y Europa, aportan un contexto y una profunda visión histórica de las obras de arte del Caribe –lugar de origen de la empresa colonial española– y de los enormes virreinatos de Nueva España (que abarcaban el actual México, América Central, el suroeste de Estados Unidos y California, así como Filipinas) y Perú (la actual Sudamérica de habla hispana).

El arte colonial, deslumbrante y sorprendente, inventó un tipo de arte nuevo, diferente y extraordinario, que desafiaba y trastocaba la estética tradicional europea y hacía gala de un ingenio y unos matices –tan sutiles como poderosos– que plantaban cara a la autoridad colonial. El Museo de Arte de Denver tiene la suerte de contar con una colección sin parangón que nos permite contar esta historia fascinante y llena de matices. Esta publicación presenta una historia del arte más plural, centrada en los flujos artísticos transculturales y en las consecuentes rupturas con los modelos establecidos.

* * *

Todo cambió en las Américas tras la llegada de los europeos en la década de 1490, con los profundos procesos de reajustes y transformaciones derivados de la conquista y colonización de la tierra. Para los pueblos indígenas, la invasión europea impregnó todas las facetas de la vida, trayendo consigo el cambio político, la destrucción de sus ciudades y monumentos, las enfermedades, la esclavitud –así como el trabajo forzado de las encomiendas–, que causaron pérdidas demográficas catastróficas y devastaron sus civilizaciones. Para los europeos fue un reto enfrentarse a las nuevas realidades resultantes de la colonización y administración de aquellos vastos territorios y de la incorporación al nuevo orden de las tantas y tan diversas poblaciones que habitaban las Américas. Fueron necesarias varias generaciones para asimilar la magnitud del cambio, sin embargo, de ese dilatado proceso surgieron nuevas expresiones artísticas, a menudo con importantes contribuciones de artistas indígenas. La llegada de africanos esclavizados a principios del siglo XVI, seguida por el comercio y la inmigración de Asia a finales de ese mismo siglo, complicó aún más la relación, ya de por sí compleja, entre las culturas visuales europeas y no europeas en las Américas.

En un intento por crear continuidad en todo el imperio, los colonos europeos organizaron su vida cotidiana y administración siguiendo las costumbres españolas, incluyendo una conexión profundamente enraizada en el catolicismo romano, pero los diferentes contextos y condiciones locales les impidieron suplantar totalmente las costumbres indígenas. Los artistas europeos tuvieron que adaptarse a los recursos locales, a las condiciones del mercado y, sobre todo, a lidiar con muchas sociedades heterogéneas, entre las que se encontraban hábiles artistas indígenas que competían con los europeos.[1] Los artistas indígenas y los mestizos no eran un grupo homogéneo. Reflejaban las complejidades raciales, la diversidad de orígenes y las diferencias de clase de la sociedad colonial. La rica producción artística de la época fue el resultado de prolongados procesos de negociación, adaptación y apropiación cultural que dieron lugar a la invención de vocabularios visuales que reflejaban las continuidades y rupturas con antiguas tradiciones artísticas, e igualmente la dinámica social y cultural de cada comunidad.

La producción artística en Hispanoamérica fue algo más que un ejercicio unidireccional de copia, traducción y adaptación de los modelos europeos. En el proceso de transferencia y reubicación de un marco cultural a otro, la creación artística adquirió nuevos contextos y significados. El intercambio cultural colonial no es solo la circulación de arte e ideas, sino también su inexorable reinterpretación y resignificación dentro de una situación transcultural. Al estudiar la cultura material, por ejemplo, los artefactos religiosos tienen connotaciones y significados diferentes según el contexto y los usuarios. Por ejemplo, las cuentas de esmeralda prehispánicas retocadas y montadas sobre una cruz de oro que en su día adornaban la corona de una estatua de la Virgen María en Colombia tenían diferentes connotaciones según el adorador que tuviera delante (CAT. 9). Para un indígena converso, las cuentas de esmeralda probablemente estaban cargadas de un valor sagrado y simbólico –asociado con la vida y la fertilidad–, que transferían un significado religioso antiguo y prehispánico a la imagen cristiana. Para un europeo, esas gemas verdes eran valiosas ofrendas a la Virgen María, pero probablemente no tenían mayores asociaciones simbólicas. Encontramos un ejemplo similar en las imágenes coloniales del arte plumario mexicano, en las que los artistas adaptaron las técnicas y los materiales antiguos para producir imágenes cristianas

(CAT. 13). Cargadas de significado sagrado y asociadas al poder y a las élites gobernantes, las plumas se incorporaron a muchos aspectos de la cultura material azteca.[2] La readaptación de esta tradición artística sugiere que el propio material, imbuido de un antiguo valor simbólico, desempeñó un importante papel en el desarrollo de las formas artísticas interculturales coloniales.

Los antiguos tipos de objetos asociados a las prácticas religiosas fueron perdiendo sus connotaciones simbólicas al pasar a ser utilizados como objetos de uso cotidiano. Por ejemplo, las vasijas rituales andinas para beber llamadas *keros* (CAT. 10) se empezaron a decorar con motivos europeos después de la conquista (CAT. 11) y, en otros casos, su forma y su decoración geométrica grabada sirvieron de modelo para los bernegales coloniales.[3] En este ejemplo concreto, se añadieron asas de estilo español (CAT. 12). En Mesoamérica se produjo un proceso de transformación similar. El antiguo tipo de recipiente para beber chocolate hecha de calabazas (*xicalli* en náhuatl) se transforma en la jícara colonial o taza de chocolate. Inicialmente fabricadas con calabazas (CAT. 14), y más tarde con semillas de coco (CAT. 15), las jícaras estaban minuciosamente grabadas y talladas. Su decoración y sus formas representan a menudo una fusión de repertorios ornamentales europeos y antiguos, y con frecuencia muestran el nombre grabado de sus primeros propietarios.

En el caso de la pintura y la escultura, los estilos y la estética europeos no tenían parangón en las culturas visuales de las antiguas Américas; en consecuencia, su combinación con los estilos y las prácticas indígenas creó nuevos vocabularios visuales adecuados al mundo multicultural que se desarrolló tras la conquista. Los artistas de Hispanoamérica se basaban a menudo en fuentes impresas o en copias de obras maestras europeas conocidas para crear sus composiciones, como *El rey Salomón y la reina de Saba*, de Antonio Enríquez (CAT. 16), basada en un grabado del mismo tema de la *Icones Biblicae*, una popular biblia ilustrada publicada por Matthäeus Merian antes de 1630 (FIG. 1).[4] En otros casos, las interpretaciones de los artistas eran más bien libres, como en un par de modestos países (paisajes) peruanos de la colección (CAT. 17 Y 18), que probablemente se inspiraron en grabados europeos, pero que se ejecutaron, sin duda, con la paleta de colores y los rasgos estilísticos de la pintura andina de finales de la época colonial.

Aunque las fuentes impresas llevaron a los artistas que nunca habían pisado Europa a abrazar estrechamente los cánones artísticos y las iconografías europeas, muchos pintores fueron más allá, desafiando el canon e inventando nuevos estilos y tipos de representación. *La Santa Rosa de Lima con el Niño Jesús y la Donante,* de Juan Rodríguez Juárez, ejemplifica la sofisticación intelectual y la inventiva de los artistas hispanoamericanos (CAT. 19). Como muestra de su familiaridad con el arte español, Rodríguez Juárez hace referencia a una conocida pintura de la santa realizada por el maestro español Bartolomé Esteban Murillo (FIG. 2), pero el artista incluyó el retrato de una donante en la parte inferior –una aspirante a monja ricamente vestida– y reelaboró muchos detalles, como la fina alfombra sobre la que se arrodilla la donante y la copiosa cantidad de sangre que gotea por la frente de la santa.[5] Durante la época española, las representaciones de la sangre evocaban a las culturas anteriores a la conquista, para las que la sangre era fundamental en los rituales religiosos y a menudo se representaba en el arte.[6] Los artistas coloniales representaron la sangre con un realismo asombroso y una abundancia exagerada, que superaba con creces las convenciones artísticas europeas. El arte religioso de la época, tan hermoso como desagradable, puede resultar escandalosamente gráfico en su representación de los sufrimientos de Cristo y la crucifixión (CAT. 20), los esfuerzos de los santos (CAT. 21) y las alegorías de la santa eucaristía (CAT. 22).

En otros casos, la inventiva de los artistas fue menos ambiciosa y se limitó a gestos más sutiles, como la sustitución de un elemento europeo en una pintura cuzqueña que representa a la Virgen María como la Inmaculada Concepción con un donante indígena (CAT. 23). El artista nativo transformó el ciprés europeo (símbolo de la inmortalidad) por la bromelia gigante, una planta andina más familiar (*titanka* en quechua).[7] Los retratos de donantes indígenas, que a menudo llevan una mezcla de ropa indígena y europea, también muestran cómo los artistas adaptaron los modelos europeos para que se ajustaran mejor a la sociedad colonial y a su compleja estructura (CAT. 24).

Las obras de arte analizadas en este breve texto abarcan más de tres siglos de apropiación e invención en las artes. Muestran el ingenio de los artistas locales y sus esfuerzos por crear expresiones originales que reflejaran la compleja sociedad en la que vivían y trabajaban. También hablan de las formas en que las ambiciones artísticas alimentaron la formación de la identidad y las ideas de nacionalismo que con el tiempo condujeron a la independencia de España.

1 En sus memorias, Toribio de Benavente (Motolinía) describe las habilidades de los artesanos indígenas mexicanos para aprender los oficios españoles observando trabajar a los europeos. Toribio de Benavente (Motolinía) y Daniel Sánchez García, *Historia de los indios de la Nueva España: escrita a mediados del siglo XVI* (Barcelona: Herederos de J. Gili, 1914), 79.

2 Sobre el arte plumario, ver Alessandra Russo, Gerhard Wolf y Diana Fane, *El vuelo de las imágenes: arte plumario en México y Europa* (Ciudad de México: Instituto Nacional de Antropología e Historia, 2011).

3 Las vasijas rituales para beber (*keros*) eran objetos simbólicos muy importantes en toda la cultura andina. Ver Tom Cummins, "Representation in the Sixteenth Century and the Colonial Image of the Inca", en *Writing Without Words: Alternative Literacies in Mesoamerica and the Andes*, editado por Elizabeth Hill Boone y Walter D. Mignolo (Durham, NC: Duke University Press, 2004), 188–219.

4 Matthäeus Merian, *Icones biblicae; praecipuas sacrae scripturae eleganter & graphice repraesentantes; Biblische Figuren, darinnen die Fuernembsten Historien, in Heiliger und Goettlicher Schrifftbegriffen* (Strasbourg: L. Zetzners, 1629). Sobre fuentes impresas europeas, ver Thomas B. F. Cummins, "The Indulgent Image: Prints in the New World", en *Contested Visions in the Spanish Colonial World*, editado por Ilona Katzew (Los Angeles: Los Angeles County Museum of Art, 2011), 203–225; y Kelly Donahue-Wallace, "Picturing Prints in Early Modern New Spain", *The Americas* 64 (2007): 325–49.

5 Para un estudio más detallado de este cuadro, ver Jaime Cuadriello, "Representaciones y ficciones transoceánicas: Representaciones marianas con personificación social", en *Tornaviaje: arte iberoamericano en España*, editado por Rafael López Guzmán (Madrid: Museo Nacional del Prado, 2021), 71–75.

6 Sobre los rituales de sangre prehispánicos, ver Giuseppe Orefici, "Bleeding Hearts, Bleeding Parts: Sacrificial blood in Maya society", en *Blood: Art, Power, Politics, and Pathology*, editado por James M. Bradburne (Munich: Prestel, 2002), 41–54.

7 Endémica de los valles altoandinos, la *titanka* (*Puyaraimondii Hams*), también conocida como "la reina de los Andes", es la mayor especie de bromelia del mundo.

Materialidad e innovación en la pintura novohispana del siglo XVII

Elsa Arroyo Lemus

La colección del Denver Art Museum reúne una selección heterogénea de pinturas novohispanas nutrida tanto de artistas señeros, que no dudaron en dejar evidencia de su capacidad técnica e inventiva, como de autores no identificados que, en conjunto, reproducen temáticas centrales a las preocupaciones intelectuales y a las creencias de su público.

En los albores del siglo XVII la pintura novohispana comenzó a perfilar su identidad gracias al establecimiento de talleres encabezados por pintores europeos o criollos que ya comprendían las exigencias de una élite local dispuesta a demostrar su poder.[1] Fue entonces cuando los maestros de imaginería comenzaron a negociar el reconocimiento de su trabajo como una actividad intelectual.

La figura del vasco Baltasar de Echave Orio (ca. 1558-1623) fue capital para proyectar las demandas y reivindicaciones de su gremio.[2] Encabezó una de las genealogías artísticas más reconocidas por su capacidad de halagar el gusto de la clientela del virreinato novohispano, reinventándose dentro de un vasto mercado local en auge, donde lo mismo circulaban obras producidas por artífices indígenas que obras bien calificadas por el pensamiento y el público de las cortes europeas de la Edad Moderna.

Las láminas de cobre de Baltasar de Echave Ibía (ca. 1584-1643) *La Crucifixión* y *El camino al Calvario* (CAT. 25 Y 26) son ejemplos de la valoración que imperaba en el mercado artístico de la Nueva España, ya que debieron competir con los numerosos envíos de imágenes flamencas que abastecían a la clientela americana vía el puerto de Sevilla.

Las láminas de cobre ocupaban un lugar privilegiado dentro de este universo de imágenes portátiles debido a su resistencia a las condiciones ambientales y a la manipulación que implicaba su traslado por el Atlántico. Otras piezas de la colección como *El nacimiento de la Virgen* de Luis Juárez (ca. 1585-1639) (CAT. 28) y *San Antonio con el Niño Jesús* de Alonso López de Herrera (ca. 1580-1675) (CAT. 27) atestiguan la preferencia de los artistas de la época por la materialidad de estos formatos que abastecían un circuito comercial global.[3]

Las estrategias en el uso del color serán también clave en el devenir de la pintura de la época. En la obra de Echave Ibía hemos identificado una importante innovación: el uso de imprimaciones rojizas y oscuras. Este cambio en la paleta operó como un acto de apertura de los esquemas de representación visual del Barroco.[4]

Aunque el papel del colorido en el desarrollo de la pintura novohispana está aún poco estudiado, algunas soluciones recurrentes nos permiten interpretar las decisiones de los artistas en sus procesos de invención. Cuando el sevillano Sebastián de Arteaga (1610-1652) pintó la *Aparición de san Miguel en el monte Gargano* (CAT. 29), seleccionó una paleta variada de colores brillantes y traslúcidos para configurar la imagen del ángel monumental. Es probable que esos paños sueltos y expresivos de tonalidades traslúcidas hayan sido plasmados mediante mezclas de laca roja de grana cochinilla, un material tintóreo de alta estima y tradición en la Nueva España que se explotaba en la zona Puebla-Tlaxcala desde tiempos anteriores a la conquista española.[5] Al aprovechar las ventajas del también llamado "carmín de Indias", un material costoso de enormes cualidades plásticas, Arteaga celebraba la inscripción de su producción en un circuito local de circulación de imágenes, consciente de su distancia respecto a los modelos europeos y capaz de aprovecharse del desarrollo económico del virreinato ya observado en la producción de las materias primas "de la tierra".[6]

Es también en las obras del maestro sevillano donde se percibe el recurso de dejar los contornos libres y sin pintura, a modo de un área de reserva apta para separar las figuras de los fondos.[7] Parece que esta solución fue compartida por artistas contemporáneos como Diego de Borgraf (1618-1686), tal como se observa en su *Santa Catalina de Alejandría* (CAT. 30). Pintar dejando las áreas reservadas se convertiría en un *leitmotiv* en los procedimientos colorísticos de la plástica posterior.

Pero la apuesta más significativa con relación a las estrategias pictóricas y los efectos del colorido se inscribe, sin lugar a dudas, en la obra de Cristóbal de Villalpando (ca. 1649-1714), uno de los artistas de mayor prestigio en la Nueva España.[8] Entre las características que singularizan su producción está su ingenio y modos de pintar, en los que confluyen notablemente las cualidades de transparencia y opacidad de las capas pictóricas. Villalpando usaba una paleta rica en tonalidades, compuesta por materiales crudos o mínimamente procesados, como el índigo, el carbón vegetal y las tierras, y también por colorantes orgánicos. De igual modo, los minerales y otros pigmentos derivados de la síntesis química están presentes en sus cuadros: azurita, malaquita, yeso, azul esmalte, bermellón, verdigrís y los obtenidos de la corrosión del plomo.[9]

En *José reclama a Benjamín como su esclavo* (CAT. 31), Villalpando integró varias acciones simultáneas. Una de ellas, el gesto de sorpresa de un personaje al fondo que mira a través de sus espejuelos, actúa como una invitación a descubrir las formas construidas mediante superposiciones de capas delgadas y fluidas de pintura. Brillos cambiantes y fulgores dorados resaltan los pliegues de las telas, dando a esta escena devocional un carácter de máximo lujo y extravagancia.

Este peculiar sistema rápido y efectista con el que Villalpando expresa su habilidad en la ejecución del colorido se constituye en una especie de marca registrada, sobre todo en la última parte de su carrera artística. A mi parecer, se trata de la defensa pública de una teoría del color basada en las variaciones de la luz y el dominio técnico.

Por otra parte, si estas estrategias de representación de Villalpando organizan un código reconocible, resulta obligado revisar algunas de las atribuciones asociadas a su pincel. En particular, la *Virgen de Valvanera* (CAT. 32) invita a comenzar una discusión abierta sobre el ambiente artístico y los modos de pintar de la década de 1680 en Nueva España. Esta obra revela una lógica distinta en el uso del color y en sus efectos plásticos que la separa de la obra del extraordinario maestro colorista que fue Villalpando. Aquí, el artista parece repetir convenciones formales que se encuentran en la obra del mismo tema que pintó el mulato Juan Correa (1646-1716), aunque aquella está cargada de detalles iconográficos, plasmados con mejor oficio, esmero y precisión (FIG. 1). Por ello esta pintura podría más bien atribuirse a Correa o su taller.

La colección del museo de Denver reúne ejemplos diversos de la rica herencia artística de la Nueva España, piezas que nos permiten comenzar a armar el enigma de la invención desde el papel expresivo y semántico que juega su materialidad y, con ello, expandir las fronteras geográficas y culturales de las fórmulas que alguna vez se concibieron solo como prácticas trasplantadas desde el Viejo Mundo.

1 Los argumentos sobre el comienzo de la tradición pictórica novohispana se deben a: Rogelio Ruiz Gomar, "La tradición pictórica novohispana en el taller de los Juárez" y Nelly Sigaut, "El concepto de tradición en el análisis de la pintura novohispana. La sacristía de la catedral de México y los conceptos sin ruido" en María Concepción García Sáiz y Juana Gutiérrez Haces, eds., *Tradición, estilo o escuela en la pintura iberoamericana. Siglos XVI-XVIII* (México: Universidad Nacional Autónoma de México/ Instituto de Investigaciones Estéticas/ Fomento Cultural Banamex, 2004), 151-172 y 219-221.

2 Jaime Cuadriello, Elsa Arroyo et al., *Ojos, alas y patas de la mosca. Visualidad, técnica y materialidad en* El martirio de san Ponciano *de Baltasar de Echave Orio* (México: Universidad Nacional Autónoma de México, 2018), 83-87.

3 Retomo esta noción de globalización temprana de: Dennis O. Flynn y Arturo Giráldez, "Los orígenes de la globalización en el siglo XVI", en Bernd Hausberger y Antonio Ibarra, coords., *Oro y plata en los inicios de la economía global: De las minas a la moneda* (México: El Colegio de México, 2014), 29-76.

4 Así lo hemos confirmado mediante el examen científico de la *Inmaculada Concepción* (Museo Nacional de Arte, inv. 3068) y más recientemente en la tabla del *Pentecostés* (pinacoteca de la casa Profesa). Ver: Elsa Arroyo, Manuel Espinosa, et al., "Variaciones celestes para pintar el manto de la Virgen", *Anales del Instituto de Investigaciones Estéticas* XXXIV, núm. 100 (2012): 85-117 y Miguel Pérez, E. Arroyo-Lemus, et al., "Technical Non-invasive Study of the Novo-Hispanic Painting *The Pentecost* by Baltasar de Echave Orio by Spectroscopic Techniques and Hyperspectral Imaging: In Quest for the Painter's Hand", *Spectrochimica Acta Part A: Molecular and Biomolecular Spectroscopy* 250 (2021): 1-16.

5 Baltazar Brito Guadarrama, "La grana en Hujotzingo. Lugar del pequeño huejote" en Georges Roque, coord., *Rojo Mexicano. La grana cochinilla en el arte* (México: Instituto Nacional de Bellas Artes/ Museo del Palacio de Bellas Artes, 2017), 74-91.

6 Arteaga empleó de manera intencional la laca de cochinilla en obras como *Virgen con Niño* y *Desposorios de la Virgen*, pertenecientes a la colección del Museo Nacional de Arte de México. Elsa Arroyo Lemus, Manuel Espinosa Pesqueira y Witold Nowik, "Paños labrados de carmín en la pintura novohispana", en Georges Roque, coord., *Rojo Mexicano...*, 158-177.

7 Para un acercamiento a los efectos plásticos del artista ver: Elsa Arroyo, "Sebastián de Arteaga y la construcción de un lenguaje pictórico en contexto". https://www.sebastiandearteaga.esteticas.unam.mx/ (consultado 27 de septiembre de 2021).

8 Juana Gutiérrez Haces, Pedro Ángeles Jiménez, et al., *Cristóbal de Villalpando ca. 1649-1714. Catálogo razonado* (México: Fomento Cultural Banamex/ Instituto de Investigaciones Estéticas, UNAM, 1997).

9 En los años recientes se ha ampliado notablemente la bibliografía especializada en la técnica de Villalpando: Mari Carmen Casas, "Técnica pictórica utilizada por Cristóbal de Villalpando en la cúpula de la Capilla de los Reyes", en Montserrat Galí Boadella, ed., *La catedral de Puebla en el arte y en la historia* (Puebla: Secretaría de Cultura, 1999), 255-261; Elsa Arroyo, "Transparencias y fantasmagorías: La técnica de Cristóbal de Villalpando en *La Transfiguración*", adenda al catálogo de la exposición *Cristóbal de Villalpando, pintor mexicano del Barroco* (México: Fomento Cultural Banamex, 2017), 1-14; Dorothy Mahon, Silvia A. Centeno, et al., "Cristóbal de Villalpando's *Adoration of the Magi:* A Discussion of Artist Technique", *Latin American and Latinx Visual Culture* I, núm. 2 (2019): 113-121; Mirta Insaurralde Caballero y María Castañeda-Delgado, "At the Core of the Workshop: Novel Aspects of the Use of Blue Smalt in Two Paintings by Cristóbal de Villalpando", *Arts* 10, núm. 25 (2021): 1-18.

Innovación, tradición y estilo en la pintura mexicana del siglo XVIII

Luisa Elena Alcalá

La colección de pintura mexicana del siglo XVIII del museo es conocida desde hace tiempo tanto por su amplitud como por su calidad. Incluye obras de los artistas más famosos de la época, así como de algunos nombres menos conocidos que actualmente atraen la atención de los estudiosos. La colección mantiene un equilibrio entre las pinturas hechas en Ciudad de México, la capital y el centro artístico dominante, y las de los centros regionales de otras zonas del virreinato. La pintura colonial del siglo XVIII difiere de la del periodo anterior, pues las primeras décadas del siglo revelan un deseo consciente por parte de los principales pintores de inclinar su paleta hacia tonalidades más claras, de estudiar el dibujo anatómico, de seguir los ideales académicos, de explorar el potencial narrativo de los gestos y las expresiones y de responder a los modelos de Italia y Francia impregnados de clasicismo barroco.

Juan Rodríguez Juárez (1675-1728) allanó el camino para estas transformaciones gracias a su gran talento. Su lúcido retrato del jesuita francés san Juan Francisco Régis (CAT. 33) ilustra su habilidad en un género en el que convergen el retrato y la pintura religiosa.[1] Rodríguez Juárez modela la figura con la elegancia que lo caracteriza, añadiendo un refinado halo sobre la cabeza para señalar su estatus. En contraste con el crucifijo y los lirios –atributos genéricos–, el trigo y el montón de grano sobre la mesa aluden a un milagro ocurrido durante la hambruna de 1638 en Le Puy, Francia: san Régis había organizado un granero de beneficencia que, al agotarse, se repuso milagrosamente.[2]

El modelado de la figura en esta obra refleja el liderazgo de Rodríguez Juárez en la academia informal de pintura creada en México en la década de 1720. Se sabe poco de ella, pero los pintores se reunían allí para practicar el dibujo de la figura humana y corregir el trabajo de los demás. Los efectos artísticos de esta academia se reflejan en numerosos cuadros de temas narrativos que incluyen múltiples figuras, poses complicadas, o bien requieren la presencia de un desnudo y se recrean en él, como en la Pasión de Cristo.[3] Un ejemplo esclarecedor es la *Lamentación sobre Cristo muerto*, de Juan Patricio Morlete y Ruiz (CAT. 37). La forma en que el cuerpo de Cristo queda extendido ante el espectador en el primer plano invita a la contemplación al tiempo que muestra el uso característico del artista de los azules y los blancos. Contra el cielo nocturno, los sucesivos pliegues de tela blanca consiguen dirigir la mirada: desde la esquina inferior derecha, a través del cuerpo de Cristo, en el vestido de la Virgen y, finalmente, más arriba, en torno a la cruz. Conmovedores y pintados con delicadeza, los cuadros de Morlete inspiran la oración devocional y, simultáneamente, muestran su habilidad, evidente también en el intenso tratamiento de los objetos brillantes aislados en el primer plano.[4]

Aunque los temas religiosos del Nuevo Testamento y las vidas de Cristo y la Virgen dominan la producción pictórica en el mundo hispánico, el Antiguo Testamento captaba la imaginación y ofrecía la oportunidad de pintar lugares exóticos e historias fantásticas. Un ejemplo de ello es *El rey Salomón y la reina de Saba*, de Antonio Enríquez (VER RIVAS PÉREZ, CAT. 16), con su trono bordeado con leones dorados y camellos desfilando por la ciudad y la plaza con un obelisco.[5] Las obras de Enríquez que han sobrevivido sugieren que se labró un nombre con ambiciosas composiciones similares, pobladas con multitudes vívidas y paisajes lejanos. Sabemos que incluso se adentró en la pintura mitológica, una rareza para aquellos artistas que, no obstante, está representada en la colección.[6]

Enríquez es uno de los pintores del museo –al igual que Pedro Noriega, en Querétaro, y Miguel Jerónimo Zendejas, en Puebla– que trabajaron en un centro regional, en su caso en Guadalajara.[7] Capital de la rica región de Nueva Galicia, Guadalajara floreció en el siglo XVIII, y ya antes los artistas nacidos en el siglo XVII, como Francisco de León, encontraron allí un mercado creciente.[8] Su *Nacimiento de la Virgen* (CAT. 36), de brillante colorido como era típico de este artista, recuerda estilísticamente las postrimerías del siglo XVII, aunque los deslumbrantes cortinajes también están en consonancia con el gusto dominante de principios del siglo XVIII, cuando el ornamento era muy apreciado en las artes. La versión de Miguel Cabrera del mismo tema, pintada décadas más tarde (CAT. 38), mantiene los rojos al tiempo que introduce una combinación tonal clásica y apagada, más típica de esta época, en las prendas rosa y azul claro de la sirvienta de la parte inferior izquierda. Además, Cabrera destaca el papel de san Joaquín tras el auge del culto a la Sagrada Familia ampliada, incluyendo los padres de la Virgen o lo que se conoce en México como los Cinco Señores.[9]

Las tonalidades de mayor sosiego introducidas en la obra de Cabrera se convirtieron en la norma en las décadas de 1780 y 1790. Varios cuadros de la colección atestiguan esta transformación, que suele asociarse con la fundación de la Real Academia de San Carlos en 1781-84 y con la llegada del gusto neoclásico. Estos cambios son evidentes en el pincel sobrio y suave de la *Coronación de la Virgen*, de Juan Nepomuceno Sáenz (CAT. 34), y en la contenida interpretación del *Martirio de santa* Águeda (CAT. 35), de José Guerrero. La arquitectura del fondo de esta última obra es la típica de muchos cuadros de la época, aunque en este caso, no se limita solamente a anclar la escena figurativa. El detalle poco común de la pared detrás de la santa ofrece un complemento simbólico para el martirio; la piedra se desprende para revelar ladrillos rojos, una segunda piel que parece hacerse eco del cuerpo sangrante.

Mientras la academia oficial intentaba controlar la educación artística –y a través de ella la forma y el estilo–, la tradición anterior seguía prosperando gracias a la demanda de los consumidores.[10] Por ejemplo, la pintura de Sáenz representa a la Trinidad en una versión antropomórfica, que era la interpretación preferida en

Nueva España desde principios de siglo. A pesar de ser duramente criticada en el Cuarto Concilio Provincial Mexicano de 1771, la iconografía sin duda persistió.[11] Del mismo modo, las composiciones de densidad simbólica del Divino Esposo, reclinado en un fantasioso jardín alegórico del amor divino, que se exhibían en los conventos novohispanos femeninos desde la década de 1740, siguieron produciéndose mucho más tarde, como la versión de Andrés López (1727-1807) (CAT. 39).

Algunas de estas monjas también adornaban sus hábitos en ocasiones especiales con grandes escudos pintados, de los que el museo posee una rica colección (CAT. 40). Los cultos locales florecieron, como es el caso de la Virgen de Guadalupe en el Tepeyac, que precisamente se ve en este escudo de monja. Debido a su popularidad, las imágenes de la Virgen de Guadalupe se convirtieron en un elemento básico de la producción de cualquier artista. Aunque las representaciones de las imágenes de culto debían copiar fielmente un original que obrara milagros para mantener a salvo a los clientes virreinales e inspirarles devoción, el gusto local era sofisticado, y los pintores prodigaban su atención en los adornos que rodeaban las imágenes, como se aprecia en la mesa del altar del *Cristo de Ixmiquilpan*, de José de Ibarra (CAT. 41).

En definitiva, el siglo XVIII fue un periodo decisivo para las tradiciones pictóricas locales, y la pintura novohispana en general adquirió un carácter más individualizado. Este carácter es especialmente evidente en el gran número de pinturas de castas que se produjeron a lo largo del siglo XVIII. Este nuevo género, iniciado por Juan Rodríguez Juárez, consistía en series de cuadros que representaban unidades familiares con padres e hijos de razas diversas identificadas a través de inscripciones (CAT. 42). En el museo abundan las pinturas de castas, incluyendo el único conjunto completo en los Estados Unidos, el cual está firmado por el pintor español Francisco Clapera (1746-1810) (CAT. 43). A través de esta serie, así como de otras obras individuales, incluida la pintura recientemente limpiada, atribuida a José de Alcíbar (1726-1803) (CAT. 44), emerge la compleja visión local sobre el mestizaje. Al mismo tiempo, estas obras ofrecen información sobre la cultura material novohispana y su particular combinación de elementos indígenas, españoles, asiáticos y africanos.[12] Por su parte, Rodríguez Juárez, sensible al creciente orgullo de la identidad local, explotó el poder de la vestimenta, específicamente la mexicana, desde muy temprano, y más allá de sus pinturas de castas. Esto es evidente en la forma en que se esmera en el *huipil* bordado del retrato de la donante en su famosa *Santa Rosa de Lima* (VER RIVAS PÉREZ, CAT. 19), una de las obras maestras de la colección.

Resumiendo, la pintura novohispana del siglo XVIII floreció y demostró tener una enorme capacidad para innovar en nuevos temas, técnicas, formatos y estilos locales. Evolucionó para satisfacer un creciente mercado y las exigencias de los comitentes, a la par que respondió a las ambiciones profesionales de los maestros.

1 La especificidad simbólica de esta obra sugiere que Rodríguez Juárez debió de desempeñar un papel importante en el desarrollo de la iconografía del santo en el virreinato. La noticia de su beatificación en 1716 viajó rápidamente de Roma a América, y en 1722 ya se le habían dedicado varios retablos en las iglesias jesuitas de Ciudad en México. Ver "El espejo pintado: retórica y práctica en el mundo hispánico", de Luisa Elena Alcalá, en *La mirada extravagante. Arte, ciencia y religión en la Edad Moderna. Homenaje a Fernando Marías*, eds. María Cruz de Carlos, Felipe Pereda y José Riello (Madrid: Marcial Pons, 2020), 542, 551–52.

2 Más allá de la intención didáctica, este atributo pudo haber resonado entre los habitantes de Ciudad de México, debido a sus propios problemas de abastecimiento de cereales y maíz, así como a las epidemias que azotaron la población durante las décadas de 1720 y 1730. Ver *Por voluntad divina: escasez, epidemias y otras calamidades en Ciudad de México, 1700-1762*, de América Molina del Villar (Ciudad de México: Centro de Investigaciones y Estudios Superiores en Antropología Social, 1996), 129-36.

3 Para una introducción a los principales artistas y al desarrollo del estilo en este periodo, ver, entre otros: Rogelio Ruiz Gomar, "Unique Expressions: Painting in New Spain", en *Painting a New World: Mexican Art and Life, 1521-1821*, ed. Donna Pierce, Rogelio Ruiz Gomar y Clara Bargellinie (Denver: Denver Art Museum, 2004), especialmente 69-75; Paula Mues Orts, "Illustrious Painting and Modern Brushes", en *Painted in Mexico, 1700-1790: Pinxit Mexici*, ed. Ilona Katzew (Los Ángeles y Ciudad de México: Los Angeles County Museum of Art y Fomento Cultural Banamex A.C., 2017), 52-75, así como la entrada del catálogo, 259-60; e Ilona Katzew, "Valiant Styles: New Spanish Paintings, 1700-1785", en *Pintura en Hispanoamérica, 1550–1820*, ed. Luisa Elena Alcalá y Jonathan Brown (New Haven: Yale University Press, 2014), 149-203.

4 Tales ejercicios de observación y naturalismo, aislando objetos en el primer plano, se encuentran también en otras obras de Morlete, como en la *Virgen de los Dolores* (hacia 1760) en el Convento de Nuestra Señora del Carmen del Santo Desierto, Tenancingo, México, analizado en *Painted in Mexico*, 261-63.

5 La firma de Antonio Enríquez y la fecha de 1732 en este lienzo son un descubrimiento reciente, lo que hace que esta obra pase a formar parte del creciente número de pinturas conocidas de este maestro. La composición se basa en un grabado de Matthäus Merian I (1593-1650) que fue reimpreso y reelaborado en numerosas estampas posteriores que se prolongaron hasta el siglo XVIII. La estampa está ilustrada en Project on the Engraved Sources of Spanish Colonial Art (PESSCA), (Proyecto sobre las Fuentes del Grabado en el Arte Colonial Español), de Almerindo Ojeda, 2623B, consultado el 4 de octubre de 2021, https://colonialart.org/artworks/2623b.

6 Las obras mitológicas están analizadas por Clara Bargellini e ilustradas en *Painting a New World*, 203–5.

7 Enríquez trabajó en Guadalajara por lo menos entre 1747 y 1760: Alena Robin, "Antonio Enríquez, *Felipe Pastor y san Ángel predicando*: un cuadro desconocido en la colección del Museo Regional de Guadalajara", en *Anales del Instituto de Investigaciones Estéticas* XLII,n.º 17 (2020): 259–87. Algunos artistas regionales viajaban a Ciudad de México y se formaban allí antes de regresar a sus lugares de origen.

8 Su conexión con Guadalajara se propuso en la historiografía anterior de Leopoldo I. Orendáin, "Francisco de León, pintor del siglo XVII", *Anales del Instituto de Investigaciones Estéticas* V, n.º 17 (1949): 17–21.

9 Ver Gomar, entrada del catálogo, *Painting a New World*, 212–15. El cuadro forma parte de una serie en el Museo de América, Madrid, analizado por Ana Zabía de la Mata, "La obra de Miguel Cabrera en España. La serie de la Vida de la Virgen del Museo de América de Madrid", en *Identidades y redes culturales. V Congreso Internacional de Barroco Iberoamericano* (Granada: Universidad de Granada, 2021), 353–64.

10 Jaime Cuadriello, "Las pinturas en el departamento de la Real Academia de San Carlos: Orígenes, tránsito", en *Pintura en Hispanoamérica* de Alcalá y Brown, 205–42.

11 Sobre la iconografía de la Trinidad en Nueva España, ver María del Consuelo Maquivar, *De lo permitido a lo prohibido: iconografía de la Santísima Trinidad en Nueva España* (Ciudad de México: Instituto Nacional de Antropología e Historia, 2006); y, más recientemente, Cuadriello, entrada del catálogo Katzew, *Painted in Mexico*, de Katzew, 411–12.

12 Para más información sobre la indumentaria, así como de la presencia del chocolate en este cuadro, ver la entrada de catálogo de Katzew en, *Painting a New World*, de Pierce, Gomar y Bargellini, 245. Y sobre pintura de castas en general, ver *La pintura de castas* de Ilona Katzew (Madrid: Turner, 2004).

Inventando la identidad: Retrato y sociedad en Nueva España

Michael A. Brown

Mientras la imponente arquitectura, la magnífica pintura devocional y –con sus orígenes en las técnicas y materiales indígenas– las espléndidas tradiciones de las artes decorativas florecieron durante los siglos XVI y XVII, el retrato se desarrolló de forma irregular en las primeras décadas del virreinato. Hubo que esperar hasta el siglo XVIII para ver este género poco conocido emerger finalmente con una gloriosa explosión de color y estilo. Hasta cierto punto, esta notable transformación reflejó las variaciones en el gusto de la corte española tras el cambio dinástico de la monarquía en 1700, que dejó atrás a los rígidos Habsburgo para abrir las puertas a los más extravagantes Borbones. Sin embargo, lo más importante es que los retratos manifestaron la identidad ascendente, la individualidad y la incipiente independencia de la sociedad mexicana.

En la España de los Austrias, el retrato –aparte de los pioneros, Tiziano (hacia 1488-1576) y Velázquez (1599-1660)– se ajustaba al impecable pero estático estilo cortesano establecido por Antonis Mor, Alonso Sánchez Coello y Sofonisba Anguissola. También reflejaba las leyes suntuarias que restringían la ostentación sartorial, como el exceso de joyas, los colores chillones y los elaborados cuellos de encaje. Los artistas españoles consagrados que viajaron a Nueva España al principio de la empresa colonial, como Baltasar de Echave Orio y Alonso López de Herrera, importaron esta tradición cortesana, especialmente en las series de retratos corporativos de estadistas y autoridades eclesiásticas que se encargaban para el palacio del virrey, el ayuntamiento y las salas capitulares de las catedrales. Por su propia naturaleza, estas series, a las que se añadía a perpetuidad cada titular del cargo, imponían un tipo de composición y una gama de atributos simbólicos consistentes y servían al propósito político específico de cimentar la legitimidad del cargo mostrando su linaje ininterrumpido.

Tres ejemplos de retratos eclesiásticos destacan en la donación de Frederick y Jan Mayer al Museo de Arte de Denver: en orden cronológico, el *Arzobispo Fray Felipe Galindo Chávez y Pineda*, de Diego de Cuentas (CAT. 45), *Don Francisco José Pérez de Lanciego y Eguilaz*, de Juan Rodríguez Juárez (CAT. 46), y *Don Fernando Navas Arnanz*, de José de Páez (CAT. 47). Este último fue jefe de finanzas de la catedral de Morelia[1], y la colección de Denver cuenta también con un raro retrato de adolescente realizado a su sobrino (CAT. 48). Las dos primeras obras, que representan a los arzobispos de Guadalajara y de México, respectivamente, siguen al pie de la letra el modelo de cuerpo entero inicialmente fundado por Echave Orio y López de Herrera para la primera serie de retratos encargados para la catedral metropolitana (posteriormente, este estilo se abandonaría en favor de la actual serie de medio cuerpo que coincide con la de los virreyes).[2] Sin embargo, el retrato de Lanciego presenta una segunda figura y, al parecer, se hizo con la intención de ser enviado a la familia del arzobispo en Navarra, España.[3] Se encargaron varios retratos de Lanciego para la catedral y otras instituciones; en conjunto, los retratos reflejan el deseo del prelado de proyectar su autoridad política como delegado de Felipe V y la política del monarca en América.

Antes del 1700, los retratos de la nobleza de menor rango eran raros, y aún más los de las mujeres de las clases mercantiles emergentes. El *Retrato de Doña Inés de Velasco* , de Echave Orio, un retrato magistral de una donante en oración, y el doble retrato anónimo de Don Bartolomé Andrés y Don Agustín Pérez (CAT. 49), que también se muestran en actitud de adoración, son excepciones notables. En el caso de este último, es aún más notable el hecho de que los donantes sean personas de la nobleza indígena tlaxcalteca, uno de ellos lleva la *tilma* (capa) prehispánica, mientras que el otro (a la derecha) viste un atuendo de estilo europeo, incluyendo un lujoso abrigo forrado de oro o plata. Es de suponer que las equivalentes femeninas de los modelos estarían ataviadas de forma similar en el lienzo colgante, ahora perdido, que habría colgado a la derecha. La decisión de los donantes de representarse a sí mismos habitando ambos mundos no refleja una crisis de identidad, sino un poderoso indicador del estatus de los modelos y de su movilidad social y cultural.

El núcleo de la colección de retratos de Denver reside en un impresionante grupo de retratos cívicos –podríamos llamarlos "de sociedad"–, todos realizados en la segunda mitad del siglo XVIII. Entre estos, cinco de ellos son considerados como los mejores ejemplos producidos en Nueva España virreinal. El primero (CAT. 50) representa a una joven de pie junto a un clavicordio, en edad prematrimonial, cuya identidad, al igual que la del pintor, aún se desconoce, vistiendo una suntuosa bata abierta de seda importada (de China o de Valencia). La posición social y la educación de la joven se muestran en sus aspiraciones musicales, ya que señala una partitura con la palabra "Sonata". Las mujeres músicas y compositoras eran muy apreciadas en los conventos de México, y las alusiones a la más famosa de todas las hermanas compositoras –sor Juana Inés de la Cruz– no habrían pasado desapercibidas a los espectadores contemporáneos. Tal vez estaba destinada a la vida religiosa, como la futura Madre Ana María de la Preciosa Sangre de Cristo, representada en 1770 con motivo de la toma de sus votos, coronada con flores (típicamente de tela) para la ceremonia (CAT. 51). El museo ha adquirido recientemente un exquisito retrato en miniatura (CAT. 52) en óleo sobre placa de plata de una joven con un fino traje de corte. El artista representa la seda y el hilo de oro del traje de la modelo, así como su tiara de plata y su mantilla de encaje negro, con una maestría y una destreza que apuntan a una tradición muy desarrollada, aunque ignorada, de la pintura en miniatura en México.[4]

Compitiendo con la moda de los lujosos trajes de las jóvenes, destaca el extraordinario retrato de *Don Francisco de Orense y Moctezuma, conde de Villalobos,* realizado en 1761 (CAT. 53), cuyo carisma y confianza personal quedan brillantemente plasmados por un

pintor aún no identificado. En general, los retratados fueron adoptando un comportamiento paulatinamente menos formal a finales del siglo, como es el caso del *Retrato de Fernando de Musitu Zalvide*, de Juan Nepomuceno de Sáenz, realizado en 1795 (CAT. 54). Musitu, procedente de una familia vasca acomodada, aparece representado en pleno apogeo de la moda madrileña del majo, desaliñado pero elegante, que se había hecho famosa en las obras de Francisco Goya.[5] De hecho, la conexión del pintor con Goya no era muy lejana. Sáenz se formó en la Real Academia de San Carlos con el director Rafael Ximeno y Planes, artista valenciano que, a su vez, había estudiado con el maestro y suegro de Goya, Francisco Bayeu, en la academia de Madrid.[6] Sin embargo, la brillante paleta y la despreocupación de la persona retratada la diferencian de las tendencias coetáneas en España y de los retratos rígidos y reglamentados de las décadas anteriores en México. La independencia de España –que llegaría en 1821– estaba a la vuelta de la esquina, y el espectador tiene la sensación de que Fernando de Musitu, como muchos de sus compatriotas, estaba preparado para ese momento.

1 La inscripción de la parte inferior derecha señala que fue nombrado prebendado (canónigo) de Valladolid (actual Morelia) en 1757. La biblioteca de tomos jurídicos refleja su formación académica, mientras que el reloj muestra la precisión y eficacia con la que desempeñaba sus funciones financieras. El pintor del sobrino de Navas Arnanz, Fernando Fraile Navas, sigue sin ser identificado, aunque es probable que la familia recurriera de nuevo a Páez o a alguien de su círculo para el encargo.

2 Michael A. Brown, "La imagen de un imperio: el arte del retrato en España y los virreinatos de Nueva España y Perú", en *Pintura de los reinos: identidades compartidas: territorios del mundo hispánico*, editado por Juana Gutiérrez Haces, Jonathan Brown, y Cándida Fernández de Calderón (Ciudad de México: Fomento Cultural Banamex, 2009), 1474.

3 Paula Mues Orts identifica al asistente como José Ansóain y de los Arcos, secretario de Lanciego y enlace con las autoridades papales en Roma. Ver Ilona Katzew, ed., *Painted in Mexico, 1700—1790: Pinxit Mexici* (Los Ángeles: Los Angeles County Museum of Art; México: Fomento Cultural Banamex, 2017), 348–49. En otro lugar, he sugerido que la segunda figura es la de Miguel Ángel Lanciego y Eguilaz, sobrino jesuita del arzobispo, que lo acompañó a México y sirvió como co-eulogista de su tío con Juan Antonio de Fábrega en 1728. Ver Michael A. Brown, *Portraiture in New Spain, 1600–1800: Painters, Patrons and Politics in Viceregal Mexico* (tesis doctoral, New York University: 2011), 91.

4 Ver Mari Carmen Espinosa Martín y Soumaya Slim de Romero, *Santuarios de lo íntimo: Retrato en miniatura y relicarios: La colección de Museo Soumaya* (México: Telmex y Museo Soumaya, 2004).

5 Ver James Middleton, "Reading Dress in New Spanish Portraiture: Clothing the Mexican Elite, circa 1695–1805", en Pierce, *New England/ New Spain*, 138–39.

6 Donna Pierce, "Portrait of Fernando de Musitu Zalvide", Denver Art Museum, 2015, https://www.denverartmuseum.org/en/object/2008.27.

Mediadores divinos en madera policromada: Escultura en la Nueva España

Franziska Martha Neff

La variada producción escultórica desde el siglo XVI a principios del XIX, cuando México y Guatemala, bajo la figura de la Nueva España, formaron parte de la monarquía española es principalmente de carácter sagrado. Estas piezas privilegian la relación obra-espectador frente a la de autor-obra, no suelen estar firmadas y más bien enfatizan su poder comunicativo y función cultual. Por esto, y por las estrategias escogidas para ello, muchos intelectuales del siglo XIX les negaron la denominación de escultura, con prolongadas implicaciones. Sin embargo, poseen múltiples discursos inscritos y son testimonios valiosos de aspectos diversos de la vida y sociedad virreinal.

La Nueva España heredó de la península la tradición de las tallas en madera policromada, caracterizadas por la colaboración entre escultor y dorador,[1] dejando así testimonio de dos manos, e incluso de otras más debido a la costumbre de actualizar las esculturas. Mientras que los primeros artífices, así como muchas esculturas, vinieron de Europa durante el siglo XVI, para 1557 y 1568 se aprobaron ordenanzas de pintores y de escultores en Ciudad de México, es decir que existieron gremios que reglamentaron estos oficios ejercidos en adelante lo mismo por españoles que castizos, mestizos, indios (entre ellos caciques) y mulatos durante el virreinato, según las fuentes documentales.[2]

Excelente calidad de talla y policromía presenta el *San Juan Nepomuceno* de procedencia guatemalteca (CAT. 59). Desde el siglo XVII, los talleres de la Capitanía General de Guatemala crearon esculturas de un preciosismo característico que fomentó su gran éxito de exportación, combinando un delicado bulto redondo con una prolija policromía de amplio repertorio formal. El santo patrono de los sacerdotes está presentado en *contrapposto* —lo cual repercute en acompasados movimientos de telas, con la cabeza inclinada dirigiendo una mirada contemplativa a un crucifijo que originalmente portaba en la mano derecha. Los recursos naturalistas como la aplicación

de pestañas postizas y ojos de cristal apoyan el detallismo de los rasgos faciales: encarnación de tonos sutiles, peleteado,[3] pestañas y cejas delineadas finamente. El estofado[4] evoca los opulentos textiles de la época, aunque adaptados a la expresión plástica[5], aprovechando técnicas como el relieve, el picado de lustre, el esgrafiado[6] y la pintura a punta de pincel, estas últimas representan con maestría la delicadeza de los encajes traslúcidos de la sobrepelliz.

Incentivar la contemplación es la finalidad de la escultura de *Cristo* perteneciente a la tipología de esculturas ligeras (CAT. 56),[7] igualmente destinadas a la exportación a gran escala. Temprano en el siglo XVI, se dio una fusión de técnicas escultóricas europeas y americanas que resultó en estas piezas idóneas para procesiones y escenificaciones de Semana Santa. El Cristo muerto (aunque con ojos entreabiertos que intensifican el impacto) exhibe sus heridas, conmoviendo al espectador y encaminándolo en sus reflexiones hacia el reconocimiento de las culpas que dieron origen al sufrimiento expuesto. La sangre, presentada de manera dramática, así como las huellas de golpes y de cuerdas en el cuerpo, incluida la espalda, enfatizan la pasión. El reducido volumen del cabello y del paño de pureza indica que en la figura se usó peluca, corona de espinas y paño de tela real con fines de mayor naturalismo.

No solo los intercambios entre las diferentes regiones de los virreinatos y con Europa determinaron el ámbito escultórico; también los productos del galeón de Manila inspiraron la producción artística local. Esta confluencia de estilos y tradiciones se percibe en la talla de dos vistas con *San Miguel, la Virgen y el Niño, santo Domingo y san Juan Bautista* (CAT. 57). Es de alabastro y está elaborada al estilo de los marfiles orientales. Los personajes ostentan rasgos asiáticos, algunos detalles recuerdan técnicas de la India y la iconografía está basada en el repertorio cristiano forjado en Europa. Se cuenta entre los pocos ejemplos de esculturas firmadas, empero las palabras "Diego Reinoso inbentor" en su base dejan en la ambigüedad si se trata del creador de la composición o de la talla.[8]

Gran parte de las esculturas se ubicaban en retablos, y por ende en un discurso iconográfico de contexto. Los retablos del siglo XVI se caracterizan por un relieve en la calle central, como el de *Cristo lavando los pies a los apóstoles* (CAT. 58), que remite a un retablo pasionario o eucarístico.[9] La composición circular aprovecha todo el espacio y contempla la posición del espectador, atrayendo la mirada hacia Jesús y el apóstol a quien se le lavarán los pies. Por el diálogo insinuado, este es san Pedro al momento de negarse, lo cual explica el asombro del resto de los apóstoles que se comunican con sus miradas y gestos. Juan asistiendo con la garrafa añade un elemento narrativo adicional.

También el *San Francisco de Asís* (CAT. 55), de buena calidad de talla y estofado, formó parte de un retablo, lo cual recalca la identidad y la misión de las órdenes religiosas, en específico los franciscanos.[10] Se le reconoce por los estigmas, el cráneo y un crucifijo (ahora perdido), así como rasgos faciales y barba característicos. Guiños que el escultor realiza hacia la verosimilitud son la boca ligeramente abierta para dejar entrever la lengua, el dedo gordo del pie derecho sobresaliendo de la peana y la posición de la capucha para divisar la tonsura, señal de los monjes. Viste hábito franciscano hecho de retazos y ceñido con el cordón de cuatro nudos, pero el delicado esgrafiado realza y embellece la tela.[11]

El estofado juega asimismo un papel importante en la escultura de tamaño natural de *San Fernando* (CAT. 60), a quien el orbe imperial, la espada y la corona (ambos perdidos) designan como rey. El estofado resalta —gracias al dorado con punzones, esgrafiado y dibujo a punta de pincel— las distintas texturas de los textiles, metales y joyas que porta el personaje. Éste está representado de manera anacrónica, dado que en el siglo XVII se había establecido el modelo iconográfico para este personaje del siglo XIII,[12] mientras que el naturalismo de las flores y los motivos tipo concha del estofado remiten a textiles rococó. La escultura pertenecía a un retablo de reyes, señal del real patronato que el monarca español ejercía sobre la Iglesia americana.[13]

Los retablos siguieron vigentes en el México decimonónico, aunque con una estética más sobria que se avecinaba desde mediados del siglo XVIII, reforzada con la creación de la Academia de San Carlos, modificándose además la enseñanza y ejecución del oficio. En este contexto se ubica la puerta de un tabernáculo (CAT. 61) que remite a la importancia de los grabados como fuente visual, ya que parte de una pintura de 1868 de Franz Ittenbach, grabada por Joseph Kohlschein (FIG. 1).[14] Ambos artistas pertenecían a los nazarenos, una corriente del romanticismo alemán con repercusión en México. La escena de la Sagrada Familia señala a través del cordero premonitorio la tarea de salvación que espera al Niño Jesús, y con ello a la sagrada forma guardada detrás de esta puerta.

Las esculturas protagonizaban también el ámbito doméstico, pues inventarios, testamentos y cartas de dote mencionan imágenes de pequeño formato, ocasionalmente con materiales valiosos como alabastro, marfil, ébano, metales y piedras preciosas, así como textiles lujosos. Entre estos objetos se cuenta la figura ingeniosa de *San Miguel* (CAT. 62) esculpida en tecali, el alabastro de Puebla. El escultor entrelazó alas, telas, espada, plumas y dragón de tal manera que logró una unidad dinámica cuyo centro es san Miguel posando con elegancia, casi en actitud de baile. La policromía morada se antoja de grana cochinilla, lo cual aumentaría el valor del objeto. Este guerrero victorioso era un patrono muy popular, tal vez aquí de una autoridad eclesiástica por el escudo circular plasmado en la base.

Los retablos domésticos constituían el marco adecuado para este tipo de esculturas. El presente ejemplo (CAT. 63) ostenta columnas salomónicas[15] con el fuste helicoidal cubierto por vides doradas. La policromía vistosa del conjunto armoniza el dorado, la imitación de telas florales y de mármoles de distintos colores. Especial esmero mereció la cortina pintada del nicho, que devela y oculta, un recurso teatral característico de la época. Aunque la *Virgen de Loreto* (CAT. 65) no es propia del retablo, permite completar la escenografía. Esta peculiar advocación mariana introducida en la Nueva España por los jesuitas se ubica en el contexto de la Sagrada Familia y marcó la geografía devocional del siglo XVIII. Su iconografía se distingue por la vestimenta campaniforme que acoge al Niño Dios, la cabellera suelta de la Virgen y las joyas regaladas por los devotos.

Una devoción del culto popular y doméstico, pero también fuertemente arraigada en los conventos femeninos,[16] era la del Niño Dios bajo diferentes iconografías. El presente caso es un *Salvator Mundi*, con gesto de bendición (CAT. 64), que portaba un globo terráqueo en la mano izquierda. Se transfieren al niño todo el poder y los significados del Cristo adulto, con la desnudez como señal del misterio del Dios encarnado.[17] Talla y policromía resaltan las características del cuerpo infantil, provocando empatía. Además, las figuras solían vestirse según la ocasión, apelando a las emociones e incentivando la interacción con la escultura.

Sea para ámbitos públicos o privados, de tamaño natural o en miniatura, de materiales preciosos o cotidianos, para legitimación de autoridades o consuelo del alma, la escultura novohispana atestigua creatividad artística, redes de intercambio y procesos transculturales aún muchos por desvelar.

1 Aunque el examen de pintor facultaba para pintar lienzos y policromar piezas de madera, muchas veces quien policromaba era el dorador, un oficio que solía pertenecer al gremio de pintores. A su vez, el gremio de escultores solía integrar también a los talladores (talla de ornamentos y piezas escultóricas menores) y ensambladores (elaboración de retablos). En muchas ocasiones un maestro dominaba varios oficios del mismo gremio o de distintos.

2 Las ordenanzas de los pintores se renovaron en 1687 [revisar Paula Mues Orts, *La libertad del pincel* (México: Universidad Iberoamericana, 2008), 378-392], las de los escultores en 1589 y 1703 [revisar María del Consuelo Maquívar, *El imaginero novohispano y su obra: Las esculturas de Tepotzotlán*, (Ciudad de México: INAH, 1999), 135-161]. También Puebla conserva ordenanzas y documentos de elecciones de los representantes del gremio. (ver Neff, "La escuela de Cora...", 2013).

3 Cabellitos pintados en la transición al cabello tallado.

4 Imitación de la vestimenta a través de la policromía con ayuda de hojas metálicas. Aunque la hoja de oro es lo más frecuente en la escultura novohispana, también se usaban hojas de plata, pero requerían ser cubiertas por una capa traslúcida de pintura (corladura) para evitar la oxidación, creando a su vez un efecto tornasolado.

5 Debido a la falta de firmas en las esculturas, los textiles imitados constituyen una ayuda relevante para datar la policromía. Respecto a la relación entre escultura policromada y textiles, ver Pablo F. Amador Marrero y Patricia Díaz Cayeros, *El tejido polícromo. La escultura novohispana y su vestimenta* (México: IIE-UNAM, 2013) y Pablo F. Amador Marrero, "A propósito de los estofados novohispanos del siglo XVIII", ponencia en Seminario de Escultura Virreinal, youtube, 3 de agosto 2020.

6 Se aplicaba una capa pictórica encima del oro que luego se rasgaba en ciertas partes para que se viera el oro, provocando diferentes efectos.

7 Antes denominadas esculturas en caña de maíz, pero por la variedad de materiales empleados (papel, madera de colorín, pasta de caña de maíz, entre otros) actualmente se opta por un nombre más genérico.

8 Existe una pieza parecida, firmada por el mismo personaje ("Diego Reinoso Inventor en Mxico 1696") en el Victoria and Albert Museum en Londres.

9 A pesar de tener faltantes de madera y policromía, aún se perciben los característicos estofados del siglo XVI. (Maquívar, *El imaginero novohispano*, 107; Pablo F. Amador Marrero ,"En busca de eslabones para el estudio de la policromía en la Nueva España: Tras los pasos de Pedro de Requena y Francisco de Zumaya", ponencia en Seminario de Escultura Virreinal, youtube, 04 de mayo 2021, https://www.youtube.com/watch?v=FvuwvW1nI24.)

10 También podría estar en un retablo dominico dada la legendaria hermandad entre las dos órdenes, por lo cual es común que el santo fundador de una de las órdenes tenga su lugar en un retablo dedicado a la otra.

11 Ya que está catalogada como procedente de la Escuela de Puebla, se presume que se adquirió en tal lugar, que fue uno de los centros productores escultóricos del virreinato, aunque quedan por definir los rasgos distintivos de la producción escultórica de la Puebla del siglo XVII.

12 El grabado de Claude Audran el Viejo (1630), inspirado en *Los Santos Reyes y Nobles* de Giovanni Battista Crespi (1587), se considera una de las primeras obras que muestra la iconografía oficial de san Fernando, donde viste armadura, manto real de armiño y cuello de lechuguilla de la época. (Manuel Jesús Roldán, "Un san Fernando sevillano, a subasta. 26 de junio de 2017. https://sevilla.abc.es/pasionensevilla/noticias-semana-santa-sevilla/sevi-san-fernando-sevilla-no-subasta-113952-1498429319-201706260021_noticia.html).

13 Según información del museo, la escultura proviene de Querétaro; su pareja, la escultura de san Luis de Francia, se encuentra en una colección privada en Ciudad de México. Esta misma fuente indica que estaba ubicado en su origen en la catedral de Querétaro (https://www.denverartmuseum.org/en/object/1956.91a-b). Sin embargo, Querétaro se convirtió en sede episcopal en 1921, por ende para las fechas de la elaboración de la escultura no tenía catedral. La actual catedral se ubica en la antigua iglesia del Oratorio de San Felipe Neri, inaugurada en 1805. Dado que la morfología de la escultura y de su estofado remiten más bien a mediados del siglo XVIII, futuras investigaciones tendrán que determinar si efectivamente pertenecía al Oratorio de San Felipe Neri.

14 El grabado de Joseph Kohlschein (1841-1915) se dio a conocer gracias a la asociación para la difusión de imágenes religiosas de Düsseldorf, Alemania. La pintura de Franz Ittenbach (1813-1879) *La Sagrada Familia en Egipto* se encuentra en la Nationalgalerie der Staatlichen Museen zu Berlin, en Alemania. Agradezco al Mtro. Israel Gutiérrez Barrios haberme notificado la existencia del grabado.

15 Este tipo de columnas marcó la elaboración de retablos en la segunda mitad del siglo XVII y las primeras décadas del XVIII. Era común que entre los ornamentos vegetales y roleos resaltaran los ornamentos cristológicos como las granadas y los racimos de uva.

16 Para el rito de la profesión se solía entregar una imagen del Niño Dios a las monjas, como se ve en el género pictórico de los retratos de monjas. Aún se conservan bastantes esculturas del Niño Dios en las colecciones conventuales.

17 Ver Ramón Avendaño Esquivel, *En este tiempo con la demasía de cosas vaciadas: El Niño Jesús de plomo en la imaginería sevillana* (tesis de maestría UNAM, 2019), citando a M. Dolz, *El Niño Jesús: Historia e imagen de la devoción del Niño Divino* (Córdoba: Editorial Almuzara, 2010).

En torno al mobiliario virreinal novohispano

Gustavo Curiel Méndez

El famoso Códice Florentino del siglo XVI[1] registra en la lámina que da inicio al Doceno Libro la llegada a las costas de Veracruz (1519) de las naves españolas, procedentes de Cuba, en las que viajaba el conquistador Hernán Cortés con su tropa. En el desembarco se observa que han arribado una caja y un baúl (FIG. 1). Se trata de los primeros muebles europeos en tierra firme de lo que posteriormente sería la Nueva España.

Antes de llegar a la gran Tenochtitlán, el conquistador extremeño hizo llegar como regalo a Moctezuma una silla de caderas (FIG. 2) para que el tlatoani de los mexicas se sentara en ella cuando los dos personajes se encontraran.[2] Una vez terminada la conquista, comenzaron a elaborarse muebles informados en el mobiliario europeo. Dice fray Toribio de Benavente (Motolinía) que los indios "labran bandurrias, vihuelas y arpas, y en ellas mil labores y lazos. Sillas de caderas han hecho tantas que las casas de los españoles están llenas".[3]

El 26 de octubre de 1568 la Audiencia de México aprobó las primeras ordenanzas para carpinteros, entalladores, ensambladores y violeros de Ciudad de México.[4] Una vez regulada la producción

de los trabajadores de la madera, dio inicio el complejo intercambio de formas, técnicas, materiales, apropiaciones e interpretaciones que desembocó en la creación de un mobiliario propio, aunque nutrido a trasmano por las formas del arte europeo.

Desde 1571, llegaron a Acapulco muebles de lujo procedentes de Manila, en las islas Filipinas (por vía del llamado galeón de Manila), producto de la primera globalización del mundo. Esta ciudad asiática fue un centro de acopio y producción de multitud de muebles; destacan los de China, Japón y la India. En este formidable intercambio arribaron los primeros biombos, que pronto se adaptaron a la realidad americana. Los biombos de pintura desplegaban temáticas locales y escenas de la vida cotidiana (VER SANABRAIS, CAT. 193). Si algo caracteriza al mobiliario del virreinato es la convivencia de tipologías y ornamentaciones derivadas de muebles de las diferentes localidades novohispanas (mobiliario de la tierra), de Europa, de Asia y de la zona andina.

En cuanto a las maderas locales del nuevo mobiliario se pueden citar las siguientes: ayacahuite, caoba, tapincerán, bálsamo, oyamel, ocote, xalocote, tepehuaje, linaloe y el sabino o ahuehuete. Los muebles de importación usaban maderas preciosas europeas y asiáticas, entre ellas nogal, cedro, narra, huanghuali, caoba china, sándalo, ébano, palo de rosa, naranjo, peral y fresno.[5]

Durante todo el periodo virreinal siguieron llegando a Veracruz muebles españoles, franceses, ingleses y alemanes, que se integraron a la producción de este nuevo laboratorio de formas. Se destacan los escritorios de Augsburgo, que dieron pie a producciones específicas como es el caso de los muebles de la Villa Alta de San Ildefonso, Oaxaca, los cuales muestran taraceas esgrafiadas, rellenas de una pasta negra conocida como zulaque (CAT. 66).[6] En estos muebles aparecen multitud de imágenes de creación local (flora y fauna) que conviven con asuntos de la mitología clásica occidental y la vida cotidiana.

Con el advenimiento del siglo XVIII el mobiliario novohispano se vio influido por el rococó francés. Posteriormente se copiaron las formas del clasicismo y el neoclásico, pero siempre con el carácter local en patas, guardamalletas, faldones, palas de respaldos y brazos de sillas y canapés. En la manera de ensamblar los muebles se recurrió a las formas tradicionales europeas, aunque también a las chinas. Otra influencia decisiva fue la llegada de mobiliario europeo con *chinoiserie*, es decir, con interpretaciones occidentales de las ornamentaciones asiáticas. Estas se reprodujeron en el virreinato tanto en maques (lacados locales) como en pintura que imita esa técnica.

Los muebles novohispanos recurrieron en numerosas ocasiones a la pintura y los dorados. Lo anterior está en clara contraposición con el mobiliario castellano, producción que se distingue por las tallas directas y no usa ni pinturas ni dorados. Con el paso del tiempo, sobre todo en el siglo XVIII, el mueble novohispano recurrió a la madera al natural. Se pueden citar los ejemplos de roja caoba, puestos de moda por las producciones de Inglaterra, Francia y España (CAT. 67).

Entre las tipologías de muebles europeos del siglo XVIII se destacan escritorios, espejos, tocadores, rinconeras, roperos, sillas, taburetes, escabeles, cornucopias, baúles, bufetes, camas, bancas, bufetillos, escribanías, cajas, cómodas, estantes, papeleras, contadores y mesas. Un conjunto de gran belleza son las sillas, cómodas y mesas informadas en los muebles ingleses de estilo reina Ana, que se reprodujeron con bastante éxito (CATS. 68 Y 69). Para el caso del mobiliario asiático se pueden mencionar mesas de maque, atriles del Japón (arte *namban*), baúles con incrustaciones de madreperla, biombos de maque, cajas doradas y escritorios del Japón. Los muebles de laca de China y del Japón dieron lugar a copias en maques americanos y muebles con pinturas a imitación de los maques de importación; los mejores fueron los de Pátzcuaro y Peribán en Michoacán y los de Olinalá en Guerrero (VER SANABRAIS, CAT. 191).[7] De igual manera, los muebles con incrustaciones de concha nácar fueron muy exitosos (CAT. 70). Son famosos también los butaques de Campeche (CAT. 71) derivados de los tures caribeños. Otras producciones importantes son los baúles y cajas de carey de Campeche (CAT. 72) y Guadalajara y los formidables muebles de Puebla, entre los que resaltan los de geometrías derivadas de la carpintería mudéjar (CAT. 73), además de las mesas y baúles de alabastro de Tecali.[8] Un grupo más es el mobiliario con geometrías incrustadas de Choapan, Oaxaca, que exhibe herrajes de primera línea.

1 Ver Biblioteca Digital Mundial, *Historia general de las cosas de Nueva España* por fray Bernardino de Sahagún (Códice Florentino), Libro XII: "De la conquista de México". https://www.wdl.org/es/item/10623/view/1/1/ (consultado 18 de agosto de 2021). Este códice se hizo entre 1547-1577.

2 Ver Bernal Díaz del Castillo, *Historia verdadera de la conquista de la Nueva España*. Introducción y notas de Joaquín Ramírez Cabañas (México: Editorial Porrúa, 2019), 64. Ver además *Lienzo de Tlaxcala, Hernán Cortés and La Malinche meet Moctezuma II in Tenochtitlan, November 8, 1519*. Facsimile (c. 1890) of Lienzo de Tlaxcala.

3 Fray Toribio de Benavente, o Motolinía, *Historia de los indios de la Nueva España. Relación de los ritos antiguos, idolatrías y sacrificios de los indios de la Nueva España, y de la maravillosa conversión que Dios en ellos ha obrado* (1541), anotado por Edmundo O'Gorman, Tratado tercero, capítulo 13, "De los oficios mecánicos que los indios han aprendido de los españoles, y de los que ellos de antes sabían" (México: Editorial Porrúa, 2007), 246.

4 En este cuerpo jurídico se estipuló que aquellos oficiales que quisieran ser maestros deberían hacer a la perfección "un escritorio con dos tapas y su basa de molduras [...], una silla francesa y una de caderas ataraceada [...], una cama de campo torneada y ataraceada [...], una mesa de seis piezas con seis cuerdas y sillas de ataraceas". Para el caso de los carpinteros de lo blanco que aspiraban a tener tiendas, se señala: "El que fuere tendero para examinarse, ha de saber hacer una caja de lazo [...] con su basa de molduras al romano; otra caja fajada de las dichas molduras y la faja medio labrada. Sepa hacer una mesa de seis piezas, con sus cabezas y bisagras; sepa hacer unas puertas con su postigo y una media moldura a dos haces" [María del Consuelo Maquívar, *El imaginero novohispano y su obra: Las esculturas de Tepotzotlán* (México: Instituto Nacional de Antropología e Historia, 1999), 46, 140]. Las primeras ordenanzas fueron modificadas y puestas al día en 1589 y 1703-1704. No se pierda de vista que las cofradías y las escuelas conventuales jugaron un papel importante en la producción de obras de carpintería.

5 Ver Gustavo Curiel, *La mansión de los condes de San Bartolomé de Xala de la Ciudad de México. Inventario y aprecio de los bienes del caudal de don Antonio Rodríguez de Pedroso y Soria. 1792.* (México: UNAM, Instituto de Investigaciones Estéticas, en prensa), en particular la Relación VII del Apéndice X.

6 Ver *Carpinteros de la sierra. El mobiliario taraceado de la Villa Alta de San Ildefonso, Oaxaca (siglos XVII-XVIII)*, Tomo I, Estudios; Tomo II, Catálogo razonado, ed. y coord. Gustavo Curiel (México: UNAM, Instituto de Investigaciones Estéticas, 2019).

7 Destacan en Pátzcuaro los muebles de maque del taller de Manuel de la Cerda, indígena noble activo en la segunda mitad del siglo XVIII.

8 Sobre el mobiliario de Puebla y Tecali, ver Gustavo Curiel, "En el cruce de caminos: el mobiliario civil virreinal en la ciudad de Puebla de los Ángeles", en *El mobiliario en Puebla: Preciosismo, mitos y cotidianidad de la carpintería y la ebanistería*, ed. Francisco Pérez de Salazar Verea (Puebla: Fundación Mary Street Jenkins, 2009), 11-32. De las canteras de la famosa piedra de Tecali, en Puebla, salieron baúles de pequeño formato y formidables cubiertas para mesas. Hubo un gusto muy especial por este tipo de piezas con vetas multicolores.

Platería de la Nueva España

Carla Aymes

En mucho, la historia de Iberoamérica está ligada a la búsqueda y extracción de metales preciosos en dicho territorio y, en concreto en el ámbito de la Nueva España, a la plata. Resulta interesante, entonces, fijar la atención en ciertas piezas de la colección del Denver Art Museum que permiten destacar algunos aspectos del arte de la platería novohispana, oficio que jugó un papel fundamental en la vida, el comercio y las artes durante esos 300 años (1521-1821).

El mundo novohispano se vio sometido a diversas influencias culturales que le confirieron una identidad propia, única y compleja. Evidentemente, los procesos de manufactura, las tipologías y muchos de los modelos ornamentales fueron legados del mundo europeo, y aunque más tarde esa influencia continuó, los plateros "de la tierra" fueron apropiándose, transformando y graduando dichos influjos —junto con otros— hasta lograr objetos netamente novohispanos, incluso generando tipologías específicas que respondían a necesidades y costumbres propias.

De la colección del Denver Art Museum, una selección de diez piezas sirve aquí para vislumbrar la importancia de este quehacer. Las obras se han escogido por su calidad técnica, tipología, marcaje, temporalidad u originalidad, procurando también ofrecer una visión equilibrada entre objetos pertenecientes al mundo religioso y otros del ámbito civil. Esto resulta significativo, ya que en las colecciones suelen abundar las piezas litúrgicas, siendo las domésticas más escasas y raras. Los tipos de objetos suntuarios del ámbito civil que aquí se exploran fueron producidos para un grupo social privilegiado que, fascinado por el boato, hacía alarde de su riqueza, lo cual era casi una obligación dentro de su escalafón social.

Comenzamos con un jarro de pico (CAT. 74) fechado hacia 1600, de excelente manufactura, con sugerente trabajo de cincelado y picado de lustre.[1] Esta tipología está presente desde el siglo XVI, aunque es interesante que aparece en inventarios de bienes solo hasta mediados del siglo XVIII, probablemente por cambios en la moda.[2] Según las ordenanzas del gremio de plateros, son cuatro las marcas que debían colocarse: artífice, localidad, ensayador e impuesto del "quinto real", equivalente a la quinta parte del valor de la pieza. El jarro ostenta dos marcas parciales. Una de ellas, claramente de localidad, presenta una estructura con una cabeza varonil entre columnas coronadas y por debajo la inicial de la ciudad donde fue marcada (esto en algunos casos consta de dos letras). Se presume que sea una pieza de Ciudad de México —a pesar de la poca legibilidad del punzón—, pues es concordante con sus platerías.[3] Sin embargo, otros centros plateros utilizaron esta misma estructura en su marcaje toponímico: Puebla de los Ángeles, Guadalajara, Zacatecas, Pachuca, Guanajuato, Querétaro, San Luis Potosí, Mérida de Yucatán y Antequera de Oaxaca, por mencionar algunos de los más importantes.

Se destaca también una salva, o salvilla, con pie (CAT. 75) —este último término es el más empleado en la época— que se usaría como bandeja para servir bebidas en vasos o jarros.[4] Ricamente trabajada y con gran personalidad, evidencia un gusto especial por la decoración profusa, en este caso elaborada a partir de un medallón central que genera radialmente ocho secciones con motivos vegetales ondulantes. Pertenece a los talleres de Ciudad de México y ostenta dos marcas: la del ensayador mayor Juan de la Fuente (activo entre 1674 y 1677), de quien se conocen pocas obras, y la del "quinto real".[5]

Capta luego nuestra atención un candelero (CAT. 76) con torneados de tipo balaustral con patas de garra y bola y ornamentación vegetal propia del Barroco con motivos de contrapuntas entrelazadas. Presentan una inscripción con fecha de 1727 que atestigua, asimismo, su patronazgo.

Una corona imperial (CAT. 77) labrada para guarnecer una imagen religiosa nos sumerge ya en el lenguaje ornamental del rococó, hacia el último tercio del siglo XVIII. El mundo virreinal gustó de este motivo, por lo que tuvo una amplia aplicación y pervivencia, y se crearon elaboradas combinaciones en torno a él.

También con rocallas observamos un bolso limosnero (CAT. 78), delicada pieza con fines religiosos. Está conformado por dos placas labradas de plata con alma de rica tela de seda e hilos de oro entorchado. De un lado, el monograma de la Virgen María; del otro, sobredorada, una custodia flanqueada por dos ángeles.

La tachuela (CAT. 79) es una especie de escudilla o recipiente por lo general hecho de plata, con o sin asas. Es una tipología recurrente en los inventarios a partir de 1700.[6] La mayoría de los ejemplares que se conocen son guatemaltecos, a los cuales es cercano el ejemplar del museo de Denver[7] (debe recordarse que la Capitanía General de Guatemala era dependiente administrativamente del Virreinato de la Nueva España).[8] Esta pieza con dos asas ha sido fechada hacia 1775 y presenta un contorno ondulado en el que alternan delgados gallones dobles cóncavos y otros más gruesos convexos.

Una elegante jofaina (CAT. 81) de las últimas décadas del siglo XVIII, de sencillas líneas y suave movimiento ondulante, sirve para comentar que muchas de las piezas novohispanas se distinguen por el empleo de una gran cantidad de plata; suelen ser obras de cierto peso. También llamada bandeja para el aseo, esta en particular fue marcada por el celebrado ensayador José Antonio Lince y González,[9] que trabajó en Ciudad de México entre 1779 y 1788.[10]

Un ciborio (CAT. 82) en plata dorada con refinado trabajo de facetado sobre su superficie recuerda al rococó guatemalteco, que quizás sirvió de modelo a las platerías de El Salvador; de hecho, el ciborio ostenta la marca de esta localidad.[11] Llama la atención que presenta en su marcaje dos juegos de coronas extemporáneas, utilizadas para atestiguar el pago del "quinto real". Una es consistente con las de San Salvador, mientras que la otra es más cercana a las de Nueva Guatemala, por lo que se intuye que pudo ser remarcada ahí.[12]

Fechada hacia 1785, una placa (CAT. 83) de gran formato lleva en el centro un motivo ornamental de una urna adornada con elementos vegetales y florales, enmarcada por una cenefa perimetral, también decorada. Es interesante considerar que pudiera tratarse

de un panel de un frontal de altar, dadas las dimensiones y el tipo de motivos ornamentales.[13]

Concluimos con una pieza (CAT. 80) situada ya en el México independiente que demuestra no solo la maestría de sus artífices, sino la pervivencia del oficio ante los avatares del siglo XIX, cuando evidentemente fue perdiendo pujanza poco a poco. En este caso, se desconoce el platero, pero por el marcaje sabemos que la pieza fue ensayada por el celebrado Cayetano Buitrón, lo que permite fecharla en los años de actividad de este en Ciudad de México, entre 1823 y 1843.[14] Se trata de un recipiente con pie y dos asas. Su tipología provoca la pregunta de si sería un frutero o quizás otra tipología utilizada en ese momento, como una copa o una tembladera.[15]

A manera de colofón, es interesante dar cuenta de otro aspecto de esta colección, pues al revisar y hacer la selección de las piezas más significativas, se pudo constatar que más del cuarenta por ciento de ellas presenta algún tipo de marca. Al considerar el cálculo de que tan solo una quinta parte de la platería novohispana fue marcada, es evidente aquí una clara intención de reunir piezas no solo de calidad, sino que cuenten con la impronta de este valor añadido.

1 El trabajo de cincelado es una de las labores en platería que requiere mayor destreza y conocimiento por parte del artífice. Consiste en añadir texturas y líneas mediante la suave incisión con cinceles a golpe de martillo sobre la superficie de la plata. El picado de lustre es un trabajo de fondo texturizado. Consiste en imprimir distintos diseños con punzones sobre la superficie del metal con la ayuda de un martillo. Estas impresiones se colocaban muy juntas y de manera uniforme para producir un efecto graneado con diferentes brillos y texturas.

2 Carla Aymes, "La platería civil novohispana y decimonónica en los ajuares domésticos. Estudio documental 1600–1850", tesis de maestría (Universidad Nacional Autónoma de México, 2010).

3 La segunda marca, también incompleta, exhibe una V. Se ignora a qué hace alusión.

4 Aymes, "La platería civil novohispana…".

5 Cristina Esteras Martín, *Marcas de platería hispanoamericana. Siglos XVI-XX* (Madrid: Ediciones Tuero, 1992), 24, 25, 108 y 180.

6 En inventarios de Ciudad de México. Véase: Aymes, "La platería civil novohispana y decimonónica en los ajuares domésticos. Estudio documental 1600–1850", Anex 1 (p. 139), 31.

7 Es una tipología arraigada en las platerías guatemaltecas. Ver: Cristina Esteras Martín, *La platería del Museo Franz Mayer: Obras escogidas, siglos XVI-XIX* (México: Museo Franz Mayer, 1992), 235, 236, 238, 239, 242 y 243. Ver también Cristina Esteras Martín, *La platería en el Reino de Guatemala, siglos XVI-XIX*, 1a ed. (Guatemala: Fundación Albergue Hermano Pedro, D.L., 1994).

8 A esta capitanía pertenecieron las platerías de Almolonga (Guatemala), Santiago de Guatemala, Nueva Guatemala de la Asunción, León (Nicaragua), Quetzaltenango (Guatemala), Ciudad Real (Chiapas, México) y San Salvador (El Salvador).

9 Lince está marcado con las iniciales LNC. El objeto ostenta otras marcas: la de Ciudad de México, la del quinto real y una última, especialmente controvertida: la R coronada que puede hacer alusión a la plata de rescate. Ver: Carla Aymes, "'R': La marca de la plata de rescate", en *Ophir en las Indias: Estudios sobre la plata americana. Siglos XVI-XIX* (León, España: Universidad de León, 2010), 241–48.

10 Esteras Martín, *Marcas de platería hispanoamericana. Siglos XVI-XX*, 180.

11 Como ya se comentó, este centro platero fue dependiente de la Capitanía General de Guatemala.

12 Ver el caso similar de una compotera en Esteras Martín, *La platería en el Reino de Guatemala, siglos XVI-XIX*, 176. Ver la marca en Esteras Martín, *Marcas de platería hispanoamericana. Siglos XVI-XX*, 126.

13 Ver ejemplos de frontales de altar en las láminas 110, 115 y 126 en Cristina Esteras Martín, *El arte de la platería mexicana, 500 años* (México: Centro Cultural Arte Contemporáneo, 1989), 94–95, 102–3, 114–15.

14 Ver Esteras Martín *Marcas de platería hispanoamericana. Siglos XVI-XX*, 85, 86, 87, 88, 89, 90, 110 y 179.

15 De acuerdo con el *Diccionario de Autoridades de la Real Academia Española*, 1726-39: "vaso ancho de plata, oro o vidrio, de figura redonda, con dos asas a los lados, y un pequeño asiento. Las hay de muchos tamaños, por hacerse regularmente de una hoja muy delgada, que parece que tiembla, por lo que se le dio este nombre".

Convergencia y divergencia de la cerámica

Philippe Halbert

Los cuadros de casta, como los del pintor inmigrante español Francisco Clapera, ahora en la colección del Museo de Arte de Denver, constituyen un cautivador registro visual del tipo de bienes que se encontraban en los hogares coloniales de Nueva España. Aunque la relativa armonía doméstica y la actividad industrial de una familia mestiza son el centro de atención en *De Chino e India, Jenízaro*, de Clapera, el artista también se preocupó por representar una variedad de piezas cerámicas, como cuencos, tazas y platos azules y blancos (CAT. 84). Estos objetos están dispuestos en un estante de madera y en el entrepaño inferior se representa una jarra de cuerpo redondo, cuyo color rojo hace juego con el de otras seis bandejas de cerámica redondas y rectangulares artísticamente colgadas en la pared. La inclusión de estos objetos no se limita a ambientar la escena o a sugerir la profundidad de la pintura, sino que nos lleva a considerar las cerámicas existentes en el Museo de Arte de Denver como una prueba más del intercambio cultural en lo que ahora es México antes de 1800.

Dos vasijas zoomorfas de barro, una con forma de mono sentado y otra de pato, hablan de la permanencia de las antiguas tradiciones que nunca llegaron a desaparecer del todo (CATS. 85 Y 86). Los ejemplos de la cerámica de Tonalá, que lleva el nombre de un pueblo de Jalisco, cerca de Guadalajara, en el oeste de México, están hechos a mano, usando una técnica de baja cocción y están equipados con picos largos en forma de embudo. La cerámica de Tonalá se producía prácticamente por parte de alfareros indígenas y mestizos, cuyo trabajo y arte sustentaron el legado de la cerámica mesoamericana bruñida y engobada. Estos objetos del siglo XVIII, aparentemente caprichosos, recuerdan las vasijas de efigie y otros antecedentes, como una vasija tarasca de Michoacán con pintura geométrica engobada (CAT. 87). Probablemente se utilizaban para almacenar agua, y están decorados a mano con engobes rojos, negros y marrones que sugieren detalles más naturalistas, además de motivos florales y vegetales más estilizados. Por otro lado, un pequeño cuenco de Tonalá adopta el perfil del bernegal español, o copa de vino (CAT. 88). Fabricado con dos pequeñas asas y adornado con engobes de colores, es probable que resultara igualmente práctico para consumir el chocolate, un alimento claramente americano. Un vaso cilíndrico de Tonalá con engobe rojo, también utilizado para beber, prescinde de cualquier adorno pintado y en cambio recurre a una combinación de líneas grabadas y formas geométricas estampadas (CAT. 90). Estos búcaros de Indias eran apreciados por su arcilla supuestamente perfumada y se exportaban a España, donde se incluían con frecuencia en las pinturas de bodegones como símbolos del exotismo del Nuevo Mundo.

La loza estannífera de la colonia española, o mayólica, también se caracteriza por la fusión cultural. La producción de mayólica floreció en la España musulmana y se cree que entró en la Península Ibérica a través del norte de África en los siglos VIII o IX. La tradición continuó en ciudades españolas como Sevilla y Talavera de la Reina, y la cerámica vidriada muy pronto se exportó a Nueva España. Fundada al este de Ciudad de México en 1531, Puebla de los Ángeles dio lugar a un gremio de alfareros en 1653 que disfrutó de una época dorada de un siglo de duración.[1] Los alfareros de Puebla produjeron artículos funcionales de mayólica, así como accesorios ornamentales, como los azulejos, para el hogar. Un azulejo cuadrado con un pájaro en vuelo, en azul cobalto, es una pieza representativa de las que se utilizaban para decorar, por igual, interiores y exteriores arquitectónicos (CAT. 89). Los azulejos vidriados con estaño se remontan a los precedentes islámicos; el jinete fantásticamente ataviado que adorna el centro de una gran pila multiusos, o lebrillo, fabricado en Puebla, bien podría ser un jinete musulmán (CAT. 92). Esta forma de cerámica, realizada en un torno de alfarero, tiene su origen en el periodo de dominio musulmán en España, y la técnica de usar puntos para rellenar el jinete con bigote y su orgulloso corcel es característica del arte islámico.

El uso de pigmentos azul cobalto por parte de los alfareros de Puebla también resalta la influencia de la porcelana azul y blanca, como el plato Zhangzhou recuperado del *San Isidro*, un barco español que naufragó frente a las costas de Filipinas a finales del siglo XVI (CAT. 91).[2] Aunque la porcelana de Asia oriental se consumía en Nueva España, la loza estannífera vidriada de Puebla, o talavera poblana, ofrecía una alternativa menos costosa que a menudo era visualmente comparable a la verdadera porcelana de pasta dura. Cinco bandas concéntricas de vides frondosas y otros follajes decoran una jarra con tapa y dos elegantes asas pintada de azul cobalto (CAT. 93). Un recipiente o maceta en forma de barril, mucho más grande, se distingue del resto por el uso de pinturas polícromas para representar borlas anudadas con lazos, así como una serie de motivos florales y cuerdas entrelazadas (CAT. 94). Si bien este objeto resalta por una paleta de colores más variada, su forma y escala se asemejan a las de los taburetes de porcelana china, además, la representación del registro central de flores y hojas estilizadas en un rojo intenso deriva posiblemente de los textiles y la artesanía en metal chinos.

Al igual que sucede con las pinturas de casta de Clapera, la muestra representativa de objetos que aquí se analizan trasciende las fronteras estéticas, materiales o tecnológicas. Más bien dan testimonio de una cultura cerámica dinámica y verdaderamente global que surgió en Nueva España a partir del siglo XVI. Cada uno de estos objetos, que trazan una vibrante trayectoria de continuidad e innovación artística, acompañó procesos más amplios de asimilación y aculturación a medida que las nuevas identidades se forjaban, literalmente, en arcilla.

1 Ver Robin Farwell Gavin, Donna Pierce y Alfonso Pleguezuelo eds., *Cerámica y Cultura: The Story of Spanish and Mexican Mayólica* (Albuquerque: University of New Mexico Press, 2003).

2 Ver Dennis Carr ed., *Made in the Americas: The New World Discovers Asia* (Boston: Museum of Fine Arts, Boston, 2015); y Meha Priyadarshini, *Chinese Porcelain in Colonial Mexico: The Material Worlds of an Early Modern Trade* (Cham, Switzerland: Palgrave Macmillan, 2018).

La pintura venezolana y el Caribe

Janeth Rodríguez Nóbrega

Gracias a la generosidad de Patricia Phelps de Cisneros podemos afirmar que el Denver Art Museum posee la mejor colección de pintura venezolana fuera de Venezuela, al reunir obras de los artistas más destacados que estuvieron activos en la provincia de Caracas desde finales del siglo XVII hasta inicios del XIX. Aproximarnos a este legado nos permite acercarnos a un área geográfica como el Caribe, usualmente relegada en la historiografía del arte hispanoamericano,[1] pese a ser un singular espacio de encuentro entre personas y objetos, comercio y contrabando, formas e ideas provenientes de distintas regiones de Europa, América, África y Asia.

Los primeros europeos que exploraron territorio venezolano pronto descubrieron que la naturaleza local no era pródiga en riquezas mineras, pero sí en tierras fértiles aptas para las labores agrícolas. No encontraron el mítico El Dorado, tampoco un imperio semejante al inca o al mexica, pero sí tribus pequeñas de gran diversidad lingüística y cultural, que fueron sometidas con prontitud. En este entorno poco atractivo, la práctica pictórica se inició en manos de colonos que tenían algunos conocimientos del oficio, pero que no hallaron en los incipientes poblados demanda suficiente para desarrollar un mercado artístico competitivo. A los puertos locales llegaban ocasionalmente cuadros y tallas de manufactura europea que satisfacían las necesidades devocionales y representativas de la población. Solo cuando se consolidaron las primeras ciudades aumentó la demanda de imágenes para el consumo doméstico y para los altares de iglesias y conventos. A mediados del siglo XVII se establecieron talleres más especializados, conformados por artistas españoles y criollos que comenzaron a formar vínculos familiares entre sí. En este reducido mercado no fue necesario fundar un gremio que supervisara los talleres, lo que impulsó una práctica artística informal, sin ordenanzas gremiales ni exámenes que evaluaran la formación de los artistas.

Hacia finales del siglo XVII, resalta un maestro anónimo que pinta en El Tocuyo, pueblo fundado en 1545 en la región centro-occidental de Venezuela. En este poblado confluyeron las rutas del comercio interregional y se concentraron los misioneros franciscanos y dominicos, que construyeron allí sus primeros conventos, por lo que no podría descartarse que se tratara de un fraile pintor. Las pocas obras atribuidas a él están fechadas entre 1682 y 1702.[2] Sus pinturas se caracterizan por una paleta de colores intensos, cálidos y terrosos, fabricados con materiales locales. Sus figuras son monumentales, ubicadas sobre fondos ocres, dibujadas con fórmulas esquemáticas y repetitivas (CAT. 95). Pese a sus imperfecciones, sirvieron de inspiración a los artesanos locales hasta bien avanzado el siglo XIX, fomentando un estilo regional, pero también impactaron a un artista caraqueño de la primera mitad del siglo XVIII.

El pintor Fernando Álvarez Carneiro (1670-1744) nació en el puerto de La Guaira, descendiente de una familia blanca de bajos recursos.[3] Se estableció en la ciudad de Caracas, donde pintó para los conventos franciscanos y dominicos. A través de esta relación con las dos órdenes religiosas más importantes, fue contratado en tres oportunidades para realizar obras en la iglesia parroquial de la Concepción y en el Hospital de San Juan Bautista, ambas en El Tocuyo.[4] Estos contratos no solo le aseguraron un trabajo estable, sino también la oportunidad de contemplar las obras del anónimo maestro, de las cuales adoptó la paleta terrosa, el dibujo de las aureolas y sus nubes de consistencia rocosa. Su obra *Santísima Trinidad* es un testimonio de este contacto, aunque no sabemos si por gusto propio o a solicitud de sus clientes (CAT. 97).

Mientras tanto, en Caracas, otros pintores competían por los encargos. Uno de ellos fue Francisco José de Lerma y Villegas (activo entre 1719 y 1753), un pardo libre. Con el término "pardo" se identificaba a las castas mixtas producto del mestizaje entre blancos, negros e indios. Pese a su condición racial, Lerma fue un artista prestigioso durante la primera mitad del siglo XVIII. En su obra predominan las figuras con formas alargadas y rostros de narices perfiladas, que se inspiran en antiguas estampas italianas y flamencas, pero con colores vibrantes y luminosos (CAT. 96).

En las mismas fechas sobresale la producción de José Lorenzo Zurita (activo entre 1727 y 1753), posible descendiente de uno de los esclavos liberados por el presbítero Lorenzo Zurita en 1692. Sus buenas relaciones con la jerarquía eclesiástica y con miembros de la élite caraqueña, a quienes retrató en diversas oportunidades, le aseguraron encargos constantes, al punto de que falleció dejando bienes de fortuna. Su obra *San José con el Niño* muestra la reinterpretación de la pintura andaluza, con una paleta bastante limitada (CAT. 98).

Hacia la segunda mitad del siglo XVIII, el mercado artístico caraqueño estaba dominado por los pardos libres, quienes ejercían la mayoría de los oficios artesanales. Un ejemplo es la extensa familia Landaeta, cuyos miembros practicaron la pintura, la escultura, la platería y la música. Entre estos sobresale el maestro Antonio José Landaeta (activo entre 1748 y 1799), quien firma una *Inmaculada Concepción* que muestra una paleta más clara y apastelada (CAT. 100), reinterpretando las formas rococó que llegaron a Caracas gracias a las imágenes traídas desde las islas Canarias, Nueva España y Puerto Rico, tanto en el comercio regular como en el equipaje de funcionarios peninsulares y misioneros que circularon por el Caribe, como el catalán José Antonio Gelabert y Garcés, cuyo retrato realizado por el cubano Valentín Arcila se encuentra en la colección del museo (CAT. 99).[5]

Desde finales del siglo XVII, se incrementó la migración de artesanos de las islas Canarias que llegaron a Caracas a probar suerte. Este archipiélago se encontraba en la ruta de navegación hacia el continente americano, por lo que se erigió en puerto de parada de las flotas españolas. Producto de estas migraciones es el pintor, dorador y escultor Juan Pedro López (1724-1787), un caraqueño descendiente de isleños, quien se convirtió en el artista más destacado de la segunda mitad del siglo XVIII, compartiendo protagonismo con la familia Landaeta.[6] El lenguaje pictórico de López,

imitado por otros artistas caraqueños, combina diversas fuentes: se inicia con una paleta oscura, característica de la pintura andaluza, que va iluminándose gradualmente con colores más vivos (CAT. 101), apastelados y formas más suaves, que parecen inspirarse en los cuadros novohispanos que arriban de manera frecuente a Caracas a través del comercio del cacao local con los puertos de Campeche y Veracruz.

La mayor parte de la pintura venezolana no está firmada. En muy pocos casos, encontramos una firma sobre la superficie pintada o al dorso de las obras. De allí que resulte una excepción el retrato de *Don José Bernardo de Asteguieta y Díaz de Sarralde* (CAT. 102), oidor de la Real Audiencia de Manila trasladado en 1788 a la Audiencia de Caracas, donde actuó como juez general de bienes de difuntos. En Caracas, fue retratado por el pintor Rafael Ochoa, un pardo libre activo entre 1787 y 1809, quien no solo firmó la pieza con una caligrafía esmerada, sino que además muestra su orgullo racial: "Rafael Ochoa, de calidad negro: lo hizo en Caracas Año 1793". Esta inscripción es la primera conocida en la que un artista local recalca su condición racial. La existencia misma de la obra testimonia que las élites, tanto peninsulares como criollas, encargaban las piezas sin importar el color de piel de los artistas. Sobre Rafael Ochoa es poco lo conocido; sabemos que trabajó para la Archicofradía de Nuestra Señora del Rosario, la más importante del convento dominico de San Jacinto, actuó como avaluador en testamentarías y donó unas arañas a la iglesia de San Mauricio, que congregaba a los mulatos de la ciudad.[7]

Los artistas caraqueños intentaron seguir los estilos dominantes en la pintura andaluza, canaria y novohispana contemporánea, adaptándose a las necesidades representativas de la sociedad. En su mayoría realizaron composiciones sencillas en pequeño formato, con muy pocos personajes, de rostros inexpresivos y representados sobre fondos neutros o con escasas referencias espaciales. Su clientela laica y eclesiástica les exigió una iconografía convencional, en la cual se repetían las imágenes de Cristo, la Virgen y los santos relacionados con las órdenes religiosas presentes en el territorio. La Iglesia local no tuvo que enfrentar los retos de la evangelización de etnias aborígenes con una cultura material sofisticada, por lo que no requirió una producción artística exuberante. Por ello se rehuyeron las escenas narrativas complejas, con numerosos personajes, características del Barroco, incluso en los cuadros de gran formato para iglesias y conventos.

1 Estas obras fueron estudiadas por Jorge Rivas en *De oficio pintor. Arte colonial venezolano. Colección Patricia Phelps de Cisneros* (Santiago de los Caballeros: Centro León; Caracas: Fundación Cisneros, 2007). Catálogo de una exposición homónima que exhibió por primera vez una amplia muestra de arte colonial venezolano fuera de dicho país.

2 Alfredo Boulton, historiador y crítico de arte venezolano, lo bautizó como el "Pintor del Tocuyo" y le atribuyó una veintena de pinturas. El investigador venezolano Carlos F. Duarte sugirió el nombre de Francisco de la Cruz, basado en el monograma que se encuentra al dorso de este cuadro, teoría que Boulton descartó al no encontrar pruebas documentales. A. Boulton, *El pintor del Tocuyo* (Caracas: Ediciones Macanao, 1985), 20-21.

3 La producción de Fernando Álvarez Carneiro había sido catalogada por Alfredo Boulton bajo el nombre de "Pintor de San Francisco" gracias a una serie de obras con un mismo lenguaje formal conservadas en la iglesia de San Francisco en Caracas. El hallazgo del cuadro *Santo Tomás de Aquino*, firmado y fechado con su nombre, en la colección del Museo Nacional de Bellas Artes de Cuba, permitió identificar la producción de Álvarez Carneiro y relacionar la información obtenida en distintos documentos.

4 Alfredo Boulton, *Historia de la pintura en Venezuela*, Tomo I, Época colonial (Caracas: Ernesto Armitano, 1975), 90.

5 Don José Antonio Gelabert y Garcés llegó a La Habana en 1748 procedente de Santo Domingo (actual República Dominicana) para ejercer el cargo de oficial del Tribunal de Cuentas en Cuba. En esta isla es retratado por el pintor Valentín Arcila en 1770. Este es el único retrato cubano del siglo XVIII conservado en un museo público norteamericano, obsequio de Frederick y Jan Mayer.

6 Carlos F. Duarte le atribuye más de 200 pinturas y algunas tallas escultóricas. Ver Duarte, *Juan Pedro López. Maestro de pintor, escultor y dorador. 1724-1787* (Caracas: Galería de Arte Nacional, 1996).

7 Ver Carlos F. Duarte, *Diccionario biográfico documental. Pintores, escultores y doradores en Venezuela. Período hispánico y comienzos del período republicano* (Caracas: Galería de Arte Nacional, 2000), 213.

Venezuela: El mobiliario en la encrucijada del imperio español

Jorge F. Rivas Pérez

Con el asentamiento de la isla La Española en la década de 1490, España ocupó un vasto territorio en el mar Caribe que abarcaba las Antillas Mayores y la costa norte de Sudamérica, que incluía vastas extensiones del litoral de lo que actualmente es Colombia y Venezuela. Por su situación geográfica, ninguna zona de América era más cosmopolita ni estaba más estrechamente ligada a España (y al resto de Europa, por extensión), a las islas Canarias y a África que el Caribe. Fue un eje central para el comercio transatlántico y regional, así como para el intercambio cultural. Las artes de la región muestran una complejidad y variedad derivadas de esta posición privilegiada.

Venezuela, en particular, se benefició de este rico diálogo cultural caribeño que incluía a Europa, México, Puerto Rico y Cuba (CAT. 103). Las nuevas modas europeas en las artes llegaban primero al Caribe. El comercio de principios de la Edad Moderna en el Cari-

be español también incluía regularmente prácticas de intercambio extraoficiales –como el contrabando– con los mercaderes británicos, holandeses y franceses, a menudo la fuente de codiciados artículos de lujo como relojes (CAT. 107), pequeños muebles, cerámica fina y textiles.

Los muebles de la segunda mitad del siglo XVIII en Venezuela muestran la fuerte influencia de los repertorios visuales españoles, ingleses y holandeses (CATS. 105 Y 106), a menudo reinterpretados en formas originales, como las patas cabriolé quebradas que se encuentran en algunas mesas y sillas (CATS. 104, 109 Y 111). Además, la inmigración procedente de las islas Canarias, entre finales del siglo XVII y principios del XVIII, influyó significativamente en el desarrollo artístico de Venezuela durante el siglo XVIII. Los hermanos Juan Francisco y Gregorio de León Quintana, de padres canarios, y el maestro Domingo Gutiérrez, nacido y formado en La Laguna, Tenerife, fueron los ebanistas más destacados de la época.[1]

Domingo Gutiérrez (1709–1793)

A partir de la década de 1730, Gutiérrez se convirtió en el principal ebanista de Caracas. Produjo una amplia gama de mobiliario doméstico que incluía sillas, mesas y pequeños muebles de caja (CATS. 110 Y 108). Sin embargo, se hizo famoso por sus numerosos encargos para la Iglesia católica, que comprendían desde grandes retablos hasta muebles como las sillas para el solio de la catedral de Caracas, que posteriormente pintaría y doraría Juan Pedro López (CAT. 114), con quien Gutiérrez muchas veces trabajaba. La excelente técnica de talla de Gutiérrez y sus sofisticadas composiciones, que combinaban intrincadas rocallas, follajes y flores con motivos arquitectónicos –a menudo expuestas en superficies curvas, como en el retablo de 1766 para la Tercera Orden de la iglesia de San Francisco de Caracas–, le valieron amplio reconocimiento. Independientemente de las dimensiones de una pieza, el sentido del equilibrio y la proporción de Gutiérrez distingue su obra de la de sus coetáneos; tal refinamiento es evidente, por ejemplo, en el pequeño tabernáculo curvo con decoración esgrafiada realizado para don José María de Tovar y Tovar en Caracas (CAT. 112). Sus repertorios ornamentales trascendieron a otros materiales; plateros como Domingo Tomás Núñez elaboraron obras que muestran con mucha claridad la influencia de Gutiérrez (CAT. 113). Gutiérrez no fue el único pionero de los estilos rococó. Desde la década de 1760 hasta la de 1780, muchos ebanistas caraqueños produjeron muebles finamente tallados y adornados con rocalla, hojas, flores y pequeños animales. Un sillón de butaca particularmente delicado de la década de 1760 es un claro ejemplo de la creatividad y la fusión de culturas que proliferaron en ese periodo (CAT. 115). Las butacas hicieron su aparición en el siglo XVII en Venezuela a partir de formas de asientos rituales de la antigua América que fueron posteriormente modificadas con elementos de diseño españoles (FIG. 1). La forma original estaba tallada en una sola pieza de madera. Más tarde, las butacas se ensamblaban a partir de varias piezas. En el siglo XVIII, el tipo de butaca siguió evolucionando, incorporando elementos decorativos europeos.[2] Este ejemplo incluye delicados detalles de rocalla y patas cabriolé adornadas con una cabeza de perro y un pájaro.

Los cambios de gustos

Aunque algunos ebanistas siguieron produciendo muebles rococós, como las sillas de José Ramón Cardozo de 1797 para el coro de la catedral de Caracas (CAT. 116), los gustos cambiaron a finales del siglo XVIII. Los diseños europeos de las décadas de 1760 y 1770, populares en Venezuela, exhibían un renovado interés del público por la influencia del diseño clásico griego y romano. Predominaban las formas rectilíneas sobrias, las patas afiladas y las formas simples pero elegantes (CAT. 118). Desde finales de la década de 1780 y hasta bien entrada la década de 1810, se puso de moda el uso de la madera enchapada, la marquetería y las incrustaciones de madera, al igual que motivos como las grecas, los guilloches, las palmetas, las columnas, las guirnaldas, las cintas, los óvalos y las placas con temas clásicos, todo ello relacionado con el gusto reinante por los ornamentos tomados de la antigüedad clásica (CAT. 117).

Conocido en vida por su elegante mobiliario y exquisita artesanía, Serafín Antonio Almeida nació en 1752 en Guatire.[3] Su estilo personal se caracterizó por sus elegantes proporciones, equilibrio, simetría y refinados motivos ornamentales de gusto clásico (CAT. 119). Almeida, que estuvo en activo en Caracas desde la década de 1780, fue la figura dominante en su oficio y produjo notables obras para la iglesia, como el nuevo coro de la catedral encargado en 1799. Permaneció activo hasta finales de la década de 1810 y murió en Caracas en 1822.

El gusto por los repertorios clásicos continuó tras la independencia de Venezuela en la década de 1820. Además de los ebanistas locales, los inmigrantes procedentes del norte de Europa y de Estados Unidos contribuyeron al desarrollo de estilos visuales apropiados para la nueva república, que a menudo seguían haciendo referencia a la antigüedad griega y romana. El ebanista de Baltimore Joseph P. Whiting se estableció en Caracas en 1825 y produjo una amplia gama de muebles de inspiración clásica para el hogar (CAT. 120), con frecuencia adornados con estarcidos doradas.[4] Gracias a su ubicación en el Caribe, Venezuela siguió desempeñando un papel fundamental en una amplia red cultural internacional que floreció durante la segunda mitad del siglo XVIII.

1 Sobre Gutiérrez, ver Carlos F. Duarte, *Domingo Gutiérrez: El maestro del rococó en Venezuela* (Caracas: Ediciones Equinoccio, Universidad Simón Bolívar, 1977).

2 Jorge F. Rivas Pérez, "Transforming Status: The Genesis of the New World Butaca", en *Festivals and Daily Life in the Arts of Colonial Latin America: Papers from the 2012 Mayer Center Symposium at the Denver Art Museum*, ed. Donna Pierce (Denver: Denver Art Museum, 2014), 111–28.

3 Jorge F. Rivas Pérez, *El repertorio clásico en el mobiliario venezolano, siglos XVIII Y XIX* (Caracas: Fundación Cisneros, 2008), 11.

4 Ver Carlos F. Duarte, "El mobiliario de la época republicana en Venezuela", en *Armitano Arte* 1 (diciembre 1982):11-42.

De la Nueva Granada a Denver: Particularidades y pluralidades de una colección pictórica

Olga Isabel Acosta Luna

Al observar la treintena de pinturas del Denver Art Museum cuyo origen ha sido identificado y atribuido al entorno neogranadino[1] y grancolombiano de los siglos XVII a XIX, resaltan indicios que invitan a pensar estas obras como un corpus sugerente que visibiliza lógicas de producción y pensamiento artístico surgidas en esta geografía desde el mismo periodo colonial hasta la fecha, y que a menudo son desconocidas fuera del entorno colombiano. El acervo del Denver Art Museum, quizá la mayor colección pictórica neogranadina existente fuera de Colombia, tradicionalmente fue atribuido al pincel de artífices activos en la Santafé del siglo XVII, tales como Gregorio Vásquez de Arce y Ceballos (1638-1711) y su hermano Juan Bautista (1630-1677), o Gaspar de Figueroa (1594-1658) y Baltasar Vargas de Figueroa (1629-1667) (CATS. 121-126). Tales atribuciones pueden leerse como una respuesta global de la historiografía del siglo XX y reciente a la hora de valorar la producción americana durante los siglos del dominio español. Es decir, el afán de identificar Vásquez, Figueroas, Medoros y Gutiérrez por doquier dentro y fuera de Colombia responde a que el reconocimiento de estos artistas, aunque tímidamente, ha permitido que las obras neogranadinas sean aceptadas en el canon de la historia del arte y, por ende, consideradas piezas artísticas.[2]

Superado en parte el miedo al anonimato y a reconocer en la ausencia de autorías la diversidad y las particularidades de una producción plural, la historiografía del arte en Colombia y Suramérica se encuentra hoy ante un interesante proceso de revisión de las historiografías de los siglos XVIII y XIX, replicadas en el siglo XX en el marco de la invención de repúblicas "civilizadas", que en el caso de Colombia tuvieron en el criollismo, sus linajes familiares y el reconocimiento externo sus principales banderas. Por ende, la defensa de un origen de corte romano y andaluz para la pintura neogranadina, que tiene eco en España y en el resto de América, representa un alegato contradictorio y violento que refleja propósitos delirantes de excluir la pluralidad. De ahí que, en las últimas dos décadas, entender cómo se ha construido la historia del arte americano se ha convertido en una prioridad enriquecedora.[3]

Por ello, quiero sugerir una breve lectura de la colección pictórica neogranadina del Museo de Denver desde diferentes indicios presentes en algunas obras que permiten pensarlas como un conjunto ajeno a un origen común y uniforme, que fue reunido en su mayoría por el coleccionista Daniel C. Stapleton durante su estadía en Colombia y Ecuador entre 1895 y 1914 y donado en 1990 al museo por la familia Renchard.[4] Esta colección visibiliza conexiones y tradiciones pictóricas y geográficas diversas, más allá de las autorías y dataciones canónicas.

A la luz de esta reflexión, llama la atención la pintura fechada en 1866 con un motivo poco común, *San Antonio Abad* (CAT. 127), obra que entrevé un interés por parte de Stapleton ante el arte religioso más allá de la tradición colonial. El autor fue Francisco Torres Medina (ca. 1841-ca. 1906), hijo de Ramón Torres Méndez (1809-1885),[5] pintor reconocido en la Bogotá decimonónica. Torres Medina siguió en su *San Antonio* el derrotero de su padre al romper con la tradición colonial y proponer modelos de religiosidad más universales. Los años que Stapleton pasa en Colombia y Ecuador son años en que, exceptuando la obra de Torres Méndez, el arte religioso se seguía produciendo bajo la iconografía del periodo colonial. Durante ese tiempo la Iglesia y el Estado estaban renovando sus votos tras los intentos de secularización del siglo XIX que llevaron en la década de 1860 a la desamortización y expulsión de comunidades religiosas del país. Si bien se había dado entonces un dramático desmembramiento en los patrimonios del arte colonial en iglesias y conventos de las comunidades expulsadas, también empezó a circular un amplio patrimonio religioso en espacios civiles, situación que pudo ayudar a Stapleton en la conformación de su colección.[6]

El gusto por la pintura religiosa en esta colección devela, además, un interés por ciertas iconografías devocionales fechables en una amplia temporalidad entre 1739 y 1830, definida por un territorio variable donde se reunieron las audiencias de la Nueva Granada y de Quito bajo un mismo virreinato hasta su separación definitiva de la Gran Colombia. Esto quiere decir que la producción pictórica diversa lograda en Quito, Popayán, Tunja y Santafé durante el siglo XVII se conjugó entonces bajo un mismo territorio administrativo y político. Las Vírgenes orantes y dolorosas de la colección son un ejemplo de esta variedad congregada. Un motivo común generalmente vinculado con la iconografía desarrollada por Sassoferrato y en el pasado atribuida a Vásquez y a su familia se presenta en la *María orante y dolorosa* (CAT. 123), cuyo sufrimiento se plasma aquí casi de manera indéxica, sin recurrir a atributos explícitos del martirio de Cristo, como sí se hace en la Virgen de comienzos del siglo XIX comisionada en Popayán "a devoción de Don José María Lemos y Hurtado" (CAT. 128), compañera de una pintura gemela de *San José* (CAT. 129). Aquí la Virgen evoca el dolor y la muerte de su hijo sosteniendo en su mano su corona de espinas, atributo que también está presente en el lienzo de la *Virgen Dolorosa* identificado como quiteño (CAT. 130). Allí, María expresa su dolor a través de los atributos de la pasión de Cristo, inscritos en una composición donde prima el colorido saturado que nos recuerda las vistosas policromías, los encarnados, los sobredorados y los apliques postizos de las imágenes de bulto quiteñas durante el mismo siglo XVIII, evocación que también está presente en *El Niño Cristo rodeado por los instrumentos de la pasión* (CAT. 131).

En particular, son dos pinturas de *Virgen de Monguí* y un retablo portátil de la *Virgen de Chiquinquirá*, todas del siglo XVIII, las obras que mejor visibilizan fenómenos propios y destacados de la producción visual neogranadina y de la circulación que pudieron

tener las imágenes devocionales locales más allá de sus límites geográficos (CATS. 132-134). Se trata de piezas que copian la indumentaria y la joyería agregadas o pintadas sobre las figuras de la Virgen y el Niño en los lienzos originarios y que reflejan la amplia devoción a imágenes marianas particulares que tuvieron su asiento en pueblos de indios en la antigua provincia de Tunja. Hoy los lienzos originarios de la Virgen de Monguí (FIG. 1) y de Chiquinquirá siguen siendo venerables y ocupando el lugar principal de sus respectivas basílicas en Monguí y Chiquinquirá.

Los lienzos que replican a la Virgen de Monguí aluden como motivo general al descanso durante la huida a Egipto de la Virgen, San José y el Niño, narrado en el Pseudoevangelio de Mateo.[7] Este texto sirvió para desarrollar una amplia iconografía en el mundo andino católico que reforzó el discurso cristiano en torno a la familia nuclear y la unidad entre madre, padre e hijos y que permitió que en estas composiciones se plasmaran preocupaciones y escenas cercanas a la cotidianidad del entorno[8]. Como también ocurre con otros ejemplos andinos, en este caso el *Reposo durante la huida a Egipto* antiguamente atribuido a Gaspar de Figueroa y a Baltasar Vargas de Figueroa (CAT. 125) muestra como José se ocupa de su familia y María no solo ha hecho una pausa en el camino para descansar, sino también para retomar su costura, que ha dejado en una canasta a sus pies mientras amamanta a Jesús.

Por su parte, la imagen de la Virgen chiquinquireña se deriva de una *Sacra conversazione* de María con el Niño junto a san Antonio de Padua y san Andrés Apóstol,[9] y es a la fecha la imagen milagrosa neogranadina más reconocida y copiada desde fines del siglo XVI dentro y fuera de Colombia. La fama de esta imagen debe mucho a su rol como Virgen venerable de la población indígena de Chiquinquirá que ha sido visibilizada en las narraciones legendarias sobre la materialidad de la pintura. El lienzo original es una manta de algodón "más ancha que larga" propia de la región y pintada al temple sin base de preparación, lo cual hizo que su imagen se desdibujara. A causa de ello, cuenta la leyenda que tras los ruegos de una mujer devota y a la vista de un niño y una mujer indígena bautizada, la tela sin imagen se renovó por sí misma en diciembre de 1586, manifestando ante sus testigos su poder taumatúrgico y su derecho a ser venerada.[10] El pequeño retablo portátil de la colección de Stapleton tiene como imagen central una versión pintada sobre madera basada probablemente en la calcografía realizada por Ioannes Pérez en 1735 (FIG. 2). En las puertas del retablillo, están representados san Francisco de Asís y san Jerónimo. Esto no es de extrañar, pues si bien la Virgen de Chiquinquirá es una representación de la Virgen del Rosario que ha sido cuidada por los dominicos desde el siglo XVII, tanto las otras órdenes religiosas como el clero secular también han sido devotos de esta imagen.

Para el caso de la Virgen de Monguí, la leyenda variable sobre su poder milagroso también menciona desde su origen la relación y la importancia de la Virgen con respecto a la población indígena local. Narra la leyenda que, durante su visita a Felipe II en España en 1557, los caciques muiscas Sogamoso y Monguí ofrecieron al monarca "piedras preciosas, los ídolos de oro y los raros animales de variadas y encendidas plumas",[11] ante lo cual el rey, en agradecimiento, entregó dos pinturas a los ilustres visitantes: la Sagrada Familia para el cacique Sogamoso y un san Martín de Tours para el cacique Monguí. Al retornar a su lugar de origen, cada cacique notó que tenía la pintura equivocada. Sogamoso intentó por diversos medios recobrar el lienzo de la Sagrada Familia. Todo fue en vano, porque en la mañana las pinturas aparecían nuevamente en el lugar equivocado. Este fenómeno finalmente fue interpretado por el cacique y su pueblo como la voluntad de la pintura de la Virgen (en el lienzo de la Sagrada Familia) de quedarse en Monguí y, con ella, la manifestación de su capacidad milagrosa.[12] Asimismo, propone la tradición que fue Carlos V quien pintó dicho lienzo,[13] y la paleta de colores utilizada por el "monarca pintor" también forma parte de la leyenda que justifica material y formalmente la obra. En 1763, el sacerdote Basilio Vicente de Oviedo explicó que, según la tradición, la razón de la diferencia en el tono de piel entre San José y su familia se debía a que el monarca, al saber "que los indios de este Reino eran de color moreno, pintó así trigueño al Patriarca san José".[14]

Hemos recorrido brevemente parte de la colección de pintura neogranadina del Denver Art Museum tratando de sugerir lógicas posibles que llevaron a un individuo a reunir este acervo. Un ejercicio de coleccionismo azaroso y ecléctico iniciado por Stapleton y retomado por el museo nos propone nuevas geografías y valoraciones del arte neogranadino a partir de objetos dispersos, hoy reunidos y convertidos en un corpus. Estos fragmentos del pasado colonial, al compartir las mismas salas y reservas, permiten visibilizar la pluralidad de la pintura colonial, que a menudo escasea en conjuntos locales que se han mantenido intactos en el tiempo.

1 Los términos "Nueva Granada" y "granadino" se utilizan tanto en alusión al Nuevo Reino de Granada (1538-1717) como a su sucesor, el Virreinato de Nueva Granada (1717-1819).

2 Con motivo de la publicación de este artículo, hemos propuesto algunas revisiones de atribuciones y autorías para estas piezas neogranadinas que han sido acogidas por el Denver Art Museum.

3 Entre otros, ver Laura Liliana Vargas Murcia, *Del pincel al papel: Fuentes para el estudio de la pintura en el Nuevo Reino de Granada* (Bogotá: ICANH, 2014); Jaime H. Borja Gómez, *Los ingenios del pincel. Geografía de la pintura y cultura visual en América colonial* (Bogotá: Ediciones Uniandes, 2021), https://losingeniosdelpincel.uniandes.edu.co; Olga Isabel Acosta Luna, "¿En el museo o en la iglesia? En busca de un discurso propio para el arte colonial neogranadino, 1920-1942" H-ART 0 (2017): 46-67, doi: http://dx.doi.org/10.25025/hart00.2017.04; Museo Colonial, *Catálogo de pintura Museo Colonial* (Bogotá: Ministerio de Cultura, 2016).

4 Agradezco la generosa información brindada por Jorge F. Rivas Pérez. Sobre la colección de Stapleton, ver Jorge F. Rivas Pérez, "Daniel Casey Stapleton. Del convento al museo: El coleccionismo norteamericano en Sudamérica a la vuelta del siglo veinte", ponencia presentada virtualmente en el Congreso Internacional *El hecho religioso en América Latina. Práctica, poder y religiosidad, siglos XVI-XX* (12-16 de abril de 2021); ver también Michael Brown, "D.C. Stapleton: Collecting Spanish Colonial Art in Colombia and Ecuador from the Gilded Age to the First World War," en *The Arts of South America, 1492-1850. Papers from the 2008 Mayer Center Symposium at the Denver Art Museum*, ed. Donna Pierce (Denver: Denver Art Museum, 2010), 168-224.

5 Efraín Sánchez Cabra, *Ramón Torres Méndez. Pintor de la Nueva Granada 1809-1885* (Bogotá: Fondo Cultural Cafetero, 1987), 34-36.

6 *Estado del arte. Pintura en tiempos de desamortización* (Bogotá: Instituto Caro y Cuervo, 2017), https://www.caroycuervo.gov.co/museos/guia-de-estudio-estado-del-arte-pintura-en-tiempos-de-desamortizacion-museos/#m; *El museo-taller. Reflexiones sobre algunas pinturas y sus pintores desatendidos* (Bogotá: Instituto Caro y Cuervo, 2020), https://www.caroycuervo.gov.co/museos/el-museo-taller-primera-edicion/#m.

7 Pseudoevangelio de Mateo 20, 1-2, en *Los evangelios apócrifos*, ed. Aurelio de Santos Otero (Madrid: Biblioteca de Autores Cristianos, 1993): 210-211.

8 Juan Pablo Cruz, "La pintura de la Sagrada Familia. Un manual de relaciones familiares en el mundo de la Santafé del siglo XVII", *Memoria y sociedad* 18, núm. 36 (enero-junio 2014): 100-117, doi: 10.11144/ Javeriana.MYS18-36.psfm.

9 Olga Isabel Acosta Luna, *Milagrosas imágenes marianas en el Nuevo Reino de Granada* (Madrid/ Francfurt: Iberoamericana/ Vervuert, 2011), 219-223.

10 Olga Isabel Acosta Luna, "La Virgen de Chiquinquirá. Reflexiones sobre una "imagen tan desblanquecida, y sin facciones" *Materia Americana*, ed. Gabriela Siracusano y Agustina Rodríguez (Buenos Aires: Eduntref, 2020), 399-401.

11 Luis Carlos Mantilla, *Franciscanos en Colombia 1700-1830*, Tomo III (Bogotá: Ediciones de la Universidad de San Buenaventura, 2000), 306. El autor cita a su vez a Basilio Vicente de Oviedo, *Cualidades y riquezas del Nuevo Reino de Granada. Manuscrito del siglo XVIII* (Bogotá: Imprenta Nacional, 1930). En línea: http://www.cervantesvirtual.com/obra-visor/cualidades-y-riquezas-del-nuevo-reino-de-granada-manuscrito-del-siglo-xviii/html/b443b182-a415-11e1-b1fb-00163ebf5e63.html.

12 Ibíd, 301.

13 Según Lucas Fernández de Piedrahita, Carlos V fue el pintor de la Virgen de Monguí, ver: Lucas Fernández de Piedrahita, *Historia General de las Conquistas del Nuevo Reino de Granada* Parte I, Libro VI, Cap. V (Bogotá: Imprenta de Medardo Rivas, 1881), 156. Según Basilio Vicente de Oviedo, se trataba de una pintura inglesa adquirida por Felipe II tras la muerte de su esposa María Tudor, ver: Basilio Vicente de Oviedo, *Cualidades y riquezas del Nuevo Reino de Granada. Manuscrito del siglo XVIII* (Bogotá: Imprenta Nacional, 1930), 123.

14 Oviedo, *Cualidades y riquezas*, 123. Conviene notar que Oviedo menciona el dato para desmentirlo, afirmando que el color de San José se debe a "estar pintado en sombra".

La pintura en los Andes

Ricardo Kusunoki Rodríguez

La introducción de lenguajes pictóricos occidentales y su paulatina transformación constituyen un importante capítulo del quiebre cultural que siguió a la conquista española de los Andes. En gran parte de la región, la presencia de los incas se había expresado en la difusión de un arte esencialmente simbólico y geométrico. Pero ni los escasos elementos figurativos de la plástica inca ni las tradiciones prehispánicas de representación naturalista tenían relación con los códigos visuales que caracterizaban a la pintura europea. De ahí que la población nativa mirase con cierta fascinación las primeras imágenes occidentales que llegaron, aun cuando estas mostraran estilos considerados ya anticuados por los círculos cultos europeos.

La escasez actual de pinturas de aquellos tiempos iniciales revela que la cultura material de la conquista pronto fue reemplazada por un arte de mayor sofisticación. Esta complejidad fue alentada por una creciente circulación de personas, pinturas, grabados y muchos otros objetos. Todo ello coincidiría con la intensificación del proceso evangelizador en el último tercio del siglo XVI. Mientras las imágenes cumplían un rol decisivo para explicar los dogmas del catolicismo, también lograban que las sociedades andinas asumiesen como suyo un universo visual compartido globalmente.

En ese sentido, el Denver Art Museum conserva una pieza fundacional de la pintura virreinal andina, la *Virgen de Belén* o *Virgen de la Leche* (CAT. 135), obra de Mateo Pérez de Alesio (1547-1606). Al igual que Bernardo Bitti (1548-1610) y Angelino Medoro (1567-1631), este artista es considerado una figura decisiva para el surgimiento de las más importantes tradiciones o "escuelas" pictóricas en la región. Nacido en Puglia, Italia, Pérez de Alesio había alcanzado notoriedad tras ejecutar, hacia 1572, un mural en la Capilla Sixtina por encargo del papa Pío V. Precedido por esa fama pasó por Sevilla antes de trasladarse a Lima en 1587. Es probable que en esta ciudad hubiera diseñado el prototipo de la *Virgen de Belén*, basado en modelos creados en Roma por el pintor Scipione Pulzone.[1] Se conocen por lo menos cuatro versiones, todas en cobre y de tamaño similar, aunque ciertas diferencias de estilo sugieren la intervención de discípulos. La versión de Denver es muy cercana a la que, según la tradición, fue imagen predilecta de santa Rosa de Lima y que hoy se encuentra en el santuario construido sobre su antigua casa.

El refinamiento cosmopolita de aquella composición explica que el artista fuera considerado arquetipo local del pintor cortesano promovido por la cultura letrada europea. Al mismo tiempo, la ausencia de su firma en todas las versiones y la lógica serial que les daba sentido remiten más bien al trabajo cotidiano de los pintores virreinales. De hecho, el ideal europeo de una práctica artística "intelectual" tendría un desarrollo discontinuo en los Andes, mientras que adquirieron verdadero arraigo dinámicas muy distintas, generalmente relacionadas con la función devocional de las imágenes.

Ejemplo de lo anterior es una *Sagrada Familia con san Juan Bautista niño* (CAT. 136). Cuando fue pintada en el Cuzco, a fines del siglo XVII, esa ciudad se había convertido en el principal centro artístico del virreinato peruano gracias al trabajo de numerosos maestros indígenas, quienes establecieron un diálogo sistemático con el arte de Flandes. Como muchas obras de la región, es probable que el cuadro fuera compuesto a partir de una estampa flamenca.[2] En todo caso, el impacto de esa escuela también se hace presente en el idealizado paisaje boscoso que sirve de fondo a la acción, así como en la forma de describir cada elemento de la escena. Aunque el prestigio de los modelos nórdicos influyó en artífices de tradiciones muy diversas, pocos lugares como el Cuzco mostraron tanto apego a estos puntos de referencia. Pero no se trataba de una relación de dependencia. Los pintores cuzqueños recombinaron los elementos de la tradición flamenca y les otorgaron una función expresiva muy distinta. Crearon así un lenguaje pictórico sumamente idealizado e irreal, el cual otorga un aspecto sobrenatural y a la vez amable a las imágenes sagradas.

El Cuzco se convirtió en el foco de procesos creativos que abarcaron amplias zonas del sur de los Andes y que también dieron origen a nuevas iconografías.[3] Por ejemplo, los ángeles adquirieron una gracia cortesana particular al lucir trajes compuestos de faldellines altos, mangas de encaje y borceguíes, o asumiendo una

apariencia similar a la de los arcabuceros de las guardias virreinales (CAT. 134).[4] En esa misma línea, la pintura religiosa incorporó frecuentes alusiones a la realidad inmediata sin contradecir un ideal artificioso y poco verista de belleza. Así, una pequeña tabla portátil muestra a san Francisco Javier como evangelizador (CAT. 138), en alusión a la labor que desplegó entre India, Japón y China, pero con una fórmula usual en la pintura americana: los pobladores asiáticos han sido reemplazados por indígenas amazónicos. Más aún, sus rostros y el registro detallado de sus trajes evidencian que tales figuras fueron tomadas del natural.

Esta particular forma de entender la pintura religiosa adquiere una formulación más radical en las impactantes imágenes de la *Inmaculada Concepción con santos franciscanos* y de *San José con el Niño* (CATS. 139 Y 140). En ambas, los elementos tomados de modelos europeos han asumido una tónica propia, hasta perder relación con sus puntos de referencia originales. Un nuevo ideal de refinamiento se hace evidente en el sobredorado que cubre varios elementos de la composición. Aunque a veces ha sido relacionado con la pintura gótica, el uso de oro en las imágenes coloniales andinas no constituía ningún rasgo arcaico. Se trataba más bien de la culminación de un gusto local consciente de su especificidad, en el que el brillo de las imágenes no solo se asociaba con lo sagrado, sino también con la ostentación que caracterizaba a las élites virreinales.[5]

El éxito de la pintura cuzqueña en la región andina no impidió el desarrollo paralelo de otras tradiciones distintas entre sí, aunque muchas veces apelasen a una misma audiencia. Las comparaciones resultan elocuentes en imágenes como los "verdaderos retratos" de esculturas con fama de milagrosas. Al difundir cultos andinos como el de la Virgen de Copacabana o el del Cristo de los Temblores, aquellas pinturas habían contribuido a consolidar un sentimiento de pertenencia compartido entre distintos sectores de la sociedad virreinal.[6] El género cumpliría una función similar para quienes buscaban mantener su identificación con lugares de origen personal o familiar muy distantes. Es el caso de *Nuestra Señora de la Victoria de Málaga* y del *Cristo de Gracia de las Navas del Marqués*, que debieron ser encomendados por peninsulares residentes en el virreinato peruano (CATS. 141 Y 142).

La carga sobrenatural que emana de la imagen de la Virgen, realizada por un anónimo maestro cuzqueño, contrasta con las intenciones veristas del autor del segundo lienzo, el altoperuano Melchor Pérez de Holguín (ca. 1665-después de 1732).[7] Activo casi cuatro décadas en Potosí, ciudad cuya riqueza era proverbial en todo el mundo, Pérez de Holguín parece haber trabajado sobre todo para una clientela de élite. Ante ella buscó encarnar el arquetipo del pintor hidalgo difundido por los tratados artísticos peninsulares, autorretratándose en varias de sus composiciones. El Denver Art Museum también cuenta con un *San José con el Niño Jesús* del mismo maestro (CAT. 137), imagen de piedad cuyo tono sentimental y anecdótico es característico de su obra tardía.

Al igual que Cuzco o Potosí, Lima fue uno de los principales centros artísticos del área andina. Tenía para ello la ventaja de ser la capital del virreinato del Perú, que hasta 1717 abarcó la mayoría de los dominios españoles en Sudamérica. Para entonces, el protagonismo de la ciudad había promovido tanto su desarrollo arquitectónico como su conversión en un centro de consumo de objetos de diversa procedencia. Los pintores limeños debieron competir así con la circulación de lienzos cuzqueños hasta que, a mediados del siglo XVIII, se consolidó una tradición pictórica en torno a la corte virreinal.[8]

Uno de los principales actores en este resurgimiento fue Pedro Díaz (activo 1770-1815),[9] cuyas refinadas imágenes de piedad suelen reelaborar modelos del clasicismo italiano o francés, como es el caso de la *Virgen con el Niño* (CAT. 144), basada en una composición de Jacopo Amigoni (FIG. 1). Lo más destacado de su trabajo se desarrolló, sin embargo, en el campo del retrato. Con toda probabilidad es autor de las imágenes de los esposos Simón de Lavalle y María del Carmen Cortés Santelizes y Cartavio (CATS. 145 Y 146), padres de José Antonio de Lavalle y Cortés, primer conde de Premio Real desde 1782. Las obras fueron realizadas poco después de que José Antonio recibiera el título, cuando la pareja ya había fallecido, lo que explica el aspecto impersonal de sus rostros. En efecto, el par de lienzos era parte de un conjunto formado además por los retratos del primer conde y de su esposa, la limeña Mariana de Zugasti, hoy en el Museo de Bellas Artes de Murcia.[10] Más que una demostración de amor filial, la función de las pinturas era acreditar el momento fundacional del nuevo linaje noble: el de la unión que lo posicionaba entre ambos mundos. Mientras que la madre criolla simboliza la pertenencia a redes de poder locales, construidas durante más de dos siglos, el padre peninsular representa el anclaje directo con las fuentes de toda legitimidad nobiliaria, sobre todo debido a su origen vizcaíno e incuestionablemente hidalgo.

Hacia fines del virreinato, las obras de Díaz reflejaban el impacto de nuevos estilos que contribuyeron a acentuar el tradicional contrapunto cultural entre Lima y el sur andino. Mientras la capital reafirmaba su papel como el principal punto de recepción de las novedades cosmopolitas, el Cuzco y el Alto Perú se mantuvieron fieles a los lenguajes artísticos que habían forjado. Llevada a sus extremos con la República, esa misma dinámica haría desaparecer todo rastro de la antigua pintura limeña de corte, mientras que las antiguas tradiciones coloniales del sur andino servirían de base para el surgimiento de las llamadas "artes populares".

1 Sobre el modelo de la *Virgen de la Leche* y su vigencia en la pintura virreinal ver Francisco Stastny, *El manierismo en la pintura colonial latinoamericana* (Lima: Universidad Nacional Mayor de San Marcos, 1981); Luis Eduardo Wuffarden, "Virgen de la Leche o de Belén", en Ricardo Kusunoki, ed., *La colección Petrus y Verónica Fernandini. El arte de la pintura en los Andes* (Lima: Museo de Arte de Lima, 2015): 30-45.

2 Sobre la influencia de los modelos impresos flamencos en el Cuzco ver Francisco Stastny, "La presencia de Rubens en la pintura colonial", *Revista Peruana de Cultura*, núm. 4 (Lima, enero de 1965): 5-35; Aaron Hyman, *Rubens in Repeat: The Logic of the Copy in Colonial Latin America* (Los Ángeles: Getty Research Institute, 2021).

3 Sobre el momento estelar de la tradición cuzqueña ver José de Mesa y Teresa Gisbert, *Historia de la pintura cuzqueña* (Lima, Fundación Wiese, 1982); Luis Eduardo Wuffarden, "Surgimiento y auge de las escuelas regionales, 1670-1750", en Luisa Elena Alcalá y Jonathan Brown, *Pintura en Hispanoamérica 1550-1820* (Madrid: Ediciones El Viso, 2014), 307-363; Marta Penhos, "'Pintura de la región andina: Algunas reflexiones en torno a la vida de las formas y sus significados", en Juana Gutiérrez, coord., *Pintura de los reinos. Identidades compartidas. Territorios del mundo hispánico, siglos XVI-XVIII*, Tomo III (México: Fondo Cultural Banamex, 2008), 820-877; Ricardo Kusunoki, "Esplendor y ocaso de los maestros cuzqueños (1700-1850)", en Luis Eduardo Wuffarden y Ricardo Kusunoki, eds., *Pintura cuzqueña* (Lima: Museo de Arte de Lima, 2016), 39-57.

4 Ver Ramón Mujica Pinilla, *Ángeles apócrifos en la América virreinal* (Lima: Fondo de Cultura Económica), 1992.

5 Ver Janeth Rodríguez Nóbrega, "El oro en la pintura de los reinos de la monarquía española", en Juana Gutiérrez, coord., *Pintura de los reinos. Identidades compartidas. Territorios del Mundo Hispánico, siglos XVI-XVIII*,

Tomo IV (México: Fondo Cultural Banamex, 2008), 1314-1375.
6 Ramón Mujica, "Semiótica de la imagen sagrada: La teúrgia del signo en clave americana", en Ramón Mujica, coord., *Orígenes y devociones virreinales de la imaginería peruana* (Lima: Universidad Ricardo Pala, Instituto Cultural Peruano Norteamericano, 2008), 163-177.
7 José de Mesa y Teresa Gisbert, *Holguín y la pintura altoperuana del virreinato* (La Paz: Biblioteca Paceña, 1956).
8 Sobre la tradición limeña ver Ricardo Estabridis, "Cristóbal Lozano, paradigma de la pintura limeña del siglo XVIII", en *Barroco Iberoamericano. Territorio, Arte y Espacio y Sociedad* (Sevilla: Universidad Pablo de Olavide, 2001), 298-316; Luis Eduardo Wuffarden, "Ilustración versus tradiciones locales, 1750-1825", en Alcalá y Brown, *Pintura en Hispanoamérica 1550-1820*, 365-401; Ricardo Kusunoki, "'La reina de las artes': Pintura y cultura letrada en Lima (1750-1800)", *Illapa Mana Tukukuq*, núm. 7 (Lima, 2010): 51-61.
9 Ver una reseña biográfica de Díaz en Anthony Holguín, "Un retrato de Santa Rosa de Lima firmado por el pintor Pedro Díaz", *Illapa Mana Tukukuq*, núm. 16 (Lima, 2019): 46-55.
10 Ver Alba Choque, "Pinturas del virreinato del Perú en el MUBAM. Retratos del comerciante José Antonio Lavalle, conde de Premio Real, y Mariana Zugasti", en María de los Ángeles Fernández Valle, Carme López Calderón e Inmaculada Rodríguez Moya, eds., *Pinceles y gubias del barroco hispanoamericano* (Sevilla: Andavira Editora, EnredArs, 2019), 229-242.

El pesebre en los Andes: Nueva iconografía y nuevos materiales

Carmen Fernández-Salvador

El pesebre, como se conoce la representación del nacimiento de Jesús en el portal de Belén, alcanzó una enorme popularidad en Europa e Hispanoamérica durante el siglo XVIII. El pesebre napolitano barroco, caracterizado por elaboradas escenografías, fue importado por Carlos III a España, desde donde se diseminó rápidamente por Hispanoamérica.[1] En los Andes, ocupó un lugar preferente en los conventos, sobre todo en los claustros femeninos, aunque también se exhibía en espacios domésticos. Lo singular del pesebre es que, al combinar escenas y personajes sagrados con elementos seculares y cotidianos, permitió a los artistas americanos introducir referencias a lo local y así reinventar los códigos del arte europeo. A través de su iconografía y materialidad, los pesebres expresaban preocupaciones relacionadas con la construcción de prestigio y el ordenamiento social.

El eje central del pesebre, denominado "misterio", está compuesto por la Virgen, San José y el Niño Jesús. A estos acompañan la mula y el buey, así como los pastores y los Reyes Magos. En ocasiones, el pesebre estaba compuesto únicamente por la escena central, que se exhibía en cajones o en pequeños retablos portátiles. Una variante de estos belenes portátiles es la que aparece en dípticos de forma esférica, tallados en marfil por artesanos quiteños, como es la pieza perteneciente al Victoria and Albert Museum (FIG. 1).[2] En este díptico, que muestra la natividad en una mitad y la huida a Egipto en la otra, se utiliza la policromía propia de la escultura quiteña del siglo XVIII. Con frecuencia, sin embargo, el nacimiento de Jesús iba acompañado de escenas secundarias que, hilvanadas entre sí, construían una narrativa más compleja, entre ellas el sueño de San José, la huida a Egipto o la matanza de los inocentes. Para estas escenas secundarias solían construirse esmeradas escenografías que imitaban la arquitectura local. Este es el caso del pesebre perteneciente al Convento del Carmen Bajo, en Quito, que muestra las fachadas de las casas quiteñas, a menudo decoradas con columnas salomónicas muy similares a las que adornan los retablos de las iglesias coloniales.

Además de las escenas religiosas, otras eran estrictamente seculares y se centraban en la representación de tipos locales, algunos cotidianos y otros curiosos. En estas esculturas, la atención al detalle en la vestimenta sugiere una preocupación por distinguir y ordenar los diferentes grupos sociorraciales que habitaban en las ciudades hispanoamericanas. Por un lado, estas figuras dialogaban con el interés de los relatos de viajeros en clasificar la sociedad americana por medio de sus trajes y costumbres. Por el otro, también materializaban el temor de los grupos dominantes hacia la creciente y empobrecida plebe. En la región andina, la segunda mitad del siglo XVIII estuvo marcada por la protesta popular.[3] En Quito, un ejemplo de ello fue la llamada "rebelión de los barrios", además de los innumerables levantamientos indígenas de las zonas rurales. A pesar de la amenaza que representaban para el orden colonial los grupos subordinados, en los pesebres se retrataba a la plebe urbana y a los indígenas de las zonas rurales desde lo pintoresco, como personajes estereotipados, dóciles y apacibles.

Un ejemplo del interés en lo pintoresco es la figura de una mujer indígena, probablemente una vendedora del mercado, de gestos reposados y expresión risueña (CAT. 147). La atención del espectador se dirige a la cuidadosa representación de su traje, de los diseños tejidos y bordados, un detalle que transforma a la mujer en objeto de contemplación. Por otro lado, la figura de un niño con su baúl, descalzo y vestido con humildes ropas (CAT. 148), nos recuerda la pobreza que azotaba a los grupos populares quiteños. No obstante, y al igual que la mujer indígena, el niño muestra una actitud sosegada, con un dejo de resignación en su expresiva mirada.

Entre las figuras de indígenas de las zonas rurales periféricas, los pesebres quiteños incluían a los yumbos. En el siglo XVIII, este término definía a los habitantes del bosque nublado hacia el noroeste de Quito y la ceja de selva hacia el este. Como se aprecia en otras imágenes de la época, los yumbos aparecían como personajes exóticos, cargando los frutos que traían para vender en los

mercados de la ciudad, a menudo con escasos ropajes, el rostro pintado y en la cabeza coloridos tocados de plumas.

Muchas veces, las figuras principales de los pesebres se manufacturaban con materiales y técnicas de decoración tradicionales. Al igual que otras esculturas quiteñas de la época, las dos figuras de San José y la Virgen (CAT. 149) están talladas en madera y policromadas. Pero a diferencia de la decoración característica del siglo XVII, en la que se eliminaban partes de la capa de pintura para descubrir el pan de oro subyacente, los artistas quiteños del siglo XVIII aplicaron el dorado directamente sobre la superficie pintada, creando diseños florales. Para los rostros utilizaban mascarillas de plomo en las que colocaban ojos de vidrio, lo cual otorga un mayor realismo a las figuras. Las manos son removibles y deben haber sido talladas por separado. En las tres figuras de los Reyes Magos (CAT. 150), también talladas en madera, las monturas de los caballos están decoradas con vistosas telas que recuerdan el recurso de la tela encolada, utilizada con frecuencia por los escultores quiteños para simular los pliegues de los trajes.

En sus diferentes estrategias de manufactura y decoración, estas esculturas revelan el complejo trabajo de los talleres escultóricos coloniales, marcado por la colaboración entre talladores, doradores y pintores. En Quito, durante el siglo XVIII, este proceso se hizo más eficiente ante la necesidad de satisfacer la creciente demanda de esculturas no solo para el mercado local, sino para compradores en ciudades como Popayán, Bogotá, Medellín e incluso Santiago de Chile. Es así que las manos trabajadas por separado sugieren la marcada especialización de los artesanos, encargados de producir en forma serializada y estandarizada las partes de una misma obra. La mascarilla de plomo y la tela encolada, por su parte, son ejemplo de lo que Alexandra Kennedy describe como "atajos" de los artesanos quiteños, con el fin de asegurar la fabricación rápida y expedita de las esculturas.[4]

Por otro lado, también es importante indagar en el valor simbólico de los materiales empleados. En Quito, los pintores de imágenes utilizaron yeso y albayalde, un pigmento blanco de plomo, para los rostros de las figuras sagradas. Con el fin de lograr el encarne brillante característico de la escultura quiteña del siglo XVIII, se frotaba la superficie con vejiga de borrego. Como ha señalado Leslie Todd, se buscaba resaltar la blancura de la piel, ocultando la identidad de los artistas y resaltando la jerarquía racial que caracterizaba al orden colonial.[5] Otros materiales también se escogían de manera consciente, como símbolos de prestigio social.

En ocasiones, la mascarilla podía trabajarse en madera o en marfil. También las manos removibles de San José y la Virgen María podían hacerse con marfil, como se observa en el conjunto escultórico del Museo Metropolitano (FIG. 2). El marfil para los artesanos locales llegaba en el galeón que conectaba a Manila con Acapulco, aunque también se importaban objetos ya tallados en Asia. Al ser un material exótico, era especialmente estimado por los artistas y coleccionistas de la época.

Si bien los pesebres quiteños tienen una importancia innegable, también en Perú se manufacturaron escenas similares, muchas veces con materiales locales. Ejemplo de ello es una figura del Niño Jesús hecha en piedra de Huamanga (CAT. 151). Este material, extraído de las canteras de Ayacucho, era apreciado por su textura y luminosidad. A pesar de su apariencia muy similar al alabastro, una vez remojado en agua se volvía blando y fácil de tallar con un cuchillo.[6] Al igual que el Niño Jesús, los bueyes del pesebre, también manufacturados con este material, estaban decorados con policromía (CAT. 152).

Las figuras de los pesebres podían ser realizadas por artesanos profesionales pero también por aficionados a la talla. Como ha señalado Alexandra Kennedy, es posible que las monjas de los claustros quiteños tallaran y adornaran las pequeñas esculturas.[7] El pesebre estaba abierto a la experimentación y en continuo proceso de ejecución. Las monjas, al igual que otros coleccionistas, añadían objetos, construían escenografías y transformaban las figuras, a las que vestían con elaborados trajes y adornaban con joyas y cabello.

Los pesebres no solo invitaban a la devoción de los fieles, sino que construían ficciones sobre la sociedad colonial y del siglo XIX. La posibilidad de interpretar lo local y de experimentar con materiales nuevos permitió a los artistas hispanoamericanos innovar, partiendo de la tradición de las natividades europeas.

1 Ver, por ejemplo, Francisco Manuel Valiñas López, *La estrella del camino. Apuntes para el estudio del belén barroco quiteño* (Quito: Instituto Metropolitano de Patrimonio, 2011); Adrián Contreras Guerrero, *Escultura en Colombia: Focos productores y circulación de obras (siglos XVI-XVIII)* (Granada: Universidad de Granada, 2019), 199-210; Ángel Peña Martín, "El gusto por el belén napolitano en la corte española", en *Simposio reflexiones sobre el gusto*, eds. Ernesto Arce, Alberto Castán, Concha Lomba y Juan Carlos Lozano (Zaragoza: Institución Fernando el Católico, 2012), 257-276.

2 Marjorie Trusted, "Propaganda and Luxury: Small-Scale Baroque Sculptures in Viceregal America and the Philippines", en *Asia and Spanish America: Trans-Pacific Artistic and Cultural Exchange, 1500-1850*, ed. Donna Pierce y Ronald Otsuka (Denver: Denver Art Museum, 2009), 160-162.

3 Ver, por ejemplo, Martin Minchom, *El pueblo de Quito 1690-1810: Demografía, dinámica sociorracial y protesta popular* (Quito: Fondo de Salvamento, 2007), 221-260. Para una discusión similar sobre las pinturas costumbristas en el siglo XIX, ver Rosemarie Terán Najas, "Facetas de la historia del siglo XIX, a propósito de las estampas y relaciones de viajeros", en *Imágenes de identidad: Acuarelas quiteñas del siglo XIX*, ed. Alfonso Ortiz Crespo (Quito: FONSAL, 2005), 63-82.

4 Alexandra Kennedy, "Arte y artistas quiteños de exportación", en *Arte de la Real Audiencia de Quito, siglos XVII-XIX*, ed. Alexandra Kennedy (Madrid: Nerea, 2002), 185-203.

5 Leslie Todd, "Reconciling Colonial Contradictions: the Multiple Roles of Sculpture in Eighteenth-Century Quito", tesis doctoral (University of Florida, 2019), 55-60.

6 Johanna Hecht, "Vision of Death of Saint Francis Xavier", en *Converging Cultures: Art and Identity in Spanish America*, ed. Diana Fane (New York: Brooklyn Museum of Art, 1996), 247.

7 Alexandra Kennedy, "Mujeres en los claustros: Artistas, mecenas y coleccionistas", en *Arte de la Real Audiencia de Quito, siglos XVII-XIX*, ed. Alexandra Kennedy (Madrid: Nerea, 2002), 109-127.

El mobiliario en los Andes

Jorge F. Rivas Pérez

Durante milenios, la rica y diversa geografía de los Andes, que se extiende hacia el sur desde el Caribe en Venezuela hasta el cabo de Hornos en Chile, moldeó el desarrollo de las culturas locales y sus historias. Cuando los españoles conquistaron el continente sudamericano durante la primera mitad del siglo XVI, se encontraron con unas sociedades complejas con ricas tradiciones culturales. El poderoso y artísticamente sofisticado imperio inca abarcaba casi toda la cordillera de los Andes, y su cultura influyó enormemente en toda la región. En pocas décadas, la llegada de colonos europeos transformó drásticamente las comunidades locales y sus tradiciones. El notable intercambio cultural que siguió a la llegada de los nuevos colonos unió a Europa, América y, a partir de la década de 1560, a Asia, a través de un dinámico intercambio de bienes, prácticas artísticas e ideas, dando lugar al surgimiento de unas sociedades únicas a lo largo de los Andes. Los orígenes de la fabricación de muebles de estilo español en los Andes se remontan a mediados del siglo XVI, cuando los ebanistas españoles se establecieron en la región y crearon sus gremios.[1] El desarrollo de la fabricación de muebles en la región presenta un caso especial dentro de las Américas, ya que algunas comunidades tenían un contacto limitado con la metrópoli colonial y permanecieron hasta cierto punto impermeables a los cambios estilísticos y las modas.

El auge del urbanismo y el intercambio comercial influyeron notablemente en la producción de muebles en la región, en parte porque las clases altas coloniales se dedicaban con frecuencia a alardear de su riqueza de forma extravagante, desafiando a menudo las leyes suntuarias que prohibían tales excesos. Los artículos de lujo y los muebles finos adornaban los interiores domésticos y simbolizaban el buen gusto y un estilo de vida cosmopolita. Los artesanos locales contaban con una clientela exigente, deseosa de equipar sus viviendas y edificios públicos con los estilos más modernos. Además de los muebles fabricados localmente, las costosas importaciones procedentes de España y de otras zonas del vasto Imperio español (CATS. 153 Y 154) llegaban a las casas, las iglesias, los edificios públicos y a los talleres de los artistas locales (CAT. 155). Los costosos muebles de marquetería fueron muy populares en el Virreinato del Perú en los siglos XVII y XVIII, y se exhibían con orgullo en el estrado (sala de estar de las mujeres) de las casas de la clase alta (FIG. 1).[2] Varias localidades se hicieron famosas por este tipo de mobiliario, entre ellas Quito (CAT. 156), algunas poblaciones de los alrededores de Cuzco y otras comunidades de la sierra andina (CATS. 157 Y 158).[3]

Al principio, los ebanistas se apegan a los tipos de muebles tradicionales españoles. Por ejemplo, desde el siglo XVII hasta mediados del XVIII, los inventarios solían incluir sillones de cuero de estilo español "de la tierra". Los registros a veces incluían pieles lisas o cueros; sin embargo, en los entornos de lujo, los documentos mostraban el uso extensivo de pieles, en ocasiones bordadas con hilos de oro y plata (CAT. 159) y otras veces repujadas y policromadas (CAT. 160). Sin embargo, uno de los aspectos más distintivos del mobiliario andino es el impacto de las tradiciones artesanales y los vocabularios visuales prehispánicos. La creación de tradiciones mobiliarias nuevas y originales con sus repertorios decorativos específicos, diferenciados de los precedentes ibéricos y prehispánicos, tuvo que esperar varios siglos y a varias generaciones de ebanistas para evolucionar y florecer. Por ejemplo, el barniz de Pasto, una técnica parecida a la de la laca producida en las actuales Colombia y Ecuador, se inspiraba en una técnica similar utilizada para decorar copas ceremoniales de madera inca, llamadas *keros* (CAT. 162) y otros objetos pequeños. Aproximadamente a partir del siglo XVII, esta técnica se utilizó en una amplia gama de objetos y pequeños muebles en los actuales Colombia y Ecuador (CAT. 162 Y VER SANABRAIS, CAT. 192).[4] Los artesanos del barniz de Pasto emplearon un estilo híbrido de decoración que mezclaba los motivos indígenas, europeos y asiáticos, un ejemplo temprano de globalización.

Algunas localidades adquirieron gran notoriedad por su producción de muebles y objetos únicos. Por ejemplo, Cuzco, la antigua capital del Imperio inca, era famosa por su carpintería ricamente tallada y dorada (CATS. 163 Y 164), un célebre estilo que tuvo su auge en la segunda mitad del siglo XVII. Huamanga (actual Ayacucho, Perú) fue uno de los principales centros de la industria del cuero virreinal.[5] Los cofres y cajas de cuero de Huamanga (CAT. 165) tienen su origen en los famosos cordobanes andaluces (cuero policromado en relieve). Las piezas suelen presentar una rica decoración en relieve con un amplio repertorio de motivos, que combinan los diseños europeos con las plantas y los animales andinos. La talla en madera fue una de las especialidades de la Audiencia de Quito, que incluía desde elaborados retablos hasta pequeñas piezas exquisitamente talladas (CAT. 166).

Al igual que en otras regiones de América, las misiones católicas desempeñaron un importante papel en la integración de la artesanía y los estilos artísticos europeos en las poblaciones indígenas. Los jesuitas activos en los siglos XVII y XVIII en Sudamérica introdujeron en las comunidades nativas un amplio espectro de prácticas artísticas en sus misiones del sur de Bolivia, el norte de Argentina y Paraguay. Por ejemplo, el trabajo en madera proliferó en las misiones de Moxos y Chiquitos (actual Bolivia); allí, los artesanos indígenas produjeron muebles y objetos tallados que combinaban repertorios ornamentales europeos y asiáticos con motivos propios de la zona que suelen incluir imágenes de la flora y la fauna locales que se exportaron a toda Sudamérica (CAT. 167).[6] Además de pequeños objetos tallados y muebles de caja, otras misiones produjeron muebles pintados, como las piezas de las misiones franciscanas de Paraguay (CAT. 168).

A partir de mediados del siglo XVIII, los gustos cambiaron en toda la región andina a medida que los consumidores buscaban el cosmopolitismo. Los ebanistas adoptaron y reinterpretaron libremente las últimas tendencias europeas en materia de mobiliario, sobre todo en las grandes ciudades como Lima, Cuzco, Quito y Bogotá. Los muebles de estilo español, británico y, en menor medida, francés del siglo XVIII llegaron a los hogares y los edificios públi-

cos (FIG. 2). Los muebles de esta época solían presentar los rasgos sinuosos asociados al estilo rococó: patas cabriolé y ornamentación tallada imitando rocalla, vegetación y elementos de formas orgánicas (CAT. 169).[7] Los muebles pintados y dorados se hicieron tremendamente populares en el siglo XVIII, y los ebanistas desarrollaron estilos de talla y repertorios ornamentales distintos que en la actualidad asociamos con ciudades y fabricantes específicos (CATS. 171 Y 172). Los interiores de la segunda mitad del siglo XVIII destacan por el uso de lujosos juegos de muebles para sentarse que incluían al menos un par de sofás (CAT. 173) para las mujeres y muchos sillones para los hombres. Todavía a finales de la década de 1790, las mujeres se sentaban con las piernas cruzadas, como dictaban el decoro y el uso heredado de la España islámica (FIG. 3).

Al igual que en Europa y Norteamérica, a finales del siglo XVIII, los repertorios asociados a la antigua Grecia y Roma se pusieron de moda en Hispanoamérica; la región andina no fue una excepción. En Lima, a principios del siglo XIX, por ejemplo, el arquitecto, pintor y escultor vasco Matías Maestro se convirtió en una figura central en la recepción y apropiación de los repertorios neoclásicos como parte de un proceso más amplio de modernización y renovación en las artes avalado por las élites locales.[8] Aunque los muebles pintados y dorados seguían de moda en esta época (CAT. 174), las clases altas preferían los muebles de marquetería adornados con repertorios ornamentales clásicos (CAT. 170). El gusto por los repertorios clásicos persistió mucho después de la independencia, en la década de 1820, cuando surgieron nuevos desarrollos del estilo, esta vez más afines a las ideas de las repúblicas libres y la construcción de la nación. En los Andes, los muebles de este periodo son en su mayoría austeros y frecuentemente adornados con incrustaciones o marquetería que representan motivos clásicos (VER MAJLUF, CAT. 203) en lugar de las elaboradas monturas de bronce dorado que se encuentran en los muebles europeos de la época.

1 Jorge Rivas, "Observations on the Origin, Development, and Manufacture of Latin American Furniture", en *The Arts in Latin America, 1492–1820.* ed. Joseph J. Rishel y Suzanne Stratton-Pruitt (Philadelphia: Philadelphia Museum of Art, 2006), 477.

2 María del Pilar López Pérez, *En torno al estrado: cajas de uso cotidiano en Santafé de Bogotá, siglos XVI al XVIII: arcas, arcaces, arquillas, arquetas, arcones, baúles, cajillas, cajones, cofres, petacas, escritorios y papeleras* (Bogotá: Museo Nacional de Colombia, 1996).

3 Jorge Rivas, "American Luxury" en *Arte Colonial: Colección Museo de Arte de Lima*, ed. Ricardo Kusunoki y Luis Eduardo Wuffarden (Lima: Asociación Museo de Arte de Lima, 2016), 77.

4 Mitchell Codding, "The Lacquer Arts of Latin America", en *Made in the Americas: The New World Discovers Asia*, ed. Dennis Carr (Boston: MFA Publications, 2015), 85–86; María del Pilar López Pérez, "El barniz de Pasto. Encuentro entre tradiciones locales y foráneas que han dado identidad a la región Andina del sur de Colombia", en *Patrimonio cultural e identidad*, ed. Paz Cabello Carro (Madrid: Ministerio de Cultura, 2007), 225-34.

5 Jorge Rivas, "Decorative Arts of the Local Baroque", en Kusunoki y Wuffarden, *Arte Colonial*, 201-2.

6 Rivas, "Local Baroque". 212; David Block, *Mission Culture on the Upper Amazon: Native Tradition, Jesuit Enterprise and Secular Policy in Moxos, 1660–1880* (Lincoln: University of Nebraska Press, 1994), 68.

7 María Campos Carlés de Peña, *A Surviving Legacy in Spanish America: Seventeenth- and Eighteenth-Century Furniture from the Viceroyalty of Peru* (Madrid: Ediciones El Viso, 2013), 331–81.

8 Rivas, "The Emergence of Neoclassicism", en Kusunoki y Wuffarden, *Arte colonial*, 253-4.

Platería sudamericana

Luis Eduardo Wuffarden

Durante la conquista de América del Sur, el asombro de los españoles ante la abundancia de metales preciosos fue unido al reconocimiento de la habilidad técnica alcanzada por los artífices prehispánicos —quimbayas, chimúes o incas— en el campo de la metalurgia. De ahí que Pedro de Cieza de León, refiriéndose al antiguo Perú, escribiera en 1553 que "los indios naturales de este reino fueron grandes maestros de plateros y de hacer oficios".[1] Para entonces, los conquistadores ya habían encontrado oro y piedras preciosas en el Nuevo Reino de Granada —donde surgió la leyenda de El Dorado—, mientras que al sur de los Andes se descubría el "cerro rico" de Potosí, el mayor yacimiento argentífero del mundo. Este último fue considerado por los escritores de la época como un hallazgo providencial para la expansión de la monarquía hispánica y del cristianismo en América.[2] Su inmensa producción no solo contribuyó a revolucionar la economía global, sino que impulsaría la aparición de vigorosas tradiciones locales de platería, en sintonía con los patrones culturales de la emergente sociedad virreinal.

Como era de esperarse, la fundación de núcleos urbanos originó una creciente demanda de piezas litúrgicas y decorativas de oro y plata para los edificios eclesiásticos que se iban construyendo. Simultáneamente, el despliegue suntuario de la vida civil y ceremonial criolla contribuyó a cimentar el difundido concepto del "lujo indiano". En ese sentido, pronto se hizo evidente que el volumen y el peso de las piezas resultaban tanto o más importantes que sus calidades formales. Otro factor determinante para la evolución del género fue la coexistencia de dos comunidades paralelas: la

"república de españoles" y la "república de indios", establecidas por la legislación del virrey Francisco de Toledo (gob. 1569-1581), que dieron lugar a tipologías bien diferenciadas. De acuerdo con su política organizativa, el propio Toledo dispuso la concentración de los pueblos o aillus indígenas dedicados a la platería en determinados espacios, con el propósito de reconvertir una mano de obra altamente especializada al tiempo que se incorporaban ciertas técnicas nativas a los usos occidentales.[3]

A través de las piezas de plata sudamericana conservadas en las colecciones del Museo de Denver, es posible seguir algunas facetas clave de esa fascinante historia de asimilación e invención. Entre las tipologías criollas más características se encuentran aquí algunos recipientes de uso extendido en España desde el siglo XVI que se arraigaron en el Nuevo Mundo y, al paso del tiempo, experimentaron importantes transformaciones. Ejemplo elocuente de ello es el bernegal o tachuela, vasija de beber de contorno redondeado con dos asas en forma de roleos. A este género pertenece un ejemplar de fines del siglo XVI (CAT. 175), de sobrio diseño, bastante próximo aún a sus modelos peninsulares. Más tarde, esta forma básica dio pie a las *cocchas* o vasijas rituales andinas de menor tamaño, con decoración cincelada o repujada sobre el fondo, además de motivos de inspiración local en las asas, que han permanecido vigentes en las ceremonias tradicionales de ofrenda o "pago" a la tierra.

Dos grandes fuentes testimonian la importancia que adquirió esta clase de objetos como elemento de ostentación, tanto en el ámbito civil como en el eclesiástico. La primera, datada en el siglo XVII, se distingue por tener un recipiente central de forma elíptica y cóncava, mientras que su amplio contorno superior desarrolla un juego de curvas y contracurvas de gran refinamiento (CAT. 176). Sus superficies lisas contrastan con las de otra fuente más tardía (s. XVIII), de uso religioso y procedencia altoperuana (CAT. 178). Es rectangular y adopta forma de artesa en el interior; sus voluminosos relieves, conseguidos por medio del repujado, albergan follajes, roleos y figuras de angelillos volantes. Se trata de un abigarrado reportorio ornamental, de claro parentesco con el gusto "mestizo" característico de la arquitectura religiosa del sur andino y el Altiplano entre 1680 y 1780 aproximadamente.

Otras piezas de carácter utilitario recuerdan el uso intensivo de la plata, incluso en objetos que en Europa solían elaborarse con otros metales. Al respecto, el corsario francés Ravenau de Lussan anotaba asombrado que en el Perú "es tanta la abundancia de este rico metal, que la mayor parte de las cosas que nosotros hacemos en Francia de acero, cobre o hierro se hacen aquí de plata".[4] Es el caso de una bacía de barbero o sangrador (CAT. 177), de fino diseño rococó en forma de concha venera, que da cuenta de la renovación estilística producida en el último tercio del siglo XVIII, cuando las corrientes estéticas asociadas con la Ilustración irrumpieron con fuerza, sobre todo en las grandes ciudades del virreinato. De época cercana, es un recipiente para popurrí, o perfumador de interiores domésticos (CAT. 179), que conjuga la pureza de su diseño con el barroquismo de las típicas asas andinas y la figurilla animal que corona la tapa calada. Su forma se inspira en recipientes europeos contemporáneos que cumplían similares funciones, pero eran hechos originalmente en porcelana o loza.

Es interesante constatar esos mismos cambios estilísticos en la evolución de los objetos de devoción privada, que alcanzaron un renovado auge en relación con los conceptos de la "piedad ilustrada". El rubro se halla presente en esta colección a través de pinturas sobre metal de factura preciosista, cuyos elaborados marcos ponían de manifiesto la opulencia de sus propietarios. El marco de *La Dolorosa* (CAT. 180), ofrece una reelaboración local del rococó entremezclado con tradiciones anteriores, mientras que el de *San Juan Evangelista* (CAT. 181) recoge un diseño neoclásico —a base de lazos y guirnaldas—, haciendo eco del liderazgo estético de Matías Maestro (1766-1835), cuya influencia irradió desde Lima hacia el sur andino y dejó huella prácticamente en todas las artes decorativas. Otro marco de plata (CAT. 182), que contiene un lienzo novohispano de la Virgen de Guadalupe, data de época anterior y procede de Popayán, en la Nueva Granada. Su ondulante perfil alterna motivos de rocalla con áreas caladas que revelan un gran refinamiento técnico. En todos estos casos, la hibridez estilística resultante reitera, una vez más, la capacidad de los artífices locales para interpretar de manera creativa los modelos europeos.

En las audiencias norteñas de Quito y Bogotá —que luego en el siglo XVIII constituyeron el virreinato de Nueva Granada— se destaca una colorida joyería que combina el uso frecuente del oro con esmeraldas, perlas y otras piedras que aportan su volumen en engastes de fina calidad. De esa región proceden algunas pequeñas joyas de factura minuciosa y preciosista, como una cruz que probablemente remataba la corona de una imagen de culto (VER RIVAS PÉREZ, CAT. 9). Su sofisticada factura y su brillante cromatismo distinguen a otras prendas de uso civil, como los dijes de la *chatelaîne* (CAT. 183), prenda de uso frecuente entre las clases altas criollas, y una imponente tiara de diseño rococó (CAT. 186), cuyo follaje calado enmarca una pedrería que supera en lujo a sus prototipos del Viejo Mundo.

Dentro de la platería que formaba parte del atuendo étnico entre las élites nativas, los tupus o tupos (*ttipqui* en quechua) representan un singular caso de disyunción formal.[5] Bajo ese nombre genérico se agrupan varios tipos de alfileres ornamentales de metal usados por las mujeres indígenas para sujetar su *lliclla* o manta. Están compuestos por un vástago punzante, que cumplía la función propiamente utilitaria y una cabeza decorativa, por lo general de notable tamaño, que adoptaba muy variadas formas. Desde tiempos preincas, dichos accesorios eran confeccionados sobre todo en plata, con toda probabilidad debido a la ancestral asociación simbólica del metal blanco con las lágrimas de la luna o *quilla* y, por tanto, con el culto a una divinidad lunar que, a su vez, se identificaba con el lado femenino del cosmos.

Después de la conquista española, el tupo lograría adaptarse a las nuevas circunstancias políticas. Su uso continuó identificando a las mujeres de la nobleza indígena y alcanzó su mayor auge durante el denominado "renacimiento inca", en el transcurso del siglo XVIII. Tras la derrota del curaca rebelde Túpac Amaru, en 1781, los tupos volvieron a experimentar importantes cambios, acentuados con el advenimiento de la república. A esta última época pertenecen los ejemplares aquí reunidos, que en su mayoría corresponden al tipo denominado "cuchara" (CAT. 184). Sus precedentes tardocoloniales fueron tolerados por las autoridades españolas al considerarse exentos del temido simbolismo inca. Estos concentran su adorno en la parte cóncava, con frecuencia decorada al buril. Sus amplios repertorios decorativos dejan entrever una inspiración romántica e incluyen desde aves, motivos vegetales y sirenas hasta representaciones del sol y de la luna (VER MAJLUF, CAT. 202).

En cambio, el bastón de *varayok* tiene un indiscutible origen hispánico, el cual los pueblos nativos transformaron dotándolo de contenidos vernáculos (CAT. 185). Son varas de forma cónica elaboradas con maderas duras, cubiertas con enchapes de plata colocados en ambos extremos, además de fajas del mismo metal que las ciñen a todo lo largo, junto con un cúmulo de cadenas, cruces y dijes en los que se despliega una gran variedad de motivos sagrados y

profanos. Su momento de mayor desarrollo fue consecuencia del paulatino resurgimiento de los pueblos y comunidades indígenas durante la república, pues constituían símbolos de la autoridad ancestral. De este modo se explica la importancia simbólica otorgada a este tipo de objetos por parte de los intelectuales indigenistas del siglo XX, quienes alcanzaron a intuir en ellos una continuidad cultural que atravesaría las diversas etapas de la historia andina.

1 Pedro de Cieza de León, *Crónica del Perú* (Lima: Pontificia Universidad Católica del Perú, 1984), 229.

2 Según el cronista anónimo de Yucay, "por tan grandes bienes como estos [la evangelización] ningún retorno invía el Pirú a España sino el fruto que saca de las entrañas de este rico y poderoso cerro". Por su parte, fray Reginaldo de Lizárraga decía que dicho yacimiento era "la riqueza del mundo, terror del Turco, freno de los herejes, silencio de las bárbaras naciones". (*El anónimo de Yucay frente a Bartolomé de las Casas* (Cuzco: Centro de Estudios Regionales Andinos Bartolomé de las Casas, 1995) 161; y fray Reginaldo de Lizárraga, *Descripción del Perú, Tucumán, Río de la Plata y Chile* (Madrid: Dastin, 2002), 220.

3 Sobre los plateros indígenas puede consultarse: Luisa María Vetter Parodi, *Plateros indígenas en el virreinato del Perú: siglos XVI y XVII* (Lima: Fondo Editorial de la Universidad Nacional Mayor de San Marcos), 2008.

4 Ravenau de Lussan, *Journal du voyage fait a la Mer du Sud avec les filibustiers de l'Amerique* (París: Jacques Le Fevre, 1705), 335.

5 Sobre los tupos, su nomenclatura y su evolución, ver: Luisa María Vetter Parodi y Paloma Carcedo de Mufarech, *El tupo: símbolo ancestral de identidad femenina* (Lima: Gráfica Biblos, 2009).

Asia e Hispanoamérica

Sofía Sanabrais

Ya en el siglo XVI, la convergencia de los mundos de la religión, el comercio y la diplomacia conectó a Asia y a Hispanoamérica y transformó la cultura material de las primeras etapas del mundo moderno. El intercambio cultural de tradiciones artísticas que reveló el impacto de la cultura material asiática en el arte de Hispanoamérica puede verse en la notable colección del Museo de Arte de Denver, pionero en la colección, la investigación y la exposición de este arte.[1]

En el siglo XVI, la expansión europea hacia Asia en busca de especias estaba muy avanzada y la cruzada por la evangelización del mundo no cristiano no tardó en llegar. Los portugueses y los españoles se hicieron con el control de los centros comerciales existentes y establecieron otros nuevos en lugares como Manila, Nagasaki, Goa y Macao. La demanda china de la plata procedente de las minas de ciudades americanas como Potosí y Zacatecas facilitó el intercambio de artículos de lujo asiáticos. Los resultados de esta expansión superaron con creces el mero intercambio de mercancías: marcaron una nueva era en el comercio global, ya que los objetos procedentes de Japón, China y la India inundaron los mercados, introduciendo un material y un vocabulario visual de influencia artística totalmente nuevos.[2]

Los gobernantes de la dinastía de los Habsburgo de España empezaron a coleccionar objetos de Asia ya en el reinado del emperador Carlos V.[3] La colonización de las Filipinas por parte de España en 1565 y el posterior establecimiento del comercio con el Galeón de Manila facilitaron a Felipe II el acceso a los bienes asiáticos. Hispanoamérica se vio profundamente afectada por la afluencia de artículos de lujo procedentes de Asia, traídos en los galeones que hacían viajes anuales de Manila a Acapulco en el virreinato de Nueva España desde 1565 hasta 1815.

La moda de los objetos asiáticos en México, y los subsiguientes intentos locales de recrear ciertos estilos y técnicas, precedieron en un siglo a la de la chinería y *el japonismo* en Europa. La alta estima que se otorgaba a estos objetos quedó expresada en un elaborado memorial de 1637 dirigido al rey Felipe IV de España y al Consejo de Indias por el procurador general de las islas, Juan Grau y Montfalcón: "En Asia y en las regiones de Oriente –escribió– creó Dios algunas cosas tan preciosas a los ojos del hombre y tan peculiares a esas provincias que, como solo se encuentran o fabrican en ellas, son deseadas y buscadas por el resto del mundo".[4]

Las materias primas exóticas como el nácar, el marfil y el caparazón de tortuga se importaron a América y despertaron el asombro de los artistas y los coleccionistas. El marfil de los elefantes se valoraba en la India y en las Islas Filipinas antes de la colonización y, como materia prima, estaba cargado de nociones de bondad, pureza y virtud espirituales y temporales.[5] Filipinas fue una de las mayores productoras de imágenes cristianas en marfil, y los artistas nativos y chinos crearon muchas de las esculturas delicadamente talladas que se exportaron a América. El marfil era ideal para dar mayor realismo a las figuras humanas mediante la aplicación de capas de pintura. Los artistas se inspiraron en la imaginería cristiana convencional e incorporaron el tratamiento estilizado del cabello, como se ve en el *Niño Jesús* (CAT. 187) y en el ropaje de la *Inmaculada Concepción* (CAT. 188), que recuerda a las tradiciones escultóricas de Asia oriental y meridional.

Como el marfil no se podía conseguir en América, los artistas encontraron sustitutos nativos. En México y Perú, los artistas sustituyeron el marfil por el alabastro local (conocido como piedra de Huamanga en Perú). Este material translúcido, blanco y suave era fácil de tallar y pintar. Esta imagen de doble cara de *San Miguel y la Virgen con el Niño y los Santos Domingo y Juan Bautista* (VER NEFF, CAT. 57), finamente tallada por Diego de Reinoso, un exquisito ejemplo de las influencias asiáticas en el arte hispanoamericano, revela que las nubes en forma de caracol que rodean a San Miguel se asemejan a las técnicas de talla indias vistas en los modelos escultóricos.

La concha, concretamente el nácar, se valoraba por su superficie brillante y se aplicaba en trozos como revestimiento sobre superficies de madera. En Japón, se utilizaba con frecuencia como incrustación en altares portátiles de laca que se exportaban a América. Esta imagen de *San Ignacio de Loyola* (CAT. 189), del artista mexicano Agustín del Pino, es un extraordinario ejemplo de enconchado, una innovación hispanoamericana que deriva su nombre de la palabra española "concha". En estas pinturas, pequeños fragmentos de concha y nácar se incrustaban en la superficie de un soporte de madera a modo de mosaico. Las imágenes de devoción, como la de *San Ignacio de Loyola*, resplandecían a la luz de las velas, realzadas por el brillo que se reflejaba en los fragmentos de concha. En *Cristo enseñando en el templo* (CAT. 190), la naturaleza luminosa de la concha en las vestimentas de cada figura añadía un nivel de preciosidad a la obra de arte. La tradición colonial del enconchado puede rastrear sus fuentes de influencia hasta Japón, Corea e India en obras de arte fabricadas tanto para uso secular como religioso.

Aunque la principal ruta comercial de los galeones de Manila se dirigía hacia Acapulco, se realizaron varios viajes entre Manila y el puerto peruano del Callao. Las mercancías asiáticas inundaban el mercado para satisfacer el insaciable apetito de los ricos consumidores peruanos enriquecidos con las minas de plata. La región del norte de los Andes (las actuales Colombia, Venezuela y Ecuador) también recibió su cuota de productos asiáticos. Los muebles de lujo se exportaban al Nuevo Mundo y tuvieron un impacto duradero en la producción artística local, especialmente en el trabajo de laca.

Cautivados por la increíble belleza y luminosidad de las lacas japonesas, los artistas utilizaron la *mopamopa*, una resina autóctona que imitaba la suavidad de la laca asiática. La *mopamopa* es una resina natural translúcida de color verde pálido que se utilizaba en la región de Pasto (Colombia) antes de la llegada de los españoles. Es el principal ingrediente de los artículos de laca conocidos como barniz de Pasto, producidos en Perú, Colombia y Ecuador.[6] Este baúl (CAT. 192) es un ejemplo notable de la tradición del barniz de Pasto. Los adornos de plata y el paisaje decorativo con flora y fauna de fantasía apuntan a un mecenas muy conocedor. Las asas de plata que lleva en los laterales y las correas reforzadas de su parte inferior sugieren que probablemente se diseñó como artículo de viaje y transporte.

La laca mexicana también está representada en la colección del museo. Este cofre (CAT. 191) de Olinalá es un ejemplo típico de la laca brillante y colorida por la que es conocida la región. Los diseños esgrafiados, o rayados, en los bordes pigmentados de plata de la superficie eran una característica común de los cofres de laca. Los cofres con elaboradas cerraduras de plata mantenían a salvo los objetos de valor.

En el centro de este comercio con Asia se encontraba un nuevo formato que transformó la pintura secular: el biombo japonés. Los biombos llegaron a América a través del comercio del Galeón de Manila y de las embajadas japonesas que los traían a México como regalo.[7] Los artistas locales adaptaron el nuevo formato, conocido como biombo, por *byōbu* (la palabra japonesa para biombo). Su versatilidad contribuyó a su adaptación a la vida cotidiana; era independiente, portátil y con varios paneles, y era ideal para pintar. Los biombos eran un elemento indispensable del interior de las casas. Los archivos coloniales los identifican a menudo como biombos de cama, que reforzaban la intimidad en torno a la cama, y como rodaestrados cuando delimitaban el espacio que rodeaba el estrado, una plataforma elevada en el salón del estrado, tanto en las residencias españolas como en las novohispanas.[8]

En el siglo XVII, los biombos representaban a menudo temas históricos, como este que muestra la conquista de México en el anverso y Ciudad de México en el reverso (FIG. 1). Normalmente, las pantallas de esta época estaban dominadas por multitud de figuras que creaban composiciones dinámicas. Sin embargo, en el siglo XVIII, las escenas de la vida cotidiana empezaron a sustituir a los temas literarios e históricos, como en este encantador biombo de diez paneles, *Garden Party on the Terrace of Country Home*, que ilustra a un grupo de asistentes a una fiesta (CAT. 193). Con el cambio de tema, hay también un cambio de figuras a escala pequeña a otras de tamaño casi natural que dominan la composición. Los asistentes a la fiesta y los jugadores de cartas dispuestos a lo largo de la pantalla parecen resaltar la progresión de la estricta jerarquía social de la sociedad novohispana.

Este breve examen de la influencia de Asia en las artes de Hispanoamérica revela que, a través de la lente del arte, es posible ver cómo la introducción de nuevos materiales y formatos, así como el deseo global de objetos de ultramar, transformaron la cultura material del mundo hispanoamericano.

1 En 2006, el Mayer Center del Museo de Arte de Denver presentó "Asia and Spanish America: Trans-Pacific Artistic and Cultural Exchange" (Asia e Hispanoamérica: Intercambio artístico y cultural transpacífico), el primer simposio de este tipo que presentó esta investigación en un foro público.

2 Para un análisis histórico más amplio, ver Sofía Sanabrais, "Desired and Sought by the Rest of the World: Asian Art in the Hispanic World", en *Art and Empire: The Golden Age of Spain*, ed. Michael A. Brown, San Diego: The San Diego Museum of Art, 2019.

3 Para el inventario de 1560 de Carlos V, que incluía, entre otros artículos, porcelana fabricada en China que mostraba su insignia real, ver Pedro de Madrazo, "Über Kronungsinsignien und Staatsgewänder Maximilian I. und Karl V. und ihr Schicksalim Spanien", *Jahrbuch der kunsthistorischen Sammlungen des allerhöchsten Kaiserhauses*, IX (1889), 45-51.

4 Ver Juan Grau y Montfalcón, *Memorial informativo al rey nuestro señor en su real, y supremo consejo de las India: pro la insigne, y siempre leal ciudad de Manila, cabeza de las islas Filipinas: sobre las pretensiones de aquella ciudad, é islas, y sus vecinos, y moradores, y comercio con la Nueva España*, Madrid, 1637. Publicado en E.H. Blair and J.A. Robertson, *The Philippine Islands, 1493–1898*, vol. 22 (Cleveland, OH: The Arthur H. Clark Company, 1903–09), 93–4.

5 Para más información sobre la escultura de marfil hispano-oriental y luso-india, ver Beatriz Sánchez Navarro de Pintado, *Marfiles cristianos del oriente en México* (Ciudad de México: Fomento Cultural Banamex, A.C., 1986).

6 Ver Mitchell Codding, "The Decorative Arts in Latin America, 1492–1820", en *The Arts in Latin America, 1492–1820*, ed. Joseph J. Rishell and Suzanne L. Stratton. (Philadelphia: Philadelphia Museum of Art, 2006), 98–121.

7 Ver Sofía Sanabrais, "From *Byōbu* to *Biombo:* The Transformation of the Japanese Folding Screen in Colonial Mexico", *Art History* 38, n.° 4 (Fall 2015): 778–91.

8 Para una introducción al interior doméstico español, ver Jorge F. Rivas Pérez, "Spanish Magnificence: Cosmopolitan Luxuries at Home in the Golden Age", in *Art and Empire: The Golden Age of Spain*, ed. Michael A. Brown (San Diego: The San Diego Museum of Art, 2019), 111–41.

Los santos de Nuevo México: El bricolaje artístico y la formación del estilo

James M. Córdova

Un estilo distintivo de santos (arte religioso pintado y esculpido) surgió en Nuevo México en las décadas anteriores al siglo XIX, un estilo identificable en sus propios términos y arraigado en un entorno culturalmente dinámico. Con imágenes estilizadas de los santos, motivos geométricos y naturales, así como una paleta colorida aunque limitada de pinturas locales e importadas, estas llamativas obras satisficieron la demanda local de arte sacro durante el periodo colonial español en los territorios de México y Estados Unidos que conformaban Nuevo México. Como formaban parte de una red más amplia de producción artística, se inspiraron selectivamente en obras locales y extranjeras, incluyendo grabados europeos y mexicanos, cerámica colonial mexicana, pinturas y cerámicas indígenas locales y otros santos.

Los frailes franciscanos fueron los primeros en introducir las imágenes cristianas en Nuevo México a principios del siglo XVII.[1] Muchas de estas obras se importaban de México y España a lo largo del Camino Real, una ruta que conectaba el norte de Nuevo México con Ciudad de México y con una extensa red de comercio mundial.[2] En algunos casos, los frailes o los artistas indígenas con los que trabajaban realizaron imágenes religiosas. Debido a que gran parte de estas obras fue destruida en la Revuelta del Pueblo (también llamada la rebelión de los indios de Nuevo México) contra los españoles en 1680, se sabe poco hoy en día sobre el arte religioso de esta primera época. Pero a finales del siglo XVIII, el arte religioso español y mexicano, junto con los santos producidos localmente, poblaban las instituciones religiosas y los hogares de Nuevo México.[3]

Los santos pueden clasificarse en retablos (CATS. 194 Y 195), paneles en relieve con yeso (CAT. 196) y esculturas cilíndricas policromadas, llamadas bultos, talladas principalmente en la raíz del álamo (CATS. 197 Y 198). Los retablos mayores y colaterales (CAT. 199) combinan retablos y, a veces, bultos con marcos arquitectónicos; solían ser encargos para iglesias y capillas privadas. Los artistas que produjeron los santos se identificaban como escultores y pintores, aunque el término santero se utiliza comúnmente en la actualidad.[4]

Las pieles de animales pintadas (CAT. 200 Y FIG. 1) se encuentran entre los primeros objetos devocionales fabricados en Nuevo México. En la década de 1630, un taller de artistas nativos de Santa Fe, la capital española, los fabricaba para exportarlos al centro de México.[5] Utilizaban el método indígena de curtido de pieles con sesos y pintaban directamente sobre la superficie de la piel para que los pigmentos saturaran el material como una mancha.[6] *La Crucifixión con instrumentos de la Pasión* (CAT. 200), del Museo de Arte de Denver, nos muestra que los artistas de la pintura sobre piel del siglo XVIII seguían utilizando los mismos métodos que sus predecesores. El fuerte sentido de la línea, el dibujo y el naturalismo aluden a una o varias imágenes impresas importadas que sirvieron de modelo a los artistas de Hispanoamérica. En las tempranas etapas del mundo moderno, las impresiones gráficas circulaban en las redes de comercio internacional en las que se encontraba Nuevo México. Sin embargo, a pesar de su impacto en el arte colonial español, los artistas locales no se limitaron a copiarlas. Esto es evidente en algunas pinturas de Nuevo México que se desvían selectivamente de sus fuentes impresas y, en algunos casos, pueden hacer referencia a los motivos de los Indios Pueblo y a la cerámica mexicana de Talavera (FIG. 1).[7]

El bricolaje hispánico-Indios Pueblo aparece en algunos santos, concretamente en diseños abstractos específicos como el remate de la terraza escalonada que corona el relieve en yeso de la *Virgen de los Dolores* del museo (CAT. 196). El bricolaje también es evidente en la representación bidimensional de figuras humanas en los retablos (CATS. 194, 195 Y 199) y en las imágenes de paisajes o de la naturaleza que son similares a los motivos de la loza azul sobre blanco importada del centro de México, así como a los murales de las kivas y al arte rupestre de los Indios Pueblo (FIG. 2).[8] Los retablos, la cerámica Pueblo y los murales de las kivas comparten ciertos rasgos compositivos, entre los que se incluyen las bandas y los marcos bidimensionales; la rotación, el reflejo, la inversión y la repetición de imágenes o motivos de diseño; y una superficie bidimensional y plana que carece de la profundidad pictórica ilusoria de una tercera dimensión.[9] A pesar de estas similitudes, el bricolaje transcultural de los santos de Nuevo México no indica una fusión de los símbolos hispanos con los de Pueblo y con sus significados, sino que apunta a un sistema gráfico y una estética compartidos, fruto de siglos de relaciones entre ambas culturas. Esto permitía una gama de interpretaciones y usos de los santos que dependía del marco cultural de referencia del espectador. Además, este margen no violaba necesariamente el mensaje cristiano y el valor devocional de los santos, sino que, en muchos casos, los habría complementado de una manera que hablaba de la diversa composición cultural de Nuevo México.

Los paneles para altares fueron el tipo de arte devocional más importante y extravagante de Nuevo México (CAT. 199). Los primeros paneles se importaron del centro de México, pero las primeras piezas hechas localmente datan de finales del siglo XVIII, cuando Bernardo Miera y Pacheco, un inmigrante español y polímata, hizo retablos para varias iglesias de Pueblo, así como para la capilla militar de Santa Fe.[10] Los anónimos Laguna Santero y Pedro Fresquís –quizás los primeros santeros nacidos en Nuevo México– produjeron retablos para las iglesias hispanas y de Pueblo y proporcionaron modelos locales para la siguiente generación de santeros. En este mismo periodo, Nuevo México fue testigo de las fuertes relaciones entre las comunidades Pueblo y las de origen hispano, el fin de las violentas incursiones comanches, un

auge económico y demográfico, y el surgimiento de cofradías locales (hermandades religiosas compuestas por laicos).[11] Además, las ciudades hispanas y jenízaras recién fundadas necesitaban santos para sus iglesias, capillas y salas capitulares, al tiempo que las estructuras religiosas más antiguas de Santa Fe también alimentaban la demanda.[12]

Hacia el 1800 surgió una nueva generación de santeros en Santa Fe y sus alrededores. Dado que en Nuevo México no existían gremios ni escuelas de arte oficiales, los talleres locales en los que los maestros enseñaban a los aprendices perpetuaron la forma de arte. Además, varios santeros conformaron lazos de parentesco entre sí y con los carpinteros profesionales mediante el compadrazgo, las relaciones sociales y sacramentales que establecían los roles de padrinos y madrinas, así como al apadrinar a una pareja en el matrimonio.[13] En este contexto surgió la segunda oleada de santeros nacidos en Nuevo México. Entre ellos se encuentran los hermanos José Aragón y José Rafael Aragón, así como Anastasio Casados y Manuel Benavides.[14] Al igual que algunos de sus predecesores, estos artistas se inspiraron tanto en imágenes importadas como en obras de arte locales, que ahora incluían la primera generación de santos hechos en la región. Además de su propia producción artística, estos santeros repararon algunos de los santos más antiguos, adquiriendo así un conocimiento inestimable del estilo, los materiales y las técnicas artísticas locales.[15] De este modo, no solo perpetuaron la tradición de los santos de Nuevo México, sino que en ese proceso también la perfeccionaron con sus propias aportaciones.

Los funcionarios de la Iglesia y del gobierno, junto con los comerciantes, los residentes privados influyentes y los devotos locales, constituían la base de clientes de los santeros. Además, la Hermandad de la Sangre de Cristo, conocida en la actualidad como la Hermandad de Nuestro Padre Jesús Nazareno, o más comúnmente conocida como "los Penitentes", aumentó significativamente esta demanda.[16] Esta influyente cofradía de laicos utilizaba los santos en sus procesiones y en las ceremonias religiosas que celebraban en sus salas capitulares, llamadas moradas.[17] Hacia 1900, seguían encargando a los cada vez más escasos santeros que ahora competían con los fabricantes estadounidenses que suministraban a Nuevo México imágenes religiosas baratas y de producción en serie. A pesar de ello, la forma de arte experimentó varios resurgimientos, uno en la década de 1920 y otro en la segunda mitad de ese siglo, que han persistido hasta nuestros días. En la actualidad, reconocemos que el estilo inconfundible de los santos de Nuevo México se debe a la apropiación selectiva de fuentes artísticas locales y extranjeras que los santeros reconfiguraron de manera nueva y creativa, al tiempo que iban añadiendo sus propias aportaciones, una estrategia que los santeros contemporáneos siguen practicando.

1 E. Boyd, *Popular Arts of Spanish New Mexico* (Santa Fe: Museo de Nuevo México Press, 1974), 96–97, 118; William Wroth, *Christian Images in Hispanic New Mexico: The Taylor Museum Collection of Santos* (Colorado Springs: The Taylor Museum of the Fine Arts Center, 1982), 37–38; Marie Romero Cash, *Santos: Enduring Images of Northern New Mexican Village Churches* (Boulder: University Press of Boulder, 1999), 9–10, 54–55.

2 James E. Ivey, "*Último Poblado del Mundo*': Evidence for Imported Retablos in the Churches of Seventeenth-Century New Mexico", en *El Camino Real de Tierra Adentro*, vol. 2, recopilado por Gabrielle G. Palmer y Stephen L. Fosberg, Cultural Resources Series 13 (Santa Fe: Bureau of Land Management, 1999), 177–195.

3 Robin Farwell Gavin, "Creating a New Mexico Style", en *Converging Streams: Art of the Hispanic and Native American Southwest* (Santa Fe: Museo de Arte Colonial Español Art, 2010), 39, 49; Marianne Stoller, "The Early *Santeros* of New Mexico: A Problem in Ethnic Identity and Artistic Tradition", en *Transforming Images: New Mexican* Santos *in-between Worlds*, eds. Claire Farago y Donna Pierce (University Park: Pennsylvania State University Press, 2006), 117–33.

4 José Antonio Esquibel y Charles M. Carrillo, *A Tapestry of Kinship: The Web of Influence of Escultores and Carpinteros in the Parish of Santa Fe, 1790–1850* (Los Ranchos de Albuquerque: LPD Press, 2004), 5.

5 Para más información sobre las pinturas de cueros en Nuevo México, ver Boyd, *Popular Arts*, 118–43.

6 Donna Pierce, "Hide Painting in New Mexico: New Archival Evidence", en Farago y Pierce, *Transforming Images*, 139.

7 Donahue-Wallace, Kelly, "Hide Paintings, Print Sources, and the Early Expression of a New Mexican Colonial Identity", en *Transforming Images*, 156–157.

8 Claire Farago, "Transforming Images: Managing the Interstices with a Measure of Creativity", en Farago and Pierce, *Transforming Images*, 165; Gavin, "Creating a New Mexico Style", 45.

9 Farago, "Managing the Interstices", en *Transforming Images*, 170–77; para un análisis alternativo de las características compositivas de los santos en Nuevo México basado en los modelos de pintura europeos medievales y modernos, véase Thomas J. Steele SJ, *Santos and Saints: The Religious Folk Art of Hispanic New Mexico*, 4th ed. (Santa Fe: Ancient City Press, 1994), 18–39.

10 Donna Pierce y Robin Farwell Gavin, "The Altar Screens of Bernardo Miera y Pacheco", en *The Art and Legacy of Bernardo Miera y Pacheco: New Spain's Explorer, Cartographer, and Artist*, ed. Josef Díaz (Santa Fe: Museum of New Mexico Press, 2013), 63–102.

11 Ross Frank, *From Settler to Citizen: New Mexican Economic Development and the Creation of Vecino Society, 1750–1820* (Berkeley: University of California Press, 2000), 70, 122–50, 182.

12 Los jenízaros eran indígenas destribalizados cautivos en Nuevo México que hablaban español y eran católicos. Ver Frances Leon Swadesh, *Los Primeros Pobladores: Hispanic Americans of the Ute Frontier* (South Bend: University of Notre Dame Press, 1974), 31–52; ver también José Esquibel, "The Formative Era for New Mexico's Colonial Population", en Farago y Pierce, *Transforming Images*, 64–79; Paul Kraemer, "The Dynamic Ethnicity of the People of Spanish Colonial New Mexico in the Eighteenth Century", en Farago y Pierce, *Transforming Images*, 80–98; y Estevan Rael Gálvez, "Coyote Convergence: Introduction through Interrogation", en Wroth y Gavin, *Converging Streams*, 13–24.

13 Esquibel y Carrillo, *Tapestry of Kinship*, 16.

14 Hasta que Esquibel y Carrillo identificaron a Benavides por su nombre, era conocido ampliamente en la literatura como el anónimo "Santo Niño Santero". Esquibel y Carrillo, *Tapestry of Kinship*, 5–9.

15 Charles M. Carrillo, "A Saintmaker's Palette (Appendix E)", en E. Boyd, *Saints and Saint Makers of New Mexico*, rev. ed., ed. Robin Farwell Gavin (Santa Fe: Western Edge Press, 1998), 99–104; Rutherford J. Gettens y Evan H. Turner, "The Materials and Methods of Some Religious Paintings of Early Nineteenth-Century New Mexico", *El Palacio* 58 (1951): 3–16.

16 Boyd, *Popular Arts*, 440–83; Marta Weigle, *Brothers of Light, Brothers of Blood: The Penitentes of the Southwest* (Albuquerque: University of New Mexico Press, 1976); Thomas J. Steele SJ y Rowena A. Rivera, *Penitente Self-Government: Brotherhoods and Councils, 1797–1947* (Santa Fe: Ancient City Press, 1985).

17 William Wroth, *Images of Penance, Images of Mercy: Southwestern* Santos *in the Late Nineteenth Century* (Norman: University of Oklahoma Press, 1991).

Hacia la modernidad: Hispanoamérica después de la Independencia

Natalia Majluf

Como todas las revoluciones, las guerras de independencia latinoamericanas prometían un nuevo comienzo. Las naciones fundadas sobre esta promesa miraban hacia un futuro aún indefinido, donde la única certeza verdadera era la idea de avanzar hacia lo que parecía un progreso inevitable. Para las élites de la región, el pasado reciente era algo que había que dejar atrás, y con él, las fronteras y los límites que la administración española había impuesto al comercio, al pensamiento y al intercambio internacional. Las tradiciones artísticas coloniales formaban parte de ese pasado.

Los historiadores han debatido sobre el impacto de la independencia. Desde el punto de vista de la economía y la sociedad, han argumentado, con razón, que la revolución política no transformó del todo las rígidas jerarquías sociales y las desigualdades de la sociedad colonial y que las promesas republicanas que impulsaron la guerra quedaron incumplidas. Sin embargo, desde el punto de vista de la historia cultural y de las artes, fue un periodo de grandes cambios. A lo largo del siglo XIX, las importaciones desplazaron la producción local de los objetos cotidianos, nuevos patrones de mecenazgo disminuyeron el dominio de la Iglesia sobre la creación artística y los nuevos lenguajes artísticos consiguieron desplazar la estética tardocolonial, introduciendo la descripción visual del paisaje, de tipos y costumbres que raramente se retrataban en el arte colonial (CAT. 201). Considerando un marco histórico más amplio, la eficacia y radicalidad de esos cambios hacen del siglo XIX un momento de profundas transformaciones culturales. Es también cierto que la modernización fue desigual y fracturada en un contexto en que las ciudades adquirieron un protagonismo excesivo y los circuitos comerciales a menudo pasaron por alto las zonas del interior. La producción artística en toda la región revela estas diferencias.

Cuzco, la antigua capital de los incas y un importante centro de producción pictórica a lo largo del siglo XVIII, entró en un periodo de declive al resultar aislada tanto de los antiguos circuitos comerciales como de los nuevos patrones internacionales de comercio costero. A diferencia de Lima y otras grandes capitales, no fue testigo de una avalancha de imágenes importadas y artistas extranjeros, de modo que sus pintores, escultores y tejedores siguieron en gran medida creando de acuerdo con las formas coloniales de producción artística. Por este motivo, el cambio llegó a Cuzco a un ritmo más lento.

La serie de retratos de gobernantes incas realizados a mediados del siglo XIX por un artista desconocido muestra la complejidad de la inserción del arte local en la modernidad (CAT. 205). El artista se inspiró en tradiciones y tipologías pictóricas anteriores, pero las reformuló para adaptarlas a las nuevas exigencias. Las pinturas de los incas habían desempeñado un papel político crucial durante el periodo colonial como parte de la compleja afirmación de las reivindicaciones de la nobleza indígena, las élites criollas y otras autoridades que buscaban apelar a lo inca como emblema de legitimidad política.[1] Tras las rebeliones de finales del siglo XVIII que sacudieron los cimientos del poder colonial, las pinturas se volvieron polémicas y su producción fue explícitamente prohibida. Sus significados, sin embargo, cambiaron para siempre por el impacto de las ideas republicanas surgidas con la independencia: a medida que las leyes específicas eliminaban los privilegios de los nobles incas y los ideales democráticos desplazaban la sucesión monárquica, el significado de esta tradición pictórica revivida también se vio alterado. Aunque desde el punto de vista formal eran similares a las series anteriores de los reyes incas, los nuevos retratos no reflejaban intenciones políticas, sino que servían como objetos de prestigio para quienes deseaban asociarse con un pasado imperial idealizado, o también como documentos históricos destinados, en última instancia, a servir de testimonios acerca del pasado inca en libros de texto y museos.[2] Al igual que muchas series similares, los retratos de Denver parecen haber sido creados en el contexto de un mercado emergente de antigüedades que se desarrolló en Cuzco y Lima para satisfacer el interés de viajeros y anticuarios.[3] Aunque enmarcadas en ideas modernas, estas obras reflejan formas visuales que estaban tan firmemente arraigadas en las tradiciones coloniales como distantes de los cambios que los nuevos ideales estéticos iban introduciendo en toda la región.

Por el contrario, el minucioso retrato de Felipe Santiago Gutiérrez de un hombre mayor refleja el rastro que el sistema moderno de las artes dejaba especialmente en los grandes centros urbanos como Río de Janeiro y Ciudad de México, donde las instituciones de enseñanza formal contribuyeron pronto al avance de los ideales académicos (CAT. 204).[4] Gutiérrez (1824-1904) se formó en la Academia Mexicana de San Carlos, y su carrera como pintor, profesor y crítico es un ejemplo de la búsqueda de la modernidad artística, emprendida con pasión y determinación durante largos viajes por México, Europa e Hispanoamérica.[5] Este estudio al óleo, que parece haber sido pintado del natural, podría datarse a principios de la década de 1870, probablemente como parte de sus estudios en la Academia de Bellas Artes de San Fernando, en Madrid, donde trabajó brevemente con Federico de Madrazo y Kuntz y Carlos Luis de Ribera. Los estudios con modelos de ancianos se estaban convirtiendo en un elemento básico de los talleres académicos, a medida que el creciente gusto por el naturalismo –informado por los avances de las nuevas tecnologías visuales– ponía el realismo barroco en el punto de mira estético. El cuadro de Gutiérrez evoca claramente su admiración por la tradición pictórica española y especialmente por José de Ribera (El Españoleto), cuyas obras había admirado en Italia, emulado en sus estudios académicos en Roma y copiado con devoción en Madrid.[6] El cuadro, realizado sobre papel, formó parte sin duda de las pertenencias que llevó a Colombia en uno de los muchos viajes que emprendió para colaborar en la creación de una academia de arte, objetivo parcialmente logrado con una academia privada que dirigió en 1873 y que, a partir de 1881, llevaría su nombre.[7]Autor de un tratado pictórico, crítico activo y promotor de las bellas artes en las numerosas ciudades que visitó,

la trayectoria de Gutiérrez ejemplifica la visión cosmopolita y el impulso casi misionero de los pintores del siglo XIX en su afán por establecer un sistema moderno de las artes.

Ese ideal, sin embargo, no llegó a plasmarse plenamente. En la mayoría de los lugares, su materialización a través de instituciones, exposiciones públicas y el debate crítico fue parcial y limitada, y aunque los nuevos lenguajes y formatos estéticos se extendieron rápidamente, su alcance estuvo a menudo mediado por tradiciones más antiguas. En algunos casos, la innovación formal transformó tipologías tradicionales en géneros como la ebanistería, la joyería y los alfileres andinos conocidos como "tupus" (CATS. 202 Y 203, Y VÉASE WUFFARDEN, CAT. 184). En otros, los lenguajes visuales no se adaptaron tan rápidamente a las nuevas modas en géneros como el retrato, que alcanzó una popularidad hasta entonces desconocida en manos de artistas formados en talleres coloniales o que operaban al margen de los preceptos académicos. Estos artistas produjeron algunas de las imágenes más impactantes de la transición a la modernidad en América Latina (CAT. 208). En muchos lugares, las formas de producción mantuvieron los antiguos patrones de consumo, distribución y lenguaje formal, como en los casos de la cerámica y el tejido, aunque las modificaciones también afectarían gradualmente a su producción (CATS. 206 Y 207). En el largo siglo XIX, cuando la región vio el fin de un régimen político y el comienzo de otro nuevo, y cuando los vastos territorios antes dominados por España entraron en los circuitos del capitalismo y el comercio mundial, pocas cosas permanecerían inalteradas.

1 Gustavo Buntinx y Luis Eduardo Wuffarden, "Incas y reyes españoles en la pintura colonial peruana: la estela de Garcilaso", *Márgenes* IV, n.º 8 (Diciembre 1991): 151-210.

2 Natalia Majluf, "De la rebelión al museo: Genealogías y retratos de los incas, 1780-1900", en Natalia Majluf, ed., *Los incas, reyes del Perú* (Lima: Banco de Crédito del Perú, 2005), 253–319.

3 La serie del Museo de Arte de Denver pertenecía originalmente a una colección británica.

4 Para una visión general de las academias del siglo XIX, ver Oscar E. Vázquez, ed., *Academies and Schools of Art in Latin America* (New York and London: Routledge, 2020).

5 Para más información sobre Gutiérrez, ver *Discursos de la piel. Felipe Santiago Gutiérrez (1824–1904)* (Ciudad de México: Museo Nacional de Arte, 2017), 132-141.

6 Para más información sobre los comentarios de Gutiérrez acerca de la obra de Ribera en Roma en 1868, así como para la copia que hizo del San Bartolomé durante su visita al Prado en noviembre de 1870, ver la entrada de Fausto Ramírez sobre el San Bartolomé en Esther Acevedo, Arturo Camacho, Fausto Ramírez y Angélica Velázquez Guadarrama, *Catálogo comentado del acervo del Museo Nacional de Arte. Pintura. Siglo XIX. Tomo I* (Ciudad de México: Instituto de Investigaciones Estéticas, Museo Nacional de Arte, 2002), 277-83. Para referencias al arte español en el siglo XIX, ver también Olga Isabel Acosta Luna, "Felipe Santiago Gutiérrez y los comienzos de la Academia en Colombia", en *Diego, Frida y otros revolucionarios* (Bogotá: Museo Nacional de Colombia, 2009), 72.

7 Según los registros del museo, el cuadro perteneció a la colección de Daniel Casey Stapleton (1858-1920) mientras vivió en Colombia y Ecuador (1895-1914). Sobre la labor de Gutiérrez en el establecimiento de la formación artística formal en Bogotá, ver Olga Isabel Acosta Luna, "Forming the National School of Fine Art in Colombia. Local Desires and External Influences", en *Academies and Schools of Art in Latin America*, ed. Vázquez, 65–78.

Fantasmas coloniales en el arte moderno y contemporáneo de América Latina

Rafael Fonseca

Desde los nombres de las avenidas y los monumentos hasta las fiestas nacionales, el fantasma del colonialismo europeo se cierne sobre América Latina, incluyendo su arte moderno y contemporáneo. En este breve texto, la comparación de dos pintores –el mexicano José Clemente Orozco (1883–1949) y el brasileño André Griffo (1979)– muestra cómo los contextos moderno y contemporáneo configuran las actitudes hacia la cultura visual colonial. Orozco es uno de los pintores mexicanos más reconocidos de la historia del arte, y Griffo es un joven artista que ha alcanzado relevancia mundial. La violencia, el dolor, la muerte y el trauma se encuentran en las obras de ambos artistas, y sus contextos históricos determinan la forma en que se apropiaron de las ideas coloniales de manera opuesta.

Como muralista, Orozco, junto con sus coetáneos Diego Rivera (1886–1957) y David Alfaro Siqueiros (1896–1974), creó un estilo moderno, dramático y expresionista para transmitir al público el pasado precolonial de México y sus posibilidades futuras, posteriores a la revolución. En el *Vía Crucis,* Orozco representa una escena cristiana familiar –Jesucristo cargando la cruz en la que será crucificado– que muchos artistas, desde la Edad Media, representaron antes que él (CAT. 209). Aunque a Orozco le interesaban los héroes y los mártires de la tradición clásica, cargó sus composiciones modernas de dramatismo, utilizando colores y pinceladas expresivas para transmitir sus temas. Alrededor de la figura central de Cristo, un grupo de devotos ataviados con túnicas se arrodillan y lo acompañan en silencio, mientras que los soldados y otras figu-

ras ejercen violencia física contra él. Al enfocar estos extremos, Orozco reflexiona sobre las contradicciones del bien y del mal.

Al abordar un tema tradicional de manera moderna, Orozco conduce a su espectador –quien ya ha experimentado los cambios existenciales, sociales y tecnológicos de principios del siglo XX– a un diálogo con la tradición del *memento mori*: recuerda la muerte, recuerda a Cristo y, si es posible, cambia tu comportamiento mientras estás vivo. La pintura de Orozco demuestra cómo los artistas modernos experimentaron con nuevos medios y formas de pintar mientras seguían apoyándose en narrativas coloniales impregnadas de cristianismo tradicional. Como muchos otros influyentes artistas latinoamericanos, Orozco reflexionó sobre la muerte tal y como la propuso el cristianismo, en medio del progreso moderno y la industrialización. Tradición y modernismo, por tanto, podían ir de la mano.

El artista contemporáneo André Griffo, nacido en Barra Mansa, en el estado de Río de Janeiro, también aborda el pasado colonial de América Latina para llamar la atención sobre el impacto de la historia en el presente. *Instruções para administração das fazendas 5* (Instrucciones para la administración de las fincas 5) pertenece a una serie de pinturas que representan varias vistas de uno de los edificios religiosos más antiguos de Río de Janeiro: la Santa Casa da Misericórdia, un hospital fundado por la Hermandad de la Misericordia en la segunda mitad del siglo XVI (CAT. 210). Es el hospital más antiguo de Río de Janeiro y sigue funcionando en la actualidad ofreciendo sus servicios al público.

Con gran realismo, Griffo representa un pasillo del hospital y vincula la caridad de la hermandad con la esclavitud negra que se extendió rápidamente en Brasil con la llegada de los portugueses, ya que fueron hombres esclavizados los que construyeron el hospital. Los benefactores de la institución, cuyos retratos cuelgan en las paredes del pasillo, estuvieron vinculados a la esclavitud negra durante siglos, eran hombres religiosos, agricultores y representantes del poder. En el suelo de baldosas en blanco y negro, Griffo pinta a hombres negros en miniatura que parecen haberse rebelado contra el trabajo forzado para construir otra realidad; hacen un agujero en el suelo y plantan un árbol similar a un baobab, un árbol ancestral que se encuentra en distintas regiones de África y que suele asociarse con la sabiduría. Con esta escena, pintada de forma realista pero onírica, Griffo recuerda al espectador la impureza de los actos de caridad de la Iglesia y la violencia física infligida durante la colonización.

Griffo no mira con nostalgia el pasado colonial de América Latina, sino que pone en primer plano cómo siglos de invasión y exterminio afectan las vidas y la memoria colectiva de los latinoamericanos contemporáneos. No retrata la violencia que se produjo en este hospital, pero sugiere un ejercicio de revisión histórica a través de sus imágenes.

Con la persistencia de las iconografías coloniales, incluidas las del cristianismo, y las críticas decoloniales más recientes de esas iconografías, los artistas latinoamericanos modernos y contemporáneos, como Orozco y Griffo, desafían a los espectadores a replantearse sus posiciones y supuestos sobre el pasado. Incluso cuando los artistas modernos como Orozco experimentan con nuevos enfoques de los medios tradicionales, como la pintura, se puede decir que son continuadores de los tropos visuales del México colonial. Los artistas contemporáneos como André Griffo, sin embargo, parecen más interesados en deconstruir los tropos coloniales y en proponer al espectador una autopsia de los traumas coloniales que se cernieron –y aún se ciernen– sobre América Latina. El poder de una colección como la del Museo de Arte de Denver reside en el hecho de que uno puede volver a los objetos más antiguos y más recientes, colocarlos unos junto a otros, y ejercer una mirada crítica para contemplar las innumerables historias no contadas y complejas de las Américas: su pasado, su presente y su futuro.

Paladia.
S. Grata.
S. Saula.
S. Vrsula.
S. Pinosa.
S. Mardia
S. Gregoria.
A devocion dela M.e Maria Manuela, de los Dolores.
año de 1734.

Selected Readings

Acosta Luna, Olga Isabel. *Diego, Frida y otros revolucionarios*. Bogotá: Museo Nacional de Colombia, 2009.

———. *Milagrosas imágenes marianas en el Nuevo Reino de Granada*. Madrid: Iberoamericana, 2011.

Alcalá, Luisa Elena, and Jonathan Brown. *Painting in Latin America, 1550–1820: From Conquest to Independence*. New Haven: Yale University Press, 2014.

Alexander, Rani T., ed. *Technology and Tradition in Mesoamerica after the Spanish Invasion: Archaeological Perspectives*. Albuquerque: University of New Mexico Press, 2019.

Amador Marrero, Pablo F., and Patricia Díaz Cayeros. *El tejido polícromo: La escultura novohispana y su vestimenta*. Ciudad de México: Universidad Nacional Autónoma de México, Instituto de Investigaciones Estéticas, 2013.

Aranda, Ana María, et al. *Barroco iberoamericano: Territorio, arte, y espacio y sociedad*. Sevilla: Universidad Pablo de Olavide, 2001.

Aste, Richard, ed. *Behind Closed Doors: Art in the Spanish American Home, 1492–1898*. New York: Brooklyn Museum and Monacelli Press, 2013.

Block, David. *Mission Culture on the Upper Amazon: Native Tradition, Jesuit Enterprise, and Secular Policy in Moxos, 1660–1880*. Lincoln: University of Nebraska Press, 1994.

Borja Gómez, Jaime H. *Los ingenios del pincel: Geografía de la pintura y la cultura visual en América colonial*. Bogotá: Universidad de los Andes, Ediciones Uniandes, 2021.

Boulton, Alfredo. *Historia de la pintura en Venezuela*. Caracas: Ernesto Armitano, 1975.

———. *El pintor del Tocuyo*. Caracas: Ediciones Macanao, 1985.

Boyd, E. *Popular Arts of Spanish New Mexico*. Santa Fe: Museum of New Mexico Press, 1974.

———. *Saints and Saint Makers of New Mexico*. Revised and edited by Robin Farwell Gavin. Santa Fe: Western Edge Press, 1998.

Brown, Michael A., ed. *Art and Empire: The Golden Age of Spain*. San Diego: The San Diego Museum of Art, 2019.

Campos Carlés de Peña, María. *A Surviving Legacy in Spanish America: Seventeenth- and Eighteenth-Century Furniture from the Viceroyalty of Peru*. Madrid: Ediciones El Viso, 2014.

Carr, Dennis, ed. *Made in the Americas: The New World Discovers Asia*. Boston: MFA Publications, 2015.

Cash, Marie Romero. *Santos: Enduring Images of Northern New Mexican Village Churches*. Boulder: University Press of Colorado, 1999.

Contreras Guerrero, Adrián. *Escultura en Colombia: Focos productores y circulación de obras (siglos XVI-XVIII)*. Granada: Universidad de Granada, 2019.

Cuadriello, Jaime, et al. *Catálogo comentado del acervo del Museo Nacional de Arte. Nueva España*. Ciudad de México: Museo Nacional de Arte, 1999.

Cuadriello, Jaime, Elsa Arroyo, Sandra Zetina, and Eumelia Hernández. *Ojos, alas y patas de la mosca: Visualidad, técnica y materialidad en El martirio de san Ponciano de Baltasar de Echave Orio*. Ciudad de México: Universidad Nacional Autónoma de México, Instituto de Investigaciones Estéticas, 2018.

Curiel, Gustavo, ed. *Carpinteros de la sierra. El mobiliario taraceado de la Villa Alta de San Ildefonso, Oaxaca (siglos XVII y XVIII)*, Tomo I, Estudios; Tomo II, Catálogo razonado. Ciudad de México: Universidad Nacional Autónoma de México, Instituto de Investigaciones Estéticas, 2019.

———. *Inventario y aprecio de los bienes de la testamentaria de don Antonio María Bucareli, Virrey de la Nueva España (1779). El ajuar de palacio y su librería*. Ciudad de México: Universidad Nacional Autónoma de México, Instituto de Investigaciones Estéticas, 2020

———. *La mansión de los condes de San Bartolomé de Xala de la Ciudad de México Inventario y aprecio de los bienes del caudal de don Antonio Rodríguez de Pedroso y Soria, 1792*. Ciudad de México: Universidad Nacional Autónoma de México, Instituto de Investigaciones Estéticas, en prensa.

Díaz, Josef, ed. *The Art and Legacy of Bernardo Miera y Pacheco: New Spain's Explorer, Cartographer, and Artist*. Santa Fe: Museum of New Mexico Press, 2013.

Duarte, Carlos F. *Diccionario biográfico documental: Pintores, escultores y doradores en Venezuela: Período hispánico y comienzos del período republicano*. Caracas: Fundación Galería de Arte Nacional, 2000.

———. *Domingo Gutiérrez: El maestro del rococó en Venezuela*. Caracas: Ediciones Equinoccio, Universidad Simón Bolívar, 1977.

———. *Juan Pedro López: Maestro de pintor, escultor y dorador. 1724-1787*. Caracas: Galería de Arte Nacional, 1996.

———. *Mobiliario y decoración interior durante el periodo hispánico venezolano*. Caracas: Armitano Editores, 1993.

Esquibel, José Antonio, and Charles M. Carrillo. *A Tapestry of Kinship: The Web of Influence of Escultores and Carpinteros in the Parish of Santa Fe, 1790–1860*. Los Ranchos de Albuquerque, NM: LPD Press, 2004.

Estella Marcos, Margarita. *Marfiles de las provincias ultramarinas orientales de España y Portugal*. 2nd ed. Monterrey, México: GM Editores, 2010.

Esteras Martín, Cristina. *El arte de la platería mexicana, 500 años*. Ciudad de México: Centro Cultural Arte Contemporáneo, 1989.

———. *Marcas de platería hispanoamericana: Siglos XVI-XX*. Madrid: Ediciones Tuero, 1992.

———. *La platería del Museo Franz Mayer: Obras escogidas, siglos XVI-XIX*. Ciudad de México: Museo Franz Mayer, 1992.

———. *La platería en el reino de Guatemala: Siglos XVI-XIX*. Guatemala: Fundación Albergue Hermano Pedro, 1994.

Fane, Diana, ed. *Converging Cultures: Art and Identity in Spanish America*. New York: Brooklyn Museum of Art in association with Harry N. Abrams, 1996.

Farago, Claire, and Donna Pierce, eds. *Transforming Images: New Mexican Santos in-between Worlds*. University Park: Pennsylvania State University Press, 2006.

Fernández Valle, María de los Ángeles, Carme López Calderón, and Inmaculada Rodríguez Moya, eds. *Pinceles y gubias del barroco hispanoamericano*. Vol. 7, Universo Barroco Iberoamericano. Sevilla: Andavira Editora S. L., EnredArs, 2019.

Galí i Boadella, Montserrat, ed. *La catedral de Puebla en el arte y en la historia*. Puebla, México: Secretaría de Cultura, Gobierno del Estado de Puebla, 1999.

García Sáiz, María Concepción, and Juana Gutiérrez Haces, eds. *Tradición, estilo o escuela en la pintura iberoamericana. Siglos XVI-XVIII*. Ciudad de México: Universidad Nacional Autónoma de México, Instituto de Investigaciones Estéticas, 2004.

Gavin, Robin Farwell, Donna Pierce, and Alfonzo Pleguezuelo, eds. *Cerámica y Cultura: The Story of Spanish and Mexican Mayólica*. Albuquerque: University of New Mexico Press, 2003.

Gutiérrez Haces, Juana, Pedro Ángeles, Clara Bergellini, and Rogelio Ruiz Gomar. *Cristóbal de Villalpando, ca. 1649-1714: Catálogo razonado*. Ciudad de México: Fomento Cultural Banamex, Instituto de Investigaciones Estéticas, Universidad Nacional Autónoma de México, 1997.

Gutiérrez Haces, Juana and Cándida Fernández de Calderón, eds. *Pintura de los Reinos: identidades compartidas en el mundo hispánico, siglos XVI-XVIII*. Ciudad de México: Fomento Cultural Banamex, 2008.

Katzew, Ilona, ed. *Contested Visions in the Spanish Colonial World*. Los Angeles: Los Angeles County Museum of Art, 2011.

———, ed. *Painted in Mexico, 1700–1790: Pinxit Mexici*. New York: DelMonico Books/Prestel Publishing, 2017.

Kennedy, Alexandra, ed. *Arte de la Real Audiencia de Quito, siglos XVII-XIX: patronos, corporaciones y comunidades*. Hondarribia, España: Editorial Nerea S. A., 2002.

Kusunoki, Ricardo, ed. *La colección Petrus y Verónica Fernandini: El arte de la pintura en los Andes*. Lima: Asociación Museo de Arte de Lima, 2015.

Kusonoki, Ricardo, and Luis Eduardo Wuffarden, eds. *Arte Colonial: Colección Museo de Arte de Lima*. Lima: Asociación Museo de Arte de Lima, 2016.

López Guzmán, Rafael, ed. *Return Journey: Art of the Americas in Spain*. Madrid: Museo Nacional del Prado, 2021.

López Pérez, María del Pilar. *En torno al estrado: cajas de uso cotidiano en Santafé de Bogotá, siglos XVI al XVIII: arcas, arcaces, arquillas, arquetas, arcones, baúles, cajillas, cajones, cofres, petacas, escritorios y papeleras*. Bogotá: Museo Nacional de Colombia, 1996.

Majluf, Natalia, Cristóbal Makowski, and Francisco Stastny. *Art in Peru: Works from the Collection of the Museo de Arte de Lima*. Lima: Asociación Museo de Arte de Lima; Promperú, 2001.

Majluf, Natalia, ed. *Arte republicano*. Lima: Asociación Museo de Arte de Lima, 2015.

Maquívar, María del Consuelo. *El imaginero novohispano y su obra: las esculturas de Tepotzotlán*. Ciudad de México: Instituto Nacional de Antropología e Historia, 1999.

Mesa, José de, and Teresa Gisbert. *Historia de la pintura cuzqueña*. Lima: Fundación A. N. Wiese, Banco Weise, 1982.

———. *Holguín y la pintura altoperuana del virreinato*. La Paz, Bolivia: Biblioteca Paceña, Alcaldía Municipal, 1956.

Mues Orts, Paula. *La libertad del pincel: los discursos sobre la nobleza de la pintura en Nueva España*. Ciudad de México: Universidad Iberoamericana, 2008.

Mujica Pinilla, Ramón. *Ángeles apócrifos en la América virreinal*. Lima: Fondo de Cultura Económica, Instituto de Estudios Tradicionales, 1992.

———, et al. *El barroco peruano*. Lima: Banco de Crédito del Perú, 2003.

———, ed. *Orígenes y devociones virreinales de la imaginería popular*. Lima: Universidad Ricardo Pala, Instituto Cultural Peruano Norteamericano, 2008.

Pérez de Salazar Verea, Francisco, ed. *El mobiliario en Puebla: Preciosismo, mitos y cotidianidad de la carpintería y la ebanistería.* Puebla, México: Fundación Mary Street Jenkins, 2009.

Pierce, Donna, ed. *The Arts of South America, 1492–1850: Papers from the 2008 Mayer Center Symposium at the Denver Art Museum.* Denver: Mayer Center for Pre-Columbian and Spanish Colonial Art, Denver Art Museum, Denver Art Museum, 2010.

Pierce, Donna. *Companion to Spanish Colonial Art at the Denver Art Museum.* Denver: Mayer Center for Pre-Columbian and Spanish Colonial Art at the Denver Art Museum, 2011.

———, ed. *Exploring New World Imagery: Spanish Colonial Papers from the 2002 Mayer Center Symposium.* Denver: Frederick and Jan Mayer Center for Pre-Columbian and Spanish Colonial Art, Denver Art Museum, 2005.

———, ed., *Festivals and Daily Life in the Arts of Colonial Latin America, 1492–1850: Papers from the 2012 Mayer Center Symposium at the Denver Art Museum.* Denver: Mayer Center for Pre-Columbian and Spanish Colonial Art, Denver Art Museum, 2014.

———, ed. *New England/New Spain: Portraiture in the Colonial Americas 1492–1850: Papers from the 2014 Mayer Center Symposium at the Denver Art Museum.* Denver: Mayer Center for Pre-Columbian and Spanish Colonial Art, Denver Art Museum, 2016.

Pierce, Donna, and Julie Wilson Frick. *Companion to Glitterati: Portraits and Jewelry from Colonial Latin America at the Denver Art Museum.* Denver: Mayer Center for Pre-Columbian and Spanish Colonial Art, Denver Art Museum, 2015.

Pierce, Donna, Rogelio Ruiz Gomar, and Clara Bargellini. *Painting a New World: Mexican Art and Life, 1521–1821.* Denver: Denver Art Museum, 2004.

Pierce, Donna, and Ronald Otsuka, eds. *Asia and Spanish America: Trans-Pacific Artistic and Cultural Exchange, 1500–1850, Papers from the 2006 Mayer Center Symposium at the Denver Art Museum.* Denver: Denver Art Museum, 2009.

———, eds. *At the Crossroads: The Arts of Spanish America and Early Global Trade, 1492–1850, Papers from the 2010 Mayer Center Symposium at the Denver Art Museum.* Denver: Frederick and Jan Mayer Center for Pre-Columbian and Spanish Colonial Art, Denver Art Museum, 2012.

Priyadarshini, Meha. *Chinese Porcelain in Colonial Mexico: The Material Worlds of an Early Modern Trade.* Cham, Switzerland: Palgrave Macmillan, 2018.

Ramírez Montes, Mina. *Pedro Rojas y su taller de escultura en Querétaro.* Documentos de Querétaro 7. Querétaro, México: Dirección de Patrimonio Cultural, Secretaría de Cultura y Bienestar Social del Gobierno del Estado de Querétaro, 1988.

Rishel, Joseph J., and Suzanne Stratton-Pruitt, eds. *The Arts in Latin America, 1492–1820.* Philadelphia: Philadelphia Museum of Art, 2006.

Rivas Pérez, Jorge F., ed. *Circulación: Movement of Ideas, Art, and People in Spanish America, Mayer Center Symposium XVI.* Denver: Mayer Center for Pre-Columbian and Latin American Art at the Denver Art Museum, 2018.

———, ed. *Materiality: Making Spanish America, Mayer Center Symposium XVIII.* Denver: Denver Art Museum, 2020.

———. *De oficio pintor: Arte colonial venezolano: Colección Patricia Phelps de Cisneros.* Santiago de los Caballeros, República Dominicana: Centro León; Caracas: Fundación Cisneros, 2007.

———, ed. *Power and Piety: Spanish Colonial Art from the Patricia Cisneros Collection.* Alexandria, VA: Art Services International, 2015.

———. *El Repertorio Clásico en el Mobiliario Venezolano, Siglos XVIII y XIX.* Caracas: Fundación Cisneros, 2008.

Roque, Georges. *Rojo Mexicano: La grana cochinilla en el arte.* Ciudad de México: Instituto Nacional de Bellas Artes; Museo del Palacio de Bellas Artes, 2017.

Russo, Alessandra. *The Untranslatable Image: A Mestizo History of the Arts in New Spain.* Austin: University of Texas Press, 2014.

Russo, Alessandra, Gerhard Wolf, and Diana Fane. *El vuelo de las imágenes arte plumario en México y Europa.* Ciudad de México: Museo Nacional de Arte; Instituto Nacional de Antropología e Historia, 2011.

Sánchez Cabra, Efraín. *Ramón Torres Méndez: Pintor de la Nueva Granada 1809-1885.* Bogotá: Fondo Cultural Cafetero, 1987.

Sánchez Navarro de Pintado, Beatriz. *Marfiles cristianos del oriente en México.* Ciudad de México: Fomento Cultural Banamex, 1986.

Siracusano, Gabriela. *Pigments and Power in the Andes: From the Material to the Symbolic in Andean Cultural Practices, 1500–1800.* Translated by Ian Barnett. London: Archetype Publications Ltd., 2011.

Siracusano, Gabriela, and Agustina Rodríguez Romero, eds. *Materia Americana: El cuerpo de las imágenes hispanoamericanas (siglos XVI a mediados del XIX).* Buenos Aires: Editorial de la Universidad de Tres de Febrero, 2020.

Stastny, Francisco. *Estudios de arte colonial.* Vol. I. Lima: Museo de Arte de Lima; Instituto Francés de Estudios Andinos, 2013

———. *El manierismo en la pintura colonial latinoamericana.* Lima: Universidad Nacional Mayor de San Marcos, 1981.

Steele, Thomas J. *Santos and Saints: The Religious Folk Art of Hispanic New Mexico.* Santa Fe: Ancient City Press, 1994.

Steele, Thomas J., and Rowena A. Rivera. *Penitente Self-Government: Brotherhoods and Councils, 1797–1947.* Santa Fe: Ancient City Press, 1985.

Stratton-Pruitt, Suzanne. *The Virgin, Saints, and Angels: South American Paintings 1600–1825 from the Thoma Collection.* Milan: Skira; Stanford: The Iris & B. Gerald Cantor Center for Visual Arts at Stanford University, 2006.

Toquica Clavijo, María Costanza ed. *Catálogo de pintura Museo Colonial.* Bogotá: Ministerio de Cultura, 2016.

Valiñas López, Francisco Manuel. *La estrella del camino: Apuntes para el estudio del belén barroco quiteño.* Quito: Instituto Metropolitano de Patrimonio, 2011.

Vázquez, Oscar E., ed. *Academies and Schools of Art in Latin America.* New York: Routledge, 2020.

Vargas Murcia, Laura Liliana. *Del pincel al papel: Fuentes para el estudio de la pintura en el Nuevo Reino de Granada (1552-1813).* Bogotá: Instituto Colombiano de Antropología e Historia, 2012.

Velázquez Guadarrama, Angélica, et al. *Discursos de la piel. Felipe Santiago Gutiérrez (1824-1904).* Ciudad de México: Secretaría de Cultura, Instituto Nacional de Bellas Artes; Museo Nacional de Arte, 2017.

Vetter Parodi, Luisa María. *Plateros indígenas en el virreinato del Perú: siglos XVI y XVII.* Lima: Fondo Editorial de la Universidad Nacional Mayor de San Marcos, 2008.

Vetter Parodi, Luisa María, and Paloma Carcedo de Mufarech. *El tupo: símbolo ancestral de identidad femenina.* Lima: Gráfica Biblos, 2009.

Weigle, Marta. *Brothers of Light, Brothers of Blood: The Penitentes of the Southwest.* Albuquerque: University of New Mexico Press, 1976.

Wroth, William. *Christian Images in Hispanic New Mexico: The Taylor Museum Collection of Santos.* Colorado Springs: The Taylor Museum of the Fine Arts Center, 1982.

———. *Images of Penance, Images of Mercy: Southwestern* Santos *in the Late Nineteenth Century.* Norman: University of Oklahoma Press for the Taylor Museum of the Colorado Springs Fine Arts Center, 1991.

Wroth, William, and Robin Farwell Gavin, eds. *Converging Streams: Art of the Hispanic and Native American Southwest.* Santa Fe: Museum of Spanish Colonial Art, 2010.

Wuffarden, Luis Eduardo, and Ricardo Kusunoki, eds. *Pintura cuzqueña.* Lima: Asociación Museo de Arte de Lima, 2016.

———. *Plata de los Andes.* Lima: Asociación Museo de Arte de Lima, 2018.

Contributors

Olga Isabel Acosta Luna is Associate Professor in the Department of Art History, Faculty of Arts and Humanities, Universidad de los Andes, Bogota, Colombia.

Luisa Elena Alcalá is Associate Professor in the Department of History and Theory of Art of the Universidad Autónoma de Madrid, Spain.

Elsa Arroyo Lemus is a researcher and professor at the Instituto de Investigaciones Estéticas, Universidad Nacional Autónoma de México, Mexico City.

Carla Aymes is a doctoral candidate in art history at the Universidad de Valencia, Spain.

Michael A. Brown is Curator of European Art before 1900 at the San Diego Museum of Art.

James M. Córdova is Associate Professor of Art History at the University of Colorado, Boulder.

Gustavo Curiel Méndez is a professor at the Instituto de Investigaciones Estéticas, Universidad Nacional Autónoma de México, Mexico City.

Carmen Fernández-Salvador is a professor of art history at the Universidad San Francisco de Quito, Ecuador.

Raphael Fonseca is the Associate Curator of Modern and Contemporary Latin American Art at the Denver Art Museum.

Philippe Halbert is a doctoral candidate in art history at Yale University.

Ricardo Kusunoki Rodríguez is the curator of colonial and republican art at the Lima Art Museum, Lima, Peru.

Natalia Majluf is an independent art historian and curator based in Lima, Peru.

Franziska Martha Neff is a researcher at the Instituto de Investigaciones Estéticas, Universidad Nacional Autónoma de México, Oaxaca.

Janeth Rodríguez Nóbrega is a professor of art history at the School of Art, Universidad Central de Venezuela, Caracas.

Jorge F. Rivas Pérez is the Frederick and Jan Mayer Curator of Latin American Art and department head at the Denver Art Museum.

Sofía Sanabrais is an independent art historian and curator based in Los Angeles.

Luis Eduardo Wuffarden Revilla is an independent art historian and curator based in Lima, Peru.

Acknowledgments

A decade after the museum published the *Companion to Spanish Colonial Art at the Denver Art Museum* (2012), and fresh from the reinstallation of our permanent galleries, I quickly came to the conclusion that a book showcasing the substantial growth of the collection in the last years and the considerable conservation work carried out on many of our masterpieces was necessary. The new galleries allowed us to think about how we understand and present art from the colonial period in Spanish America. The expansive depth and breadth of the collection offered the opportunity to provide a different perspective on this type of art—one more inclusive and diverse that addressed the thorny subject of colonialism and its long-lasting impact on the region. I want to extend my most profound appreciation to the Mayer Center for Latin American Art staff, Lilly Barrientos, curatorial assistant; Raphael Fonseca, associate curator of modern and contemporary Latin American art; Maria Luisa Minjares, former curatorial assistant; and Maria Trujillo, former interpretive specialist, who assisted with outlining this view that helped me to shape some of the ideas and content presented in this publication. Their relentless efforts were crucial in bringing this book to fruition.

I am grateful for the generosity and new scholarship of colleagues from all over the Americas and Europe for this volume: Olga Isabel Acosta Luna, Luisa Elena Alcalá, Elsa Arroyo Lemus, Carla Aymes, Michael A. Brown, James M. Córdova, Gustavo Curiel Méndez, Carmen Fernández-Salvador, Raphael Fonseca, Philippe Halbert, Ricardo Kusunoki Rodríguez, Natalia Majluf, Franziska Martha Neff, Janeth Rodríguez Nóbrega, Sofia Sanabrais, and Luis Eduardo Wuffarden Revilla.

The museum's Conservation Department provided significant support. I sincerely appreciate the efforts of Aaron Burgess, Emily Brzezinski, Gina Laurin, Sarah Melching, Pam Skyles, and Yasuko Ogino. I also want to recognize the great endeavors of our Photographic Services Department for contributing to the completion of this volume. Christina Jackson, Eric Stephenson, Bruce Fernández, and Jeff Wall produced most of the lavish images illustrating this publication.

In preparing this volume, I am deeply grateful to Valerie Hellstein, Kati Woock, and Chris Patrello from the Publications Department for their management and editing work and Renée Miller's invaluable assistance in securing image rights. Special thanks are due to María Eugenia Hidalgo and Alberto Márquez, our Spanish copyeditors and proofreaders.

I wish to thank our partners at Hirmer Publishers, Elisabeth Rochau-Shalem, Rainer Arnold, Hannes Halder, David Sánchez, Laura Puy Rodríguez, Jane Michael, and Amaia de Navascués for the exquisitely designed and produced book.

The Carl & Marilynn Thoma Foundation generously provided funding for this book.

I want to express my special gratitude to the late Frederick Mayer, and his wife Jan, for their generosity and commitment to the field of Spanish colonial art that made this book possible. I am also grateful to Christoph Heinrich, Frederick and Jan Mayer Director; his ongoing support was crucial to making this project happen.

Jorge F. Rivas Pérez

MIRANDVM SANÉ!
SEMESTRIS ACERRIMVS LABOR
ERIT IN MONIMENTVM

REINANDO
CARLOS IV. Y LUISA

Index

Imprint

Appropriations and Invention: Three Centuries of Art in Spanish America, Selections from the Denver Art Museum is made possible through the generous support of the Carl & Marilynn Thoma Foundation as well as the residents who support the Scientific and Cultural Facilities District (SCFD).

Published by

Hirmer Verlag GmbH
Bayerstrasse 57-59
80335 Munich
Germany
www.hirmerpublishers.com

Denver Art Museum
100 West 14th Avenue Parkway
Denver, CO 80204
denverartmuseum.org

The Denver Art Museum is located on the homeland of the Arapaho, Cheyenne, and Ute people, along with many people from other Indigenous nations that call this place home. Learn more about our commitments to better represent, elevate, and support Indigenous cultures and people, past and present, on our website.

Bibliographical data of the Deutsche Nationalbibliothek:
The Deutsche Nationalbibliothek lists this publication in the Deutschen Nationalbibliografie; detailed bibliographic information is available on the Internet at https://www.dnb.de.

ISBN: 978-3-7774-3968-6

Library of Congress Control Number: 2022942571

Project Management, Editing, and Proofreading Valerie Hellstein, Kati Woock, and Christopher Patrello
Curatorial Assistants Lisbet Barrientos and Maria Luisa Minjares
Manager of Rights and Reproduction Renée B. Miller
Photography Christina Jackson, Eric Stephenson, and Jeff Wells
Translation David Sánchez (Spanish to English), Laura Puy Rodríguez (English to Spanish)
Spanish Copyeditors and Proofreaders María Eugenia Hidalgo and Alberto Márquez
Additional Proofreaders Jane Michael (English), Amaia de Navascués (Spanish)
Index David Sánchez
Project Management Hirmer Publishers Rainer Arnold
Senior Editor Hirmer Publishers Elisabeth Rochau-Shalem
Layout, Typesetting, and Production Hannes Halder
Prepress and repro Reproline Genceller, Munich
Printing and Binding Cuno Druck, Calbe
Paper Magno Matt 150 g/sqm
Fonts Gotham, Egyptienne

Printed in Germany

Cover: Detail. Cat 141, p. 165 **p. 2** Detail. Cat. 29, p. 39 **pp. 4/5:** Detail. Unknown artist, *Death Portrait of Don Thomas María Joachín Villaseñor y Gómez*, Guadalajara, Mexico, 1760. Oil paint on canvas, framed 52¼ × 74½ in. (132.7 × 189.3 cm). Gift of the Collection of Frederick and Jan Mayer, 2013.316 **pp. 8/9:** Detail. Cat. 5, p. 14 **pp. 26/27:** Detail. Cat. 17, p. 24 **pp. 32/33:** Detail. Cat. 26, p. 36 **pp. 76/77:** Detail. Cat. 57, p. 74 **pp. 88/89:** Detail. Cat. 70, p. 91 **pp. 100/101:** Detail. Cat. 83, p. 103 **pp. 114/115:** Detail. Cat. 96, p. 118 **pp. 140/141:** Detail. Cat. 135, p. 159 **pp. 196/197:** Detail. Cat. 165, p. 192 **pp. 206/207:** Detail. Cat. 178, p. 204 **pp. 212/213:** Detail. Cat. 201, p. 235 **pp. 248/249:** Unknown artist, *Head of Saint John the Baptist*, Cuzco, Peru, 1640–70. Oil paint on canvas, 25⅞ × 36½ in. (65.7 × 92.7 cm). Gift of Dr. & Mrs. Seymour Rubenfeld, 1978.178A-C. **pp. 282** Detail. Pedro de Noriega, Mexican, active 1700s, *Saint Ursula and the 11,000 Virgins*, Querétaro, Mexico, 1734. Oil paint on canvas, 30 × 39 in (76 × 99 cm). Gift of Dr. Belinda Straight, 1983.596 **pp. 290/291:** Detail. Unknown artist, *Construction Plan for Bridge of San Francisco in La Paz, Bolivia*, Bolivia, ca. 1786. Watercolor and ink on paper, 18½ × 13 in. (47 × 33 cm). Gift of W. Sherwood Schoch, 1983.599 **Back cover:** Detail. Cat. 143, p. 167
Every effort has been made to supply complete and correct credits; if there are errors or omissions, please contact the publisher so that corrections can be made in any subsequent edition.